1998

Merry Christmas, Jeanette!

Love,
Carol

Behind Every Man

Behind Every Man

The Story of Nancy Cooper Russell

BY JOAN STAUFFER

Daljo Publishing, Tulsa

Daljo Publishing
Post Office Box 35919
Tulsa, Oklahoma 74153-0919

Library of Congress Catalog Card Number 90-084294
ISBN 0-9627823-0-0
Manufactured in the United States of America

Designed and produced by Carol Haralson

This book is dedicated, first and foremost, to my best friend and, in my opinion, the world's greatest researcher — my husband, Dale, who wouldn't let me give up even when I said, "I can't." He always said, "Yes, you can."

Second, to Ginger Renner and the late Fred Renner, renowned authorities on Charles Russell, who generously shared not only their information, but also their enthusiasm about this endeavor.

Third, to Jack Cooper Russell, who said on our first meeting, "My mother deserves a book."

Contents

Preface

This is the story of one extraordinary woman. It is the drama of the quest for success, the attaining of the American dream, and the price paid. It was not written for scholars but for everyone who enjoys a good tale of love, ambition, passion, jealousy, frustration, joy and sadness – all that makes us human. If you want the story of a fascinating woman, then read on – for this book was written for you.

It was also written in the hope that, even if you have never heard of Charles Marion Russell, this book will inspire you to seek out his paintings so that you may enjoy them.

Although writing in the first person required that I take some artistic liberties, this is a novel based on fact. It is based on information gathered from interviews, letters, court records, and other documents, and it is as true a story as I could tell.

J. S.
August, 1990

Acknowledgments

Hundreds of people have helped my husband Dale and me. We are deeply grateful to each of them. If anyone has been neglected inadvertently, I sincerely hope that he or she will forgive me. We sincerely thank the late Earl C. Adams; Eugene B. Adkins; Riley Allen; Robert Archibald, former Director of the Montana Historical Society; Lois Ash; Norma Ashby; Douglas Baker; Dorothy Dickinson Ball; Jean Baucus; Marian Bovaird; Tom Brayshaw, Director of the C. M. Russell Museum; Charles L. Brown; Dr. James Burke, Director of the St. Louis Art Museum; the late Alice Calvert; Ethel Calvert; Olive Carey; Ross Case; Betty Russell Crawford; Susan Chaput, Director of Medical Records at the Huntington Memorial Hospital; Juni Clarke, of the Rosenstock Gallery; Evelyn Cooper; Kay Courtnage; Harold Davidson; Flo Lynn Dickinson; Brian W. Dippie; Sara Dobberteen; Mike Dortch; Michael Duty, Director of the Eiteljorg Museum; Dr. Russell and Shirley Edwin; Francis Flaherty; Lee Forest; Elsie Fowlerholf; William Foxley; Ruth Frohlicher; Christine Gabheart; the late Dr. A. M. Gibson, University of Oklahoma History Department; Dr. William Goetzmann, University of Texas History Department; Betty Jane Mitchell Gorin; Jerry Goroski, Mr.and Mrs.Ted Gullette; Katherine Haley; L. N. Hamilton; Shirley Hamilton; Peter Hassrick, Director of the Buffalo Bill Historical Center; Sarah Hatfield;

Patrick Houlihan, former Director of the Southwest Museum; the late Earl L. Jenson; the late Dr. Otey Johnson; O'Neil Jones; Dean Krakel, former Director of the National Cowboy Hall of Fame; Peter Kriendler; Carolyn Linden; Verne Linderman; Fred and Anne Long; Ken Ludtke; Conrad Lundgren; Victoria Gray and Malcolm S. (Bud) Mackay, Jr.; Dr. W. R. Mann; Alice May; Ann McDonald, Librarian of the Kentucky Historical Society; Frances McKnight; Irma McLuskie; Harriett Meloy; Daniela Moneta, Librarian of the Southwest Museum; Jenson Monroe, Education Director of the Rockwell Museum; Robert Morgan; Jan Keene Mullert, Director of the Amon Carter Museum; Fred Myers, Director of the Gilcrease Institute of American History and Art; Dr. Van Kirke and Helen Nelson; Ed Neitzling; Dick Pace; Vivian A. Paladin; Ward and Merceina Parker; Harold Paul; Dr. Roger Paul; Raymond Pisney, former Director of the Missouri Historical Society; Don Reeves; Ginger and the late Fred Renner; Frank and Dee Repetti; Doris Reynold; William and Loraine Roberts; Robert and Hertha Rockwell; James Rogers; Will Rogers, Jr.; Steven L. Rose of the Biltmore Galleries; Elaine and Sam Rosenthal, Jr.; Jack Cooper Russell; Frances Sanborn; Bill P. Sherman; Dr. Clement M. Silvestro, Director of the Museum of Our National Heritage; Martha Gabrielson Soho; Beverly Spencer; Elizabeth (Peg) and the late Milton Sperling; Frances Spurling; Ray Steele, former Director of the C. M. Russell Museum; John and

Rhoda Stephenson; Elmer Stewart; Guynette Sullivan; Mrs. Randall Swanberg and the late Mr. Swanberg; Thomas K. Thompson; Arthur Townsend, former Director of the Rockwell Museum; Margaret Coulter Verharen; Mrs. Neal Wahlberg; David Walter, Consultant, Historical Research, Montana Historical Society; Helen Warhine; Roy Wieghorst; W. D. Weiss; Joseph S. Wolff; Lyle and Aileen Woodcock; Carol and the late Margaret Word; Jim Yaple; and Harriette Young.

A number of organizations and institutions have assisted in our research. We thank in particular the Alaska Historical Library, Juneau; Los Angeles Public Library; Los Angeles County Hall of Records; Natural History Museum of Los Angeles County; Orange County California Court House; Pasadena Court House; Pasadena Public Library; Santa Barbara Public Library; Southwest Museum, Los Angeles, California; Los Angeles County William S. Hart Park Museum, Newhall, California; Ada County, Idaho, Clerk of District Court; Boise Idaho Public Library; Paxton Illinois Public Library; Campbellsville Kentucky Public Library; Casey County Kentucky Court House; Green County Kentucky Court House; Kentucky Historical Society, Frankfort; Liberty Kentucky Public Library; Marion County Kentucky Court House; Taylor County Kentucky Court House; Taylor County Kentucky Historical Society; Library of the Museum of Fine Arts, Boston, Massachusetts; St. Louis County Missouri Public Library; Missouri Historical Society, St. Louis, Missouri; Boulder

County Montana Court House; Cascade County Montana Court House; Cascade Montana Public Library; Chouteau County Montana Court House; Flathead County Montana Court House; C. M. Russell Museum, Great Falls, Montana; Church of Incarnation, Great Falls, Montana; Great Falls Historical Society; Great Falls Public Library; Montana Historical Society, Helena; Jefferson County Montana Court House; Lake County Montana Court House; Madison County Montana Court House; Polson Montana Public Library; Toole County Montana Court House; Lewis and Clark County Montana Court House; Rockwell Museum, Corning, New York; University of Nebraska at Lincoln Library; National Cowboy Hall of Fame Museum, Oklahoma City, Oklahoma; Gilcrease Institute of American History and Art, Tulsa, Oklahoma; Oklahoma Historical Society Library, Oklahoma City; Sapulpa Oklahoma Public Library; Church of Jesus Christ of Latter Day Saints, Tulsa Oklahoma Stake, Branch Genealogical Library; Tulsa City-County Library; Amon Carter Museum, Fort Worth, Texas; and the Buffalo Bill Historical Center, Cody, Wyoming.

A very special thank you to Millie Ladner Thompson not only for proofreading this book, but also for her constant encouragement and unwavering faith and support in this endeavor.

A Russell Family Album

The Mann family: From left to right, George Alfred Mann, Texas Mann, Fletcher Mann, John Bluford Mann, Ed Frank Mann, Nancy Bates Mann, Carrie Mann. Ca. 1872, Taylor County, Kentucky. Courtesy of Dr. W. R. Mann.

Nancy Cooper Russell, ca. 1900. Great Falls, Montana. Courtesy of Carol Word.

Nancy and Charlie at Bull Head Lodge in 1924. Courtesy of Dr. Russell Edwin.

William S. (Bill) Hart and Charlie Russell, ca. 1914, in a photograph inscribed by Bill Hart to Joe De Yong. Courtesy of the C. M. Russell Museum, Great Falls, Montana.

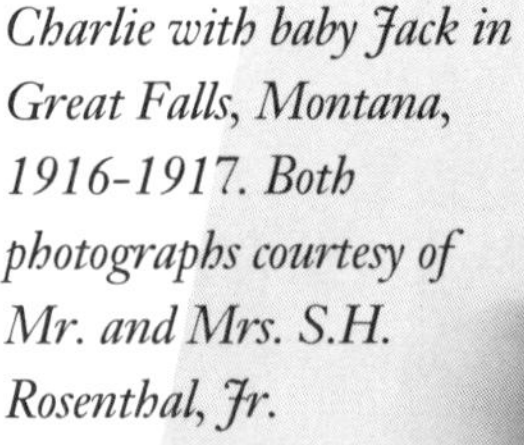

Charlie with baby Jack in Great Falls, Montana, 1916-1917. Both photographs courtesy of Mr. and Mrs. S.H. Rosenthal, Jr.

Above, facing page: From left to right, Mrs. Fernald, Nancy Russell, Charlie Russell, Ted Taylor (preparing the fire), Margaret Trigg, Josephine Trigg, "Banty" De Yong. Bull Head Lodge, the Russell's cabin at Glacier National Park, 1926. Courtesy of Stanley O. Jones.

Below, Facing page: Jack with Margaret Trigg. Courtesy of William B. Roberts.

Above: Nancy, ca. 1916. Courtesy of Mr. and Mrs. S. H. Rosenthal, Jr.
Below: Nancy in Charlie's studio in Great Falls, 1908. Courtesy of Edwin H. Magruder.

Above, facing page: Bert Sinclair, Charlie, and Nancy in front of Charlie's Great Falls log cabin studio in 1906. Courtesy of Mr. and Mrs. S. H. Rosenthal, Jr.

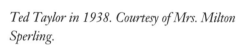

Ted Taylor in 1938. Courtesy of Mrs. Milton Sperling.

C.O. Middleton with Lindley Anderson (left) and his wife Nin. Courtesy of Carol Word.

Jack Russell with Josephine and Margaret Trigg and Nancy (at right), ca. 1929. Courtesy of William B. Roberts.

Left to right: The Russells' nephew Austin, Charlie, Frank and Ella Ironsides, Josephine Trigg, and Nancy at Bull Head Lodge. Courtesy of Stanley O. Jones.

Ella, Nancy, and Charlie, in the studio at Great Falls, ca. 1908. Courtesy of Stanley O. Jones. Below: Trail's End, the Russell home in Pasadena, California. Courtesy of William B. Roberts.

Nancy Russell at the World's Fair, 1904. Courtesy of Alice and William Marks, Seatttle, Washington.

I

At Grandpa Blue's

I CLOSED THE WINDOWS IN THE PARLOR, but only as an excuse to look down the river road and try to catch a glimpse of him. The chill of evening was not yet in the air. Earlier that afternoon, I had opened the windows to bring the wonderful smell of fall into the house. It was still warm though it was October. We'd had a light snow the week before, but its foretelling of winter was forgotten in the sunshine of Indian summer. The reds and yellows of the trees, the blue, blue endless sky and the splashing of the river lulled us into a complacency which ignored the coming of a Montana winter.

I went back into the kitchen and reset the dishes on the table. They didn't match, but I liked the array of colors and patterns. They said he was an artist, so he might notice. I rearranged them again, trying to hide the chips and cracks. I put a bouquet of the last of summer's wildflowers in the center of the table.

I had known that it was a special day when I awoke that morning. There was something in the air I could almost taste. I had been feeding Vivian his oatmeal, although he was plenty big enough to feed himself, because I really wanted to help. Ma and Pa Roberts had been so good to me. When Ma Roberts announced that Charlie Russell was coming to dinner, I dropped the spoon.

"What's wrong with you, girl?" Ma Roberts asked.

My face reddened and I felt faint. I couldn't wait to meet Charles Russell, the cowboy artist.

"Now you watch out, Mamie. He's got a fuzzy reputation and with the wrong kind of women, if you know what I mean. He drinks too much. He's too old for you. Why, you're only seventeen and he's thirty-one."

The more Ma Roberts told me to "watch out for Charlie," the more excited I got. The Roberts kids, Gorham, Hebe, and Vivian, were as excited as I was, for they knew Charlie. Hebe made up a song about Charlie's coming. She was only five so it was a simple sing-song verse she would say as she danced around the house, twirling in circles. "Charlie's coming. Charlie's coming. Uncle Charlie's coming to supper tonight." Vivian, who was three, mimicked her like a little shadow. Gorham was nine and too old for singing and skipping but I could tell he was as excited as the others. No wonder my stomach was tied up in knots.

I had just turned to rearrange the dishes and the flowers one more time when I heard the creak of the back door and the jangle of spurs. There he stood. The sun was beginning to set behind him, so he was outlined in a halo of golden rays. The Roberts kids heard the door shut and came running into the kitchen, Vivian trailing because his fat little legs couldn't keep up. They ran to Charlie and threw their arms around his legs. Charlie lifted them up one after the other and tossed them in the air. There were continuous bursts of laughter.

"Mo, mo," Vivian pleaded.

But when I looked up into Charlie's blue-gray eyes I could see that he wasn't listening to Vivian. He couldn't take his eyes off me.

Ma Roberts came away from the stove, wiping her hands on her white apron. She gave Charlie a hug and said that supper was nearly ready. Then she pointed him out the back door where there was a bench and a wash basin next to the pump and told him to wash up as if he were one of the kids.

I stood at the back door with a towel while Charlie primed the pump and filled the basin. Charlie's shoulders were broad, his back was straight, and I could see the ripple of muscles through his soft shirt.

He turned and caught me staring. My face grew hot, and I could suddenly hear the sound of my heartbeat. Charlie smiled, took the towel and dried his face and hands. I don't remember what we ate that night.

All I remember was trying not to look into those blue-gray eyes because each time I did they were looking at me.

After dinner, while the Robertses put the children to bed, I cleared the table and picked up the bucket to go out to the pump. Charlie took the bucket from my hand and went to the pump himself, then lifted the filled bucket onto the stove to heat. I put a slab of soft lye soap in the bucket, then began scrapin bits of food from the plates into two piles, one for the dogs and one for the chickens. We didn't waste anything. Once the water was steaming, I began washing the dishes. Charlie dried them.

"Why do they call you Mamie? Is that your real name?" Charlie asked.

"No, my real name is Nancy, but about everyone calls me Mamie Mann."

"Once an Indian friend of mine asked me what 'Charlie' meant," Charlie said. "I said I didn't know. Then he asked me what 'Russell' meant and I said I didn't know that either. Then my friend said, 'White man got heap of book learning and don't even know what his own name means.'"

We both laughed. Charlie could tell a story like no one else could. Before I knew it, I was telling him all about myself. He listened and understood. He had a way about him that made everyone feel important, as if they were somebody. I was nobody.

After we did the dishes, Charlie suggested we

take a walk along the river. There was still a little light left. I took a shawl off the hook by the stove and wrapped it around my shoulders. We walked along the bank, then crossed the bridge and stopped to watch the red and gold leaves fall into the water, float down the river and disappear as the water flowed around the bend. It was the first of many, many walks we would take along the river and across the bridge.

As autumn became winter, we watched snowflakes fall into the water. At first they melted, then as more and more came they gained a foothold along the banks. As the north wind blew we watched ice form along the banks, break off in huge hunks and float down the river following the path of the leaves around the bend. Suddenly, without our knowing when it had begun, there were patches of green in the snow and a few crocuses were blooming.

We became such good friends. I could tell Charlie anything, and he understood. I told him that I hadn't had much schooling. He laughed and said that was all right because he hadn't had much either.

I told him about my ma, which was hard because it still hurt. My ma and my pa had married real young. Ma was only seventeen and Pa was nineteen when they got hitched in '77 on the twenty-sixth of March. The wedding was at my grandpa's house, near Mannsville, Kentucky. My grandpa was dead set against the marriage. He didn't think James Al Cooper was good enough for Ma. I doubt if Grandpa Blue — everyone called him Blue although his real name was John Bluford Mann — thought anyone was good enough for his little girl, Texas Annie. He wouldn't even set his mark on the marriage license. He thought Al was just trying to get away from a bad situation at home. Al's ma had died and left his pa with a house full of kids, the youngest only two. She wasn't three weeks in the grave when Al's older sister died. What could his pa do but marry fast? He had to have someone to take care of those kids. Al and his step-ma didn't get along, so Al had to get away. And my ma was pretty.

Grandpa Blue was right. My ma and my pa fought all the time. Finally Pa had had all he could take and he packed up and left. My ma found out she was carrying me. She went home to the Manns.

Although times were hard, Grandpa Blue took her in. He had always had a place in his heart for his sweet little girl, and he convinced Grandma Jennie that family was family. My step-grandma, Jennie, resented having more mouths to feed. She liked it even less when I was born and my ma named me Nancy, after her own real ma, Nancy Bates Mann. Every time someone called me Nancy, Grandma Jennie bristled. And it was a bad thing to get on the wrong side of Virginia Parker Mann, so I was glad that people usually called me Mame or Mamie Mann. Grandpa Blue always called me Nannie.

From the time I was old enough to walk, I was out in the tobacco fields. Everyone had to help, from sunup to sundown. After a long day in the fields, when supper was over, Grandpa Blue would light his pipe, pick me up on his knee, and tell me the story of the Mann family. He knew the story by heart, for he had heard it from his father, who heard it from his father, who had heard it from his father.

The first Mann to come over from the old country was John Mann in 1735. He brought his wife and three sons, John Jr., Moses, and William. They settled in Orange County, Virginia, where Thomas, his fourth and last son, was born. They were devout Presbyterians, and had left Ireland because they were tired of being persecuted by the Catholics.

"But Grandpa, I thought both Presbyterians and Catholics loved Jesus," I said.

"Maybe they loved Jesus, but they sure hated each other. John Mann had to leave Ulster and free himself and his family from those black-hearted Catholics. He wanted a better life for his boys. But only two of the three lived to enjoy it. Moses was captured and killed by the Indians in 1756. Later his brothers avenged him when they fought the Shawnees and won. In his memory both John Jr. and William named their first-born sons Moses. Then the boys went on to fight with honor in the French and Indian war. Later they founded Mann's Fort on the Jackson River.

"William's boy, Moses, formed the Mann Rangers and fought under 'Light-Horse Harry' Lee. After the Revolutionary War, John Jr.'s boy Moses and his brother Asa struck out for Kentucky. Now, that Moses was my pa's pa. He already had kin out here. A nephew, come to Kentucky, by the name of Nathanial Carpenter. He founded Carpenter's Station over in Lincoln County. Well, ol' Moses came out and founded Mannsville. He picked a spot that had a salt lick for he knew how important salt was to man and beast. Some folks called it Mann's Lick.

"One day his son, also named Asa, Nathanial Carpenter, and a hired hand came upon a bunch of Indians. Those savages killed Asa and the hired hand. They sure thought they had killed Nathanial for they scalped him."

"Grandpa, how could he lay still and let them scalp him and not move a muscle?" I always asked when he told me that part of the story.

"It was better to lie still than be killed. Ol' Nathanial was tough. Then he crawled back to Moses and told him his boy had been killed. Well, Moses got his gun and stalked that band of renegades and wiped them out. If you're a Mann, you never let anybody take anything away from you that's yours. Remember that, child.

"Moses only had one boy left. That was John, my pa. My pa met my ma, who was a Bryant. Her name was really Sarah, but everyone called her Sally. They fell in love, got hitched and had fourteen kids. I was number eight. At one time ol' Grandpa Moses had two thousand acres. When he died, it was divided amongst his four younguns. My pa had three sisters. Well, when my pa died, his land was divided fourteen ways; of course, the older boys got the first pick. Some say our land here on Robinson's Creek ain't worth a damn. It's too rocky and hilly to grow much tobaccy, but I always say all it takes is just a little more sweat."

I loved those evenings when I would sit on my Grandpa Blue's lap with my head against his chest and listen to the Mann stories. He told them to me over and over.

"It's too hard to remember," I'd complain. "There are too many Moseses, Johns, and Asas. I can't keep them straight."

"All you have to remember, child, is that you come from a fine family. A family who made a name for themselves out in the wilderness. Hell, the town here is named after your great-great grandpa, Moses Mann. I know we ain't got much right now, with the price of tobaccy down. But don't you ever be ashamed and don't ever forget you are a Mann."

"Stop putting ideas in that child's head. Pride don't put food on the table," Grandma Jennie said. "She does nothing but sit around and daydream as it is. Ever since she was sick, she hasn't been pulling her own weight around here."

I remembered little about the time I was sick. Only about lying in my bed thinking I was going to die. I felt like I had swallowed fire and I was burning up. Then my teeth would chatter and I'd shake so that my body ached. One night I woke up so hot I thought my head would pop like popping corn. Then I felt something cool on my brow. I opened my eyes to see my mother squeezing out rags in a bucket and putting them on my body. She was crying.

"Honey, don't die, don't die. You're all I've got," Ma cried.

I tried to talk but nothing came out. I heard my Grandpa Blue praying. He was kneeling by my bed with his head in his hands.

"Lord, please spare this child. I know she's special and has somethin' special to do."

They say it was a miracle I lived through that bout with diphtheria for many who weren't nearly as sick as I was died, but I guess I had to live for my ma. I had to make things better for her, for if I heard it once, I heard it a thousand times from Grandma Jennie that if Ma hadn't been so hard-headed she would have never married that no-count Cooper, and Grandma Jennie wouldn't have another mouth to feed. Well, this 'other mouth to feed' was five years old, and I knew I could do plenty to help.

Tobacco was our only cash crop. We grew corn and pumpkins, but that was to feed the chickens and hogs. We grew wheat and took it over to the mill at Elkhorn but that was exchanged for flour. The only real hard cold cash we ever got was from tobacco.

"Come on girl. Don't dawdle. You've got brush to pick up. We need a big pile," Grandma Jennie ordered.

"But my fingers are stiff. They hurt," I cried.

"If you work, they'll warm up. Hurry up, now," Grandma Jennie said.

"Here," said Aunt Carrie. "Put your hands inside my hands and I'll rub them. That will warm them up." Aunt Carrie was my ma's younger sister, but she was only nine years older than I was. Her hands weren't much bigger than mine.

"Come on. I bet I can find more brush than you." Aunt Carrie made everything seem like a game.

Everyone helped and when Grandpa Blue thought the pile was big enough, we stopped. Then he set fire to the brush.

"Why do we always have to burn the brush?" I asked.

"It gets the ground ready for the seeds. See the tobaccy seeds," Grandpa said as he poured some out in his hand. The seeds were no bigger than ground pepper. "I got to mix these seeds with ashes, so when I cast them, the wind can't pick them up and blow them away." After Grandpa Blue mixed the seeds with ashes and cast them on the ground, we all gathered around him and bowed our heads.

"Dear Lord," Grandpa Blue's deep voice filled the air. "We have gathered the brush, burned it, cast the seeds, and now we pray for rain and sunshine to make them grow. When the baby plants come up, we will gently cover them each night with fine brush so the frost won't get them. When they are as big as my hand, we will be careful to transplant them. Texas, Carrie and little Nannie B will carry the plants to the tobaccy patch and gently place them on the ground equal distance apart. George, Ed, Fletcher and I will come after them and with our tobaccy pegs, will make a hole, then pick up a plant, put it in the earth and press the dirt tightly around each little stem.

"When the plants bloom, we will top the blossom, leaving the flowers on a few of the strongest, best stalks for next year's seeds. We will pick off those suckers which will sprout after the topping. The men will hoe the weeds, so they won't take over the plants. Texas and Carrie and even Nannie will pick off the tobacco worms. Yes, Lord, give Nannie the courage to pick off those squirming worms. We will do all we can. But we can't make the stalks grow. Only you can, Lord, so we ask you to bless this crop."

When Grandpa Blue had finished, we all raised our heads and said Amen.

And every one of us did what he said we would do. I even picked off those hateful worms that squirmed in my fingers and turned them dark brown with tobacco juice. I had to, for I had to prove that I was brave and that the crop was blessed.

Come August or September, it was time to harvest. The men would cut the tobacco stalks, split them, then hang the stalks on a stick. These sticks were taken to the tobacco shed and hung on the tier poles. From ceiling to floor row after row of tobacco hung to dry.

Always some leaves would break off when the tobacco was harvested, and it was my job to pick up every last one of the fallen tobacco leaves, for each was precious. I would hang them between the boards of the tobacco shed, so they too could dry. We had to wait for nature to cure the tobacco. Everyone waited for the tobacco to come "in order," which meant it was ready to take out of the drying shed to strip. This was usually done the first of December. We had to catch a misty day, so the tobacco would be moist and not crumble to pieces when the men took the sticks down. The sticks with the tobacco were laid in neat rows on the ground and covered with quilts to keep the moisture in while the stripping began.

The first leaves were called "trash" because they were small. They were taken off and tied by a tobacco leaf into a "hand." This was Uncle Fletcher's job. The next leaves were Uncle Ed's, then Uncle George's and finally Grandpa Blue trimmed the biggest and best. He was always the fastest at tying a hand of tobacco. He said it was because he had more practice. Aunt Carrie and I stripped the tips because that was the easiest job. Aunt Carrie was good at tying her tips into hands, but my fingers weren't big enough or strong enough, so Aunt Carrie always tied mine too.

After the tobacco was all stripped and tied, we would lay the hands in the wagon very carefully according to grade, then Grandpa and Uncle George would drive the wagon over the gap to Lebanon. They would borrow another team because the wagon was too heavy for one hitch. They always said the coldest place on earth was the warehouse in Lebanon. After the auction, Grandpa would take the money and buy goods and supplies. He'd always buy a present or two. We all watched the road from Lebanon looking for Grandpa Blue's wagon. When he and Uncle George returned, it was time to celebrate.

One year we heard Grandpa singing at the top of his voice as he returned. It had been a very good year. On the back of the wagon, with the supplies, tied down so it wouldn't bounce off, of all things was a Shoninger pump organ. We couldn't wait for the men to unload it and carry it into the house. After much struggling, it was finally inside. I sat on the floor and pumped the peddles while Aunt Carrie brought forth beautiful sounds as she touched the keys. Aunt Carrie had a natural gift and could play by ear. What wonderful times we had singing hymns around the organ, our voices blending from Ma's sweet soprano to Grandpa Blue's bass.

There were other years when the tobacco crop was not so good, and there was little brought home from Lebanon. And there was that awful year. Grandpa came up the road from Lebanon. He wasn't singing or even whistling. His head was hanging. There was nothing in the wagon — no goods, no presents.

"Grandpa, where's the beans and bacon and sugar? Where's the presents?" I asked as I slowly climbed down after peering into the wagon. Grandpa hitched the horses to the porch rail and dragged himself across the porch into the parlor. He slumped down into his big chair next to the fireplace.

"There ain't goin' a be no presents this year. I have to go out to the barn and kill some chickens and take them back to the warehouse to pay our floor expenses. We didn't even make our floor expenses. We owe them." He spoke just above a whisper.

"Oh, no!" moaned Grandma Jennie as she put her head in her hands and began to cry.

"Nannie B," Grandpa Blue said as he lifted me up. "The price of tobaccy is way down. We owe for floor space and the auction fee. We didn't make enough from our sale to pay our bill at the warehouse."

"It's not right. After all our work, we should get somethin'. It's just like stealin'," I wailed.

"Now listen, girl. Nobody ever steals from John Bluford Mann. I want you to listen to a honest to God true story that happened before you were born. You know that hole that's cut into the side of that corn crib out back? That hole is just big enough that I can stick my hand in and pull out a few ears at a time. Well, I noticed that someone else must be sticking his hand in, a hand that don't belong, for corn was disappearing mighty fast. So I sat a bear trap in that corn crib right on the other side of the hole. Sure enough, that night I heard the trap snap and a scream of pain. But I left that thief there all night no matter how he howled to be let free or how your grandma Nancy begged me to go get him out. The next morning, I went out and got him out of the trap. I even put him in the wagon and took him into the Doc's. He lost that hand. He wouldn't have, had he not put it where it didn't belong. Nobody has ever stolen from me since. Remember, Nannie B, when you work hard for something don't let *nobody take it away*. Also remember, if you owe a rightful debt, you got to pay it. We owe the auction house. We will pay. Now, I got to go out back and kill me some chickens."

"But what will we do, Grandpa Blue," I asked, "without any cash?"

"We'll get by. There are good years and there are bad. It's already January, and we need to think about next year. We got to gather the brush up and burn off the field so that we can start planting." Then he went out back to wring some chickens' necks.

He was right. Before I knew it, the time had come to gather the brush, pile it high, burn it, cast the seeds, protect the baby plants, transplant them, pray for rain, top the tobacco, pick off the worms, hoe the weeds, cut the stalks, then hang it to dry. That was the best part of the year, when the tobacco was hanging up. Let God's own air do the work and cure that tobacco. The evenings were still warm for winter was many weeks off, yet the blistering heat of summer was gone. We could sit on the front porch. I sat on the steps, being careful not to get a splinter in my legs.

Creak, squeak, creak, squeak, Grandpa Blue's rocker would rub back and forth on the wooden boards of the porch. He'd rock back and forth smoking his pipe till the strong sweet odor of burning tobacco filled the early evening air. For the rest of my life whenever I smelled a really strong cigar, the memories of sitting on that porch would come flooding back. A breeze with a slight chill in it would ruffle the leaves and always someone would comment that winter was not far away.

We sat on the porch listening to the katydids sing. Grandpa Blue said they made their song by rubbing their wings together, but I couldn't believe they could make so much noise that way. One would start up and from far off he would get an answer, then suddenly from all directions the unseen chorus would join in. Suddenly they would all stop, and just as suddenly start up again.

One evening in the early fall of '84, the katydids suddenly all stopped singing. I waited and waited for them to start up, then realized that they weren't singing because a stranger was coming up the road. He was a stranger to me, but Grandpa Blue recognized him.

"Is that you, James Thomas Allen?" Grandpa Blue called out when he could clearly see the man. "It's been a long time, son. I ain't seen you since your pa Zadock got you from your grandpa and took you to Montana in '66." Grandpa Blue got up from his rocker, stepped off the porch and walked up the road a short distance. The two men stopped and looked each other over. Grandpa Blue took the young man in his arms and gave him a bear hug.

"Yes, it's me, Uncle Blue," Cousin Thom said. "With Grandpa Allen gone, I've come back from Montana to get my share of land. But they've cut it up so many ways that my piece ain't worth a tinker's damn. I'm not going to stay on a Godforsaken farm and work my fingers to the bone to raise tobacco when in Montana folks are finding gold or picking up sapphires just lying out on the ground. As soon as I get a grubstake together, I'm going back. It's not my fault I didn't make it rich before. Plenty that didn't work as hard as me got smiled on by Lady Luck. But she was cruel and fickle to me. She even took my wife and babies."

"That's too bad, son," Grandpa Blue said. "I lost two wives myself and I know how it hurts. And your dear mother is gone too. You stay for supper and the night. In the morning the boys and I will take a look at your place and maybe we can help you out some. We don't have much, but what we have we gladly share. I'll do what I can for my sister Rachel's boy."

"My wife didn't die. She up and left me. Divorced me. Said I swilled from the bottle too much. Everyone knows that a nip or two don't hurt. Boy, I sure could use a swallow right now. I'm mighty dry. How about a swig before supper? I'm sure you got a jug hid somewhere," Cousin Thom said.

"Texas," Grandpa called into the house, "look up on the top shelf, blow off the dust and bring us a jug and two tin cups."

"I don't need no cup," said Cousin Thom. "I'll

drink mine straight from the jug."

Ma came outside onto the porch carrying the jug and cups.

"My, my, my, can you be Texas Annie? You've grown into a mighty good looker," said Cousin Thom as he accepted the jug from my ma and took a big swig. I noticed he slipped his free hand around her waist.

On November 17, 1884, my ma, Texas Annie Mann, and James Thomas Allen were married. Grandpa Blue put his mark on the marriage license this time. This time it was his own sister's boy marrying Texas. Grandpa had been paying taxes for years on some land right next to ours that his sister Rachel had left. He talked ZadockAllen into giving that land to Cousin Thom, and Cousin Thom into letting Zadock have his piece of land in Casey. This way Grandpa Blue could have Texas closer and make sure that Cousin Thom took good care of us.

But Cousin Thom wanted no part of me.

As soon as the wedding was over, Ma explained to me that for right now I was to stay with Grandpa Blue for Cousin Thom didn't have much yet. As soon as times got better she'd send for me.

"Oh, Nannie, darling," Ma said as she held me close, the tears running down her face. "This is just for a short time. Pretty soon Thom will want you to come live with us."

"But, Mama, I don't want you to go. Why did you have to marry Cousin Thom?" I cried as I held her tightly.

"A woman can't make it on her own, baby. She has to have a man. Thom's family. He'll feel obliged to treat us good. We'll be on the next farm over. I'll see you all the time. And it won't be for long. As soon as we get settled and things are better, we'll be together. I promise." And she gave me one last hug.

But the days became weeks. Every night when I was in bed and I thought no one could hear me, I cried. I was six years old and everyone said "growed up" for my age, but I couldn't help it. I wanted my ma. One night, Grandpa Blue heard me and came into the bedroom I shared with Aunt Carrie.

"Girl, what's wrong?" he asked.

"I want my mama," I cried. "Why does Cousin Thom hate me? Why won't he let me live with my mama?" I hugged Grandpa Blue and he picked me up and carried me to the big chair next to the fireplace.

"Right now, he doesn't feel obliged to take care of you, Nannie B, since you're another man's kid, but he'll come around. You'll see. Now you mustn't think on it. You need to get your mind on something else. You know that sorrel mare that you've been dying to learn to ride?

"You mean Purdy Mare?" I asked and my eyes were suddenly dry.

"Yes," Grandpa Blue answered. "I think tomorrow morning, first light, we'll go out and I'll teach you. Now, you get some sleep." He carried me back and laid me down, covered me up and gave me a kiss.

First thing the next morning we went out to the barn and got Purdy Mare. Grandpa Blue put a rope halter on her and led her over to a big tree stump. He told me to crawl up on the stump then on to Purdy's back. He gave me a little shove, and there I was, on Purdy.

"Now, hang on to her mane and squeeze as hard as you can with your knees. You have to be a part of her back like you're a tick on a dog and no one can pull you off," said Grandpa as he led Purdy around.

Pretty soon I could get the rope halter down myself and crawl up the rails of the fence and put it on Purdy. I could lead her to the stump and crawl on. When I came back from riding, I would rub her down with straw. She'd even eat grass out of my hand, always nibbling very carefully. Her favorite treat was June apples from Grandpa Blue's orchard. If I didn't have one to give her she'd nudge me with her nose. We played a game where I would hide an apple behind me. Only when she nudged me would I bring it around as a surprise for her to eat. The months passed. I learned how to dry apples to store so Purdy and I could still play our game when the summer apples were no more. I grew taller. I could stand on the stump and lay my hand against Purdy's neck and stroke it.

Still Cousin Thom didn't send for me. He said his farm was too poor. He said that he was barely scratching out a living for himself and Texas. Grandpa, Uncle George, and Uncle Fletcher helped him. After putting in a full day's work at home, they would go over to Cousin Thom's and help plant, hoe and harvest his tobacco. It was hard work, especially for Grandpa.

In '86, we had the worst winter anyone could remember. There was an epidemic of influenza that spread throughout the whole country. Grandpa Blue was just worn out. He came down with the flu and couldn't shake it. He laid in his bed and just got weaker and weaker until his big strong heart finally stopped. They had to take axes to the frozen ground to chop a hole to bury him. We picked a spot he loved under a big tree high on the hill behind the house where he could look down on his orchard, his house, the barn, and the tobacco fields. He could watch over us from the top of that hill.

After the funeral, I was terrified. What would I do? Ma and Cousin Thom had gone back to their place. Aunt Carrie took my hand and led me back to Grandpa Blue's house, but he wasn't there. He'd never be there again. He'd never again take me on his lap and tell me stories of the Mann family.

"What am I going to do without Grandpa Blue?" I asked Aunt Carrie.

"You'll be all right," she said. "In his will, he said that Fletcher is to make a home for you and me and Grandma Jennie right here. He also left you a two-hundred-and-fifty dollar note. Remember I'm here. I'll look after you, Nannie."

But Aunt Carrie didn't stay long. A new school

master named Joseph Morris came to our one-room schoolhouse and he had eyes for no one but Carrie from the time he arrived. At seventeen, Aunt Carrie was in the full bloom of womanhood. Her love for Joseph Morris was stronger than her desire to stay and take care of me.

"You still have your Uncle Fletcher and Grandma Jennie," she said.

Uncle Fletcher was gone from sunup 'til sundown, working in the fields. Grandma Jennie spent all her time trying to figure out when George, Ed, and Fletcher could come up with the fifteen hundred dollars that Grandpa Blue had promised her in his will so she could leave and go back to her family. All I had was Purdy.

Finally, in January of '88, they had the money together. Grandma Jennie decided to sell everything that was legally hers and go back to her people. I found out she was going to sell the Purdy Mare.

"Oh, no! Grandma Jennie, you can't sell Purdy," I cried.

"You come up with twenty dollars and she's yours. That's what I'm asking," she answered.

"Grandpa Blue left me a note for two hundred and fifty dollars. I can use some of that," I answered.

"Haven't you heard, child? James Allen was appointed your legal guardian yesterday. With Carrie married and me gone, there's no one to look after you. When I leave they are going to come and get you.

You'll have to ask James Thomas Allen for the twenty dollars," Grandma Jennie said.

I was torn between fear and happiness. I was finally going to get to be with my ma. But I had to have that twenty dollars to buy Purdy. I rushed out, put a bridle on Purdy and rode all the way over to Ma's and Cousin Thom's. As soon as I got there, I jumped off of Purdy and ran into the house.

"Cousin Thom, I got to have twenty dollars to buy Purdy Mare," I cried.

"Are you crazy, girl?" Thom asked.

"But Grandpa Blue left me two hundred and fifty dollars, and I need twenty. Don't you see? Grandma Jennie is going to sell her, and I'll never see her again."

"Your Grandpa Blue left your ma two hundred and fifty dollars too, and she's not asking me to waste it on anything as foolish as buying a broken down ol' horse. I'm savin' that money for somethin' real special. It's our grubstake to leave this place. We're going back to Montana where I'm going to strike it rich as soon as your ma drops this baby she's carrying and it's big enough to travel."

In '88, on an icy February day, my half-sister, Ella Carrie Allen, was born. Aunt Carrie had come over several days earlier to be with Ma for she knew her time was near. The night before Ella was born, we had a terrible snow storm. The roads had all disappeared under a blanket of snow and ice. When Ma started into labor,

Aunt Carrie told Cousin Thom he'd have to saddle up and fetch the midwife. Cousin Thom was furious that Ma would pick that time to have the baby. Weren't the roads covered with snow? Wouldn't that be just his luck? Ma's pains went on and on, and I could hear her cry out all day. I was so glad Aunt Carrie was there. Although I was nearly ten and would do anything for my ma, I knew nothing about bringing babies into this world. I prayed over and over, "Lord, please let my ma be all right."

The midwife finally arrived and just before dawn Ella was born. It had been a long, hard delivery and Ma was never really strong afterwards. I knew I could help with the baby, the house, the cooking and cleaning. Aunt Carrie would come over once a week to see how everything was going.

The next year, early in the summer of '90, Uncle George took sick. I had thought that nothing could happen to him, for he was so big and strong. He was the one everyone leaned on. He was only thirty-seven, not like Grandpa Blue, who had been old. They buried Uncle George in the Mann Cemetery, near his pa, John Bluford Mann; and his ma, Nancy Bates Mann; not far from the small headstones of his brothers, Union and Squire, who had died in childhood.

But the Angel of Death was not through with us. It stole my Aunt Carrie away. Joseph Morris only survived her by a few weeks. Everyone said he died of a broken heart. They were all buried up on the hill near

Grandpa Blue's grave.

After Uncle George, Aunt Carrie, and Uncle Joseph died, CousinThom was terrified. He was afraid that the dreaded illness that had clutched them would reach out and grab him too.

He decided it was time to leave Kentucky. If ever he were to make his mark, he had to move on. He was forty. Ma was thirty. Ella was two and plenty big enough to travel. I was twelve. Most important, my note for two hundred and fifty dollars, and my ma's legacy of the same amount, had finally been paid. Cousin Thom took that money and what he got for his poor farm and bought one-way tickets to Montana.

It was hard to catch our breath in the August heat as we stood on the wooden platform in front of the Campbellsville depot waiting for the L&N train. I looked down the tracks both excited and afraid. Excited to ride a train and afraid to leave Kentucky. Ma was crying. I think she knew she would never again lay flowers on the graves of Grandpa Blue and Aunt Carrie. Uncle Fletcher and Uncle Ed had come to Campbellsville to see us off. I heard the train before I saw it. As it came into view, the heat rays rising from the baked ground made it look unreal, like a ghost. But the black smoke belching from the engine and the clanging of the engine's bell made me know it was real. I was really leaving Kentucky. Ma and Uncle Fletcher clung to each other. Uncle Ed hugged me as I started to cry and said, "Mamie, you're a big girl now. You help your ma out with Ella."

We climbed aboard. With a shrill whistle and the clang of a bell the train lurched forward, almost knocking me off our hard wooden bench. Black smoke poured in the open window. It stung my eyes and made me cry, or maybe I was crying because Ma was. Long after Uncle Ed and Uncle Fletcher had disappeared from view she was still looking out the window and waving.

2

Helena, Montana

"WELL, WE'RE FINALLY LEAVING this hell-hole. Finally shaking the dust of Kentucky off our feet. There were times I was scared I'd never get out of there." Cousin Thom pulled a jug of sour mash from the picnic basket under the seat and pulled the cork out with his teeth. "Here's to never seein' another tobaccy plant again. Here's to Lady Luck smilin' on me and leadin' the way to a big strike. Here's to gettin' rich quick." He took a long swig. "All right, woman, let's have some food."

Ma pulled up the basket. She had packed loaves of bread in damp cloths to keep them from drying out. With the bread there was fried chicken, boiled eggs and dried apples. Ma knew the food wouldn't last the entire trip but she planned to parcel it out and stretch it as far as it would go.

I looked out the window. The seats faced each

other and I was sitting backwards so I could see where we had been rather than where we were going. Even though I was twelve I had never been on a train before. In half an hour I saw more countryside than I had known existed.

I had heard about the Green River Bridge, but I had never seen it. When I did, I couldn't believe it. I knew we were crossing when the sound of the wheels on the tracks suddenly changed key. I got up and looked out the window, then grasped the sill in fright because the view was straight down. How could such a long bridge, made only of wood, support a train filled with people? I held my breath and crossed my fingers until we reached the other side. But this was nothing compared to the terror I felt as the train entered the Muldraugh's Hill Tunnel. When the sunlight disappeared and all was black, every voice hushed. I knew people were still there, for I could hear them breathing. Maybe they were also crossing their fingers. Maybe, like me, they were wondering what was holding Muldraugh's Hill up and why it didn't crash in on the train. Maybe they, too, had heard the story of the witch that was buried at the end of the tunnel. When the sunlight streamed back through the windows, everyone began talking at once — a little louder than usual.

As the countryside slipped by, so did my excitement. As the green hills began to flatten, so did my spirits. It was hot and crowded. The cinders from the engine soon covered our clothes, hands and faces and everything became dirty and blackened, but we had to leave the window open or we would suffocate. A group of men sat at one end of the car playing cards and drinking. As the hours passed their voices became louder, their words more slurred. By nightfall between outbursts of drunken laughter, curses from unlucky cardplayers, and the cries of babies awakened from troubled sleep, there was no quiet in which to rest. The coal oil lamps smoked and added a foul odor to the already miserable air. My body ached from bouncing on the hard seat, my eyes burned, I felt sick at my stomach and my head ached. I was afraid I was going to have one of my fainting spells.

Cousin Thom got up to join the men playing cards. He'd had enough sour mash to be confident that he could beat them at their own game.

"Be careful, Thom."

"Nag, nag. That's all you ever do, woman."

As Thom left, Ma looked at my ashen face and patted the seat next to her. I slipped into it. She put her arm around me, and I laid my head on her shoulder. Although not big for two, Ella took up all of Ma's lap. She was fretful and could not lay still.

"Woman, you've got enough on your hands with the baby. You don't need an almost growed woman leaning on you. You'll just spoil her until she's no good," Thom said as he started up the aisle toward the card game. He didn't expect an answer so he didn't look back.

It was comforting to have my head on Ma's shoulder. My stomach quieted and the noise of the card game faded. My last thought before drifting off was that this was only the first day of our trip to Montana.

The jerk of the train woke me with a start. I was wondering where I was when the smell of the air, the stiffness of my body, and the screeching of the wheels on the rails brought it all back. I was again sitting on the seat facing backwards. Ma must have moved me during the night. Cousin Thom was across from me snoring in the deep sleep of a man who has had too much to drink.

Ma pulled out the picnic basket. The cloth around the bread had dried and the bread was already stale, but I told Ma it tasted good. The chicken was gone, so I chewed on some dried apple. Only three more days to Chicago where we would change trains for St. Paul. There we would catch the Northern Pacific for Helena.

We had read the flyers and ads printed by the Northern Pacific. They offered a special rate to anyone who would settle in what they referred to as "The Great New Northern Pacific Country" from the Great Lakes to the Pacific Ocean. In bold print the ads said, "Best Wheat Lands, Best Farming Lands, Best Grazing Lands, in the World" and went on to promise "all the people are prosperous, while large numbers have secured a competency, many have acquired wealth, AND THOUSANDS HAVE MADE FORTUNES THIS YEAR." In equal size print, it lauded "THE RICH GOLD AND SILVER SECTION" through which the Northern Pacific traveled. I looked around at the people in the car, and I knew they all believed in the ads. It had to be true.

Finally we arrived in Chicago. We picked up our grips and got off the train. Everyone was pushing and shoving to get off. When I stood on the platform, I had the sensation that I was still swaying and rolling down the railroad line. Everything was strange. There were hundreds of people on the platform. They were sitting and standing. Some were pacing, some sleeping from exhaustion, their heads resting on the bundles that held all their worldly possessions. Babies were screaming and mothers were rocking back and forth on invisible rockers.

There were groups of foreigners encircling an emigration agent and listening to him with every fiber of their beings so as not to miss one word of instruction.

There wasn't one railroad track, as at the Campbellsville depot, but so many I couldn't count them all. There were engines, trains, whistles, and bells. I choked from all the smoke mixed with the overwhelming stench of cattle cars from the stockyards.

One of the cattle trains pulled in and stopped on a track across from us. It jerked forward, screeched to a halt, then backed up. The cattle were packed in so tightly they couldn't move. There was an occasional bawling in protest. One poor cow had dropped her calf, but it was so crowded the calf had been trampled to death. The sight of that crumpled, bloody body made me sick and I knew I was going to retch. Suddenly, tears were running down my face. I didn't know whether I cried for a dead calf, or from loneliness at being so far from Kentucky, or in fear of this strange place.

"That's a fool thing to do, girl. That calf was going to the slaughter house anyway," said Cousin Thom. "There's no use all of us standing out in the heat. I'm going into the station to see about our next train. I'll be back in a little while."

Ma took my hand and held it tight. She was carrying Ella in her other arm. Ella was holding on for dear life. Ma led me away from the sight of the trampled calf and pointed out another train that had stopped along a sidetrack. It had a beautiful dining room. She pointed out the tables with their crisp, white cloths and silver bud vases, each holding a rose. Waiters in starched white jackets were setting the tables with crystal and silver. I knew she was trying to distract me from the cattle car, and I let her think that she had.

As we made our way down the platform, we saw that a crowd had gathered. They were taking turns peering in the window of a private car. Although no one was in the car, I could well imagine the handsome people in their lavish clothes who belonged there. The overstuffed chair and sofa were covered in red silk damask. The mahogany paneling had been hand rubbed until it shone. Gaslights on the side walls glistened and their many hanging prisms of crystal caught the sunlight in a rainbow of color. I knew no smoke would dare escape from those gaslights. I was trying to imagine what it would be like to ride in such a car when Ma said we needed to make our way back before Thom came.

Cousin Thom wasn't looking for us. He was nowhere to be seen. His "a little while" became longer and longer. Just as Ma was beginning to worry we saw him staggering through the crowd. He said he had happened on some of his card playing friends from the train who were passing the time with a few hands.

Finally our train for St. Paul came and everyone pushed and shoved to get aboard. I held Ma's hand, not wanting to be separated from her. We found a place, but this time the train was so crowded we didn't have the luxury of two seats. We all had to squeeze into one, and it was the backward seat. The family across, a father, mother, two young sons, and a baby, were German immigrants. They didn't speak much English, but they understood enough to realize that Cousin Thom didn't like it one bit that all these foreigners thought they could come to this country and take what didn't belong to them. What made them think they had earned the right to the best seat? They got up and offered to change seats.

Cousin Thom immediately slid across into the seat facing forward. As we settled in, Ella began to cry. The German mother offered her a piece of apple, but Cousin Thom said she couldn't have it because foreign food upset her stomach.

After that, we rode in silence.

Every evening at eight o'clock Northern Pacific pulled out of the St. Paul depot for the four-day trip to the coast. The train we caught was even more crowded than the one from Chicago. You could hear German, Swedish, Danish, even Russian. I guess those Northern Pacific ads had found their way into every corner of the world. The ads also boasted of a dining car, but none of us in the coaches could afford such elegance. We bought food from vendors who wandered up and down the aisles, selling their often old and spoiled wares for high prices. But what were we to do? The contents of our picnic basket were gone. Our life in Kentucky seemed long ago, almost a dream.

Finally the train chugged into the depot at Helena. We picked up our bundles and grips. Ma carried Ella so she wouldn't be trampled in the rush to get off the train. We were hot, tired and dirty, and we were in a strange place — all except Cousin Thom, who'd come back to find his fortune. Cousin Thom knew he'd be rich by now had he not wasted those years in Kentucky.

Helena had the hustle and bustle of a mining town. There were storekeepers and farmers, cowboys and Indians, saloon keepers and dance hall girls. You could tell by a single look what everyone did. As we walked down Main Street, I couldn't help staring at the people. I kept looking for someone I knew, but that was silly. I didn't know anyone in all of Montana, much less Helena. I looked in the distance and saw the mountains reaching up to the blue, blue sky. It was the bluest sky I had ever seen and it looked larger and deeper than the sky of Kentucky. I knew it couldn't be, yet it looked that way to me. As I walked down the street looking at the sky, I bumped into Ma, who had stopped in front of a white frame house with a sign in the window saying "Rooms." Suddenly all I wanted was a bed to lay down on. Ma said, "Just washing off that soot from the train will make me feel like a new woman."

But inside we discovered that if we wanted a bath we had to pump the water, put it on the stove to heat, then haul it up the stairs and pour it in a metal wash tub. Cousin Thom, too tired to help, said, "A little bit of dirt never hurt."

I helped Ma. After she bathed herself and Ella, it was my turn. Ma was right, nothing ever felt better. By the time I'd finished, the water was the color of ink. The rooming house had an outhouse in the back. I thought I would take the used bath water and pour it there, but when I opened the door, I changed my mind. It was August and still hot. The odor made me gag. There were flies everywhere. The landlady obviously had not cared about keeping it clean and the boarders had cared as little. The sooner we left there, the better.

We found a little house to rent on Highland Street, in the five-hundred block. Ma and I scrubbed it from top to bottom. After the dirt and filth of the rooming house, we wanted something clean. Cousin Thom had worked in the mines in Pony before he left Montana, but he found that they had played out while he was gone. Then he heard of another strike further west. From then on, he was gone most of the time chasing one rainbow after another. We had to move from the house on Highland to a smaller one on Eleventh Avenue. Thom came and went, either filled with excitement over a new strike or filled with despair at false rumors. We learned we couldn't count on him.

Ma started taking in sewing to make ends meet. I soon learned Helena, for I walked from one end of town to the other to pick up what needed to be mended; then it was my job to deliver the better-than-new pieces with Ma's perfect stitches. Word soon got around and before I knew it, I was picking up work at some of the fanciest homes in Helena. My favorite customer was Mrs. Chadwick who always had a smile and a kind word for me. She told me what "a fine young lady" she thought I was for helping my ma. The little Ma made from sewing barely made ends meet, so we also had a garden and a few chickens. When Cousin Thom did come to town, he'd take what Ma had in ready cash, always with promises that when he struck it rich we'd thank him for investing in our future.

Times were getting harder. Everywhere in Helena people were being laid off from their jobs. Most didn't even have the few pennies Ma charged for her painstaking needlecraft. We had to move again. With each move the house was smaller and the neighborhood shabbier. Cousin Thom came back and announced that since all the good strikes had already been made in Montana, he was going to Idaho, where there were new discoveries being made in silver. When he had made his fortune, he would send for us. He took the little money we had, saying he would need it more than we did since Idaho was far away. Anyway, Ma's sewing would take care of us until he sent for us.

Weeks turned into months and no word came from Cousin Thom. The Panic of '93 hit with full force. The bottom dropped out of the gold, cattle, and farm markets. What had appeared to be hard times the year before now seemed paradise. Our little houses seemed grand compared to the place we now had to move to on Eighth Avenue. But we were not alone. Families whose fathers had once had good jobs and who had lived in fine houses joined us in squalor and poverty.

Ma took in washing for there wasn't enough sewing to keep us fed. Now my job was not only to pick up the clothes for mending, but also the heavy bundles for washing and to return them neat and clean. I helped Ma make the strong lye soap we used. When we washed we'd build a fire in the back yard, then put on the large black metal tub. We fetched water from the pump, hauling it in buckets to the tub time and again until it was full. My hand was often raw from the rope handle of the bucket. We'd pour in the soft soap. When the water began to steam, we put the dirty clothes in, then took turns stirring with the big wooden paddle. We had a battling board where we laid the dirty clothes and beat them, trying to beat the dirt out. The grime from the mines and railyards didn't come out easy. Some nights my shoulders ached so I couldn't lay on my back, and I had to sleep on my stomach.

I could add to the family income by hiring out for the day for fifty cents. There were still a few families that could afford a hired girl, but most were desperate, especially the immigrants. There were many German girls younger and stronger than I was who would work for less than fifty cents a day. And, as if to punish us, the winter that year was even more severe than usual. Winters in Montana are never easy.

I was lucky to get a day job on a January day. It had started out bright, blue and clear, but by afternoon the sky darkened and the first big snowflakes began to fall. By mid-afternoon the winds were howling and the snow was packing into deep drifts. I thought I had better leave to get home to Ma and Ella.

The woman who had hired me said she expected a full day's work for a full day's wage, and that since I was leaving early, I couldn't expect my full fifty cents.

With the quarter she had given me tucked safely in my pocket, I trudged home. The snow was blowing so hard that I was blinded and bent almost double. My face stung and my fingers and toes ached. The cold cut like a knife to my very bone. Suddenly, I looked around and I was lost. A wave of panic engulfed me. Oh, no, I thought, I've got to keep my head. I'm fifteen. I can find my way home.

By the time I got home, I was half-frozen. My

feet hurt with each step. All I wanted to do was crawl into bed, pull up the covers and escape into sleep.

"Where have you been?" Ella screamed in her high five-year-old voice. "Ma's sick. I've been here all by myself."

Ma was in bed. Her body was on fire. She was thrashing about in delirium and coughing in spasms. I ran to the door and scooped up snow in a pan. As it melted, I dipped a cloth in the cold water to bathe Ma's head, trying to bring down her fever. I did this over and over again all night until, just before dawn, the fever finally broke. As the first rays of the winter sun broke the darkness of a cold night, I crawled onto the bed I shared with Ella and drifted to sleep, still hearing Ma's racking coughs.

As Ma got a little better, she became able to pull herself out of bed to do some sewing, but she wasn't strong enough to do wash. Her coughing kept getting worse. It seemed she couldn't have a minute's peace, for her body would shake with constant coughing. She got thinner and thinner. Her skin hung on her skeleton like clothes on a hanger. Her eyes sank back into dark circles. But she was so brave. She dragged herself along with a crutch under one arm, not having the strength to stand alone. I prayed for the warmth of summer to come, thinking it would make her feel better. When spring finally came, I insisted that she sit outside in the sunshine. I put an old rocking chair outside, then I'd half carry her out, thinking the fresh air would make her feel better, but nothing helped. When I could, I'd sit by her and remember with her the times we had sat on Grandpa Blue's front porch in the summer evenings and listened to the katydids. She needed more and more medicine, but it was expensive. I was working as a hired girl in the day and doing mending at night. We couldn't afford to lose the few sewing customers Ma had left. I knew my stitches didn't look as neat as Ma's but no one ever said anything.

By late summer, Ma couldn't get out of bed. I'd carry her outside and put her in her chair before I left for work. It wasn't hard for she weighed almost nothing. Then one of the neighbors would carry her in. We had good neighbors. I guess when you have nothing, everyone is bonded together by need. It was Ella's job to stay with Ma all day and fetch for her when she wanted anything. She would run get one of the neighbors when Ma was ready to come inside.

The Keiths lived across the street and the Wards lived around the corner. Both were a Godsend for I knew while I was at work that Grandma Keith would come over to check on Ma and Ella. Grandmere, as they called her, had left France as a young girl, but her thick accent still lingered and when she became upset or excited, she would slip into her native tongue. She came in the morning, sat and visited with Ma and when Ma tired Grandmere would have Ella fetch her strong grandson, Adelphus, to carry Ma indoors and lay her in her bed.

In the afternoon, Mrs. Ward came by, always bringing something for Ma and Ella to eat, a little soup, a piece of cold chicken, maybe even some of her famous pumpkin pie. In happier times, before the Panic of '93, Mr. Ward had had a good job selling Singer sewing machines, and people had had the money to buy them. The Wards had lived in the better part of town, where Mrs. Ward was well-known for her hospitality. Of all the good dishes she made, her best was pumpkin pie; in fact, her youngest son loved it so much, he got the nickname Punk Ward. Punk, who was a little older than Ella, often came with his mother when she checked on Ma.

It was a long summer but by early September there was a hint of autumn in the air. The early mornings were cool and crisp and as soon as the sun set, evening's chill set in. When I took Ma outside and wrapped her shawl around her bony shoulders, I realized how much she had shrunk for the fabric could easily have wound round her twice. She reminded me of a scarecrow out in the fields.

We'd had one light freeze, then the September weather warmed into what everyone said was an Indian Summer. The leaves were suddenly a glorious rainbow of color. The bright reds, yellows, and oranges seemed to brighten Ma's spirit and the return of warmth strengthened her. When I left for my day work on the morning of September twenty-fourth, I felt better about Ma than I had in weeks. I was late returning and the house was dark. When I went in I could hear her coughing. I hurried to her room and lit a lamp. The dim light reflected from a thin shiny trickle of blood oozing from the corner of her mouth and dripping off her chin. I screamed and screamed for Ella. Where was she? I rushed out into the street as Ella came around the corner with Carrie Keith, who was also six. They had been up the street playing.

"Where have you been?" I cried. "Don't you know you're not ever to leave Ma? She's sick. She's coughing up blood. How could you?"

I didn't realize it but I was shaking Ella violently by the shoulders.

"Stop it, Mamie. You're hurting me. I was just up the street playing with Carrie. I wasn't gone long. I never have any fun."

"Fun. Ma may be dying. Now, you get in there. Don't you move. Don't you take your eyes off of Ma. I'm going to run and get Dr. Barbour."

I ran all the way up Hoback to Sixth Street and all the way down the big hill on Sixth Street to the Power Building. I had a catch in my side. With each breath, there was a sharp pain in my chest. My legs felt as if they were made of rubber, but I couldn't stop. I willed one foot in front of the other as I ran. A light shone under the door of Room 203, so I knew Dr. Barbour was still there. I pounded on the door. The moment it opened, I grabbed his hand and began pulling him after me.

"It's Ma, Dr. Barbour. She's real sick."

"Just a minute, child, I have to get my bag."

When we got home, Grandmere Keith was there. She was holding Ella in her arms and rocking her. Mrs. Ward was sitting next to Ma's bed.

Dr. Barbour set down his black bag. He opened it and pulled out his stethoscope to listen at Ma's chest. He took Ma's wrist and felt it, then he shook his head.

"I can barely get a heartbeat or pulse. I'm afraid there's not much I can do."

I sat in the chair where Mrs. Ward had been next to Ma. I took her hand hoping that strength would flow from my body to hers. The minutes dragged on into hours. I must have dozed off, for a sudden movement awoke me. Dawn was creeping across the heavens and turning the black room pale gray. Ma's hand had dropped out of mine.

"Oh, no!" I screamed.

Dr. Barbour walked to the bed, felt for Ma's pulse, then ever so gently pulled the sheet over her head as if not to awaken her from a deep sleep.

I jerked the sheet out of his hand, pulled the covers back, grabbed Ma and held her in my arms. She was already cold. Her eyes stared up at me, but they saw nothing. I held her and rocked her back and forth like a baby. Her poor hair was so thin and straggly. I remembered how the Kentucky sunshine had once gleamed on it.

Dr. Barbour was writing in a little book. "She

died of phthisis," he said.

"Phthisis?'" I repeated numbly.

"It means simply wasting away due to consumption."

"But I gave her the medicine. I spent almost every penny I earned on her medicine. Why didn't it stop her from dying?"

"Come on now, Mamie," said Mrs. Keith, "You got lots to do. You've got to make arrangements for the funeral and burial. You've got to get the minister to say a few words at her grave. Holding your ma in your arms won't bring her back. You need to lay her back down so we can put pennies on her lids so they'll stay closed."

I didn't see what difference it would make whether her lids were open or closed. The beautiful blue eyes I remembered would never see anything again.

The next morning I went to Herrmann and Company. When I opened the front door, the bell above it tinkled. No one came. I guessed Mr. Hermann was in the back room. I walked down the sawdust aisle. There was furniture stacked on either side and display tables piled high with gloves and candles, hats and laces, bolts of material. You could buy just about anything at Herrmann and Company's Furniture and Funeral Parlor. In the back room they stored the coffins and did the embalming. I knocked on the back room door. I didn't want to go in there in case it had a strange body. Mr Hermann opened the door.

"I'm Mamie Mann. I've come to see about a

coffin and burial for my ma."

As I walked into the room, I noticed a form covered with a sheet, lying on a table in the middle of the room. Soon Ma would be lying on that very table. I wondered what they did to a body before they put it in a coffin. Suddenly, I felt faint but I couldn't think about that. I had lots to do so Ma could have a proper burial.

I looked over all the coffins. There was one was made of rosewood that looked warm and polished. I thought Ma wouldn't get so cold and lonely in that box. I told Mr. Hermann I wanted the rosewood coffin.

"I'm sorry, girl, but Lewis and Clark County will only pay twenty dollars and fifty cents for a pauper's burial and that covers a pine box. The rosewood is twenty-two dollars and fifty cents."

I didn't have two dollars, but I knew Ma deserved the rosewood box.

"That's all right, Mr. Hermann. I'll get the other two dollars. Ma's not going to be buried in a plain pine box. She's to have the rosewood."

With all the dignity of my sixteen years, I turned and walked out of the back room down the long aisle. I heard the bell again as I opened and closed the front door. I hurried down the street. I didn't want Mr. Hermann to ask me how I was going to pay the other two dollars for I didn't know.

I felt that it was only fitting for Ma to have an obituary in the newspaper. I walked to the *Helena Daily Herald*.

When I entered I was overwhelmed by the strong smell of ink and the loud voice of the hand-cranked press. I stood by the counter until a balding man appeared. He had on a green visor, thick glasses and he was coatless. I could see the wide rubberbands that held up his once-white shirt sleeves. Ink was smeared on his shirt, and on his cheeks and hands as well.

"What can I do for you?" he asked as he wiped his hands on a dirty towel.

"I've come to tell you of the death of T. Annie Allen. Her funeral is tomorrow at two o'clock at the Helena Cemetery, and she leaves two grieving daughters, and I want that in today's newspaper."

The man looked at me for a moment, then he took a pencil from behind his ear, pulled out a piece of paper and started writing.

I thanked him and left for the Methodist Church. The Manns had always been Methodist. We had been a lot more active before we moved to Montana and Ma had gotten sick. I knew she'd want a minister to say a few words, and I knew she'd rest better if he did.

I visited with the minister and asked him if he would recite the verse that went, "In my Father's house there are many mansions," for Ma deserved to be in one.

I had only one more task that day. I walked to the cemetery. The grave digger was already on plot number two-twenty-three in the Glendale paupers' section of the cemetery where weeds grew knee-high. For those who had money, there were headstones. I knew Ma would not have a headstone. It would be all I could do to beg pennies and nickels from the neighbors to collect the two dollars for Ma's rosewood box. I turned and walked home. I wasn't a beggar and I didn't want to do it, but Ma had to have that rosewood coffin. The neighbors understood. It was hard times, but they shared what little they had. They seemed even to understand my determination for Ma to be buried in a rosewood coffin.

The next morning, I was up early. I lit a fire in the cook stove, pumped a bucket full of water, and put it on to heat. When the water was boiling, I spooned in some soft lye soap, then plopped in Ella's and my best dresses. I scrubbed them, then hung them out to dry. I poured out the dirty water and pumped a fresh bucket. After hauling it and heating it, I called for Ella. I poured the warm water into a wash tub.

"Ella, we're going to be shining clean for Ma's buryin'."

Ella screamed as I scrubbed her elbows and knees, even louder as I washed her hair, crying that I was getting soap in her eyes.

"If you'd stay still, it wouldn't get in your eyes," I explained through clenched teeth while I tried to hang on to her slippery, squirming body.

"Oh, you're always so bossy, Mamie."

Finally, Ella was clean. Her hair squeaked as I pulled it through my forefinger and thumb to make sure all the soap was out. I toweled her hair then rolled it on rags to dry. Ella's hair was dark chestnut like Ma's while mine was honey blonde, but we both had Ma's big blue eyes. "Now, Ella, don't you go outside and get dirty."

I knew I had to keep an eye on her even while I bathed and washed and rolled my own hair for she would slip outside to play and get all dirty. She didn't understand. She didn't understand that Ma was dead, and was to be buried at two o'clock today. She didn't understand that we had to look our best.

The hours crawled by. I knew Ella and I would have to leave early for the cemetery if we were going to have time to pick a few wild flowers that were still in bloom along the road out to the graveyard. I unrolled Ella's hair from the rags and as if by magic her head was covered with bouncing curls. I dressed her in her stiff starched dress and tied the bow at the back at her waist, then I dressed.

We arrived at the cemetery long before any one else. There weren't many flowers and the few that we could find were scraggly and pitiful, the last hanging on before winter. The Wards and the Keiths arrived. A horse-drawn hearse could be heard before we saw it, for it had a wheel that loudly protested the rough cemetery road. The grave digger jumped down from the seat next to the driver and helped him lower the rosewood box.

They hauled it over to the freshly dug grave, then each took the end of a heavy rope. Inch by inch, they lowered the coffin into the ground. When it was no longer visible, I heard it hit bottom. They loosened the rope and pulled it free. After dropping the rope, the grave digger picked up a shovel and started shoveling dirt back into the hole.

"No," I cried. "We must wait for the preacher to say a few words."

"Girl, I can't wait. I've got two more burials today," The grave digger replied as he threw dirt on Ma's rosewood coffin.

I watched his dirty hands heaving the shovel back and forth, back and forth in a long practiced rhythm.

The grave was full and he was patting the mound of dirt with the back of his shovel when we heard the preacher's buggy bouncing up the road.

"Sorry to be late, but a longtime regular parishioner needed me," the preacher said as he slowly climbed out of his buggy. He walked over to the grave and opened a well-worn Bible. He began in his singsong voice.

Soon, I wasn't listening to him at all for the words inside my head were too loud.

What will I do? I'll never see Ma again. I'll never look into her eyes or hear her voice. I was suddenly back on Grandpa Blue's front porch and I could hear the squeak of his rocking chair and the song of the katydids, and could smell the smoke of his pipe.

I was jolted to the present by the preacher's Amen. Ella's little arms were wrapped around my legs, and she was shaking with sobs. I got on my knees and put my arms around her.

"We'll be all right, Ella. We've got each other."

The preacher came over and patted us both on the head.

"The Keiths tell me your pa's gone to Idaho to work in the silver mines."

"He's my step-pa. Ella's pa."

"Well, we'll get word to him about your ma's death." The preacher got back into his buggy, picked up the reins and clucked to his old sway-back gray nag, who knew well the way back to town.

The Keiths and the Wards clustered around patting us and giving us words of encouragement. Ella clung to Grandmere Keith. They said it was time to leave, but I couldn't.

"Mamie, I want to go home," cried Ella, clutching Grandmere Keith's neck.

"You go on. I can't leave yet. I'll be along in a little bit."

When everyone was gone, I laid the wild flowers on Ma's grave one by one. I could feel the tears dripping off my chin and could taste their strange salty twang on my tongue. Soon my crying became body shaking sobs and my sobbing turned to wailing.

"Oh, Ma, what am I going to do?"

I threw myself on her grave and sobbed until I had dry heaves.

Then suddenly I knew I would make it, no matter what it took.

"Ma, you'll never be cold again. You'll never hurt again from coughing. I know you and Grandpa Blue are together, warm and happy."

The gray twilight had engulfed the streets by the time I reached the Keiths. Ella was sound asleep in Grandmere Keith's ample lap.

Somehow the preacher's grapevine reached Thom Allen, for in a few days he showed up at our front door.

Ella ran to hug him excitedly.

He didn't say anything about Ma's illness, nor her death. He didn't want to know anything about it.

"Ella, I'm ashamed to see you in such rags. Nancy, can't you dress her better than that? It's okay, Ella honey, you're coming back to Idaho with me."

"Isn't Mamie coming with us?" Ella asked.

"She's no blood kin of mine. I don't have to be burdened with her. She's sixteen and can take care of herself if she has any gumption at all," he said.

"It will be all right, Ella. I can take care of myself. You have to go with your pa because he is your pa. Maybe he can take better care of you than I can." Ella came running to me and threw her arms around my legs. I pried the little fingers loose and held her hands, looked into her teary eyes and explained, "It's not forever and ever. Before you know it, you'll be grown, and we can see each other. You need to go to school and learn to read and write, so you can write me a letter. I need to find a job, a full-time place, not just day work."

I went in and packed her few things. I knew the sooner they left the better, for to prolong their leaving would make it harder. Soon all of Ella's things were in a cardboard box that I tied with a string. Ella picked up the box and started out the door behind Thom Allen. Halfway out the door, she put the box down, ran back and threw her arms around me.

"It's not forever and ever. I'll learn to write real quick." She picked up her box and ran after Thom Allen.

The house was so quiet. I kept listening for Ma's coughing from the other room. No sound came. I kept listening for Ella's high voice to ring out throughout the house, but it was still. I was sixteen and plenty old enough to take care of myself, but that didn't chase away the lost feeling.

I laid awake most of the night trying to figure out what I could do. When I did doze off, Ma was there in my dreams, but she wasn't sick and frail and in pain. She was strong and healthy, happily singing one of her favorite songs as she worked in a garden filled with beautiful flowers. When I woke, the songs, the flowers and Ma all vanished. I snuggled under the covers, not wanting to get out of the warm spot in the bed and into the chill of morning. But waiting wouldn't make it any easier. I knew I had to leave this house and start a new life. I shivered as I dressed, not only from cold but from fear.

I went to the Keiths after I had dressed and they asked me to stay and share their breakfast. Their kitchen was always warm and welcoming. I started to say no for I knew no one had anything extra to spare in our neighborhood, but the smell of Grandmere's bread baking and the little pains of hunger betrayed me. Before I knew it, I was sitting at the kitchen table breaking off the hot end of a loaf and feeling the soft center of the piece melt in my mouth at first taste.

"I've got to find a full-time job. I can't live in that little house any longer all alone, and I don't need a house when it's just me. I need a live-in job for a hired girl."

"Well, you will stay with us until you find work," Mrs. Keith insisted.

"I couldn't do that." I said.

"I won't take no," Mrs. Keith said determinedly.

So I packed up my few things and moved in with the Keiths. I did all I could to help out in order to repay them for their hospitality, but I knew I had to get a job soon. One day Mr. Keith came home with word from Mrs. Chadwick that Ben and Lela Roberts were in town from Cascade looking for a hired girl to help out in the kitchen and with their three children. Mrs. Chadwick had recommended me for the job.

"Mr. Keith, I want to leave for Cascade today. I've got to get that job before someone else."

Mr. Keith said he'd take me to Cascade and put

a good word in for me since he also knew the Robertses.

I rode up front with Mr. Keith on the buckboard with my few belongings bouncing in the back. I looked ahead, waiting for Cascade to appear. I didn't look back. I remembered that when I was a little girl in Sunday School they said if you look back you could be turned into a pillar of salt. I was never ever going to look back.

3

Charlie

THE ROBERTSES HIRED ME. And they were so good to me that I called them Ma and Pa Roberts. It's funny when I think back on it, but both Ma and Pa Roberts were only two years older than Charlie. I never thought about calling Charlie "Pa." There was something about being with Charlie Russell that made me feel special. When I was with him, I could tell him anything, and he seemed to understand. He didn't make fun of me for the way I talked when I told him I hadn't had much "schoolin.'" He just laughed and said he hadn't had much "schoolin'" either. How could adding numbers help him capture the glowing rays of sunset or spelling a word make a wild bronc any easier to put on canvas?

"Schoolin' ain't important. It's what you know and feel that is."

But schooling was important to Charlie's folks.

Charlie's pa had gone to a big school back East called Yale University. Charlie's ma and pa always hoped Charlie would get a good education at that Yale University and come into the family business. But it never meant anything to Charlie. All he ever dreamed about was being a cowboy and an artist. When he was only four years old, he followed a man with a trained bear. When he came home, he took some mud off of the heel of his shoe and fashioned himself a bear. He showed it to his sister Sue. She giggled with delight. Charlie was surrounded with brothers but had only one sister and it was a joy to have her love his mud bear.

"Oh, Charlie, you're so smart," cried Sue. "How'd you ever make a bear out of mud? And it looks just like a bear."

He took it in and gave it to his mother, and she patted him on the head and gave him a hug and told him how smart he was.

As the years passed and he spent his time drawing pictures of cowboys and Indians, horses and bears, on his school papers, his mother's delight in his drawings lessened.

"Charlie, you have a God-given ability to draw, but that will never earn you a living. You must get an education if you are going to come into the family business. The Russells have an important place in this community. They have always accepted their responsibility, and you must accept yours and go to school and learn. Drawing is a hobby. You've got to stop being so wrapped up in it all the time. Your teacher has talked to your father about the poor quality of your work. He said you are often absent. And when you are in the classroom, your mind is someplace else. Charlie, you must stop this daydreaming and get down to work or they will never accept you at Yale."

The more his mother scolded, the more Charlie retreated into his world of make-believe.

When he was nine, he got his first pony. Charlie could get on his pony and make believe he was a cowboy as he rode all over the Russells' land on Oak Hill.

Oak Hill was his family's home. Charlie's grandpa, James Russell, came from Virginia to Cape Girardeau. After his first wife died, he went on to St. Louis where he bought hundreds of acres of land from his brother, William. That was in 1811. There, he not only discovered a beautiful young woman twenty years his junior, but he also discovered coal on his lands. Countless immigrants, also seeking a new beginning, were happy to come and dig his coal. They lived in little narrow white wood frame houses with bright blue, or yellow or green trim shutters. From sunup to sundown they worked in the coal mines. On warm summer evenings, they would sit out on their front porches and remember the old days in Germany or Italy. Someone would start singing an old familiar song. Soon their neighbors' voices would join in, for the singing made their homesickness go away. Or maybe hearing their native tongue made this new world seem less foreign. They could close their eyes and make believe they were back home. In the winter, they would sit by their fireplaces, trying to keep warm, and decide it was better to go to bed early and snuggle with the wife to keep warm. Always there were lots of children born in the late summer.

Lucy Bent Russell, Grandpa James' beautiful young wife, decided a school must be built in Oak Hill for all the children. Because of the vast difference in their ages, it wasn't surprising that James Russell left this earth years before Lucy. Lucy called her son Charles Silas home from Yale and his formal education was terminated for it was time he accepted his responsibility and came into the family business. She also called upon her son-in-law, George Ward Parker, who had married her youngest child, Russella Lucy. Even if you had not been born a Russell but merely married one, you owed the family an obligation to help in the business. Lucy called them together and laid out a plan whereby the family business would not only survive but flourish. Lucy had brought a family-owned wholesale-retail jewelry firm to the Russells when she married. Now was the time to expand into an import-export business. She turned acres and acres of Oak Hill into vineyards and established the Oak Hill Fruit Company and a wholesale grocery. Afraid that someday the coal would play out, she expanded the Fire Clay Works, reasoning that the Russells owed these immigrants a future with a job, for hadn't they come half around the world to work for them? And if you were a Russell, you met your responsibility.

Grandma Lucy died just a few days before Charlie's seventh birthday. He heard his folks talking about the letter she had left with instructions for her funeral. She authorized the Probate Court to pay one hundred and fifty dollars for a metal casket, ninety dollars for the rental of five carriages, twenty-five dollars and fifty cents for a hearse, seventeen dollars for the purchase of silk gloves and a cape and ten dollars for digging her grave at Bellefontaine Cemetery.

Charlie rode in one of the carriages with his mother and father, his sister Sue, older brother Silas and younger brothers, Ed and Guy. His mother was holding baby Wolfert, wrapped heavily in a blanket It was bitterly cold but it was their responsibility to all stand next to the open grave and listen to the minister from the Episcopal Church say the last words. Charlie's teeth were chattering. As they covered the one-hundred-and-fifty-dollar metal casket with earth, tears rolled down his face. He remembered not the matriarch of the family who wisely managed its business, but a kindly old woman smellingwonderfully of perfumed face powder who held him on her lap and tell him stories of her brothers.

Grandma Lucy had told Charlie about her brother Robert, who was captured, killed, and scalped by wild Comanche Indians in Colorado Territory. The story never bored Charlie, and he wanted to hear it over and over. But Grandma Lucy would move on to another story about brother George, who was a fur trader with the American Fur Company and went into wild and untamed wilderness in search of furs. Her brother Charles became governor of New Mexico, but his fame and success was cut short by Pueblo Indians who killed and scalped him in Taos. Brother William had founded Bent's Fort, married an Indian woman and had a half-breed son.

When Charlie rode his pony in Tower Grove Park, he would make believe he was with his Uncle Robert. It was so wooded in Tower Grove that you couldn't see the wild Comanches sneaking up behind the trees, but Charlie could, and he saved his Uncle Robert just in time. He'd jump off his horse, throw himself on the ground, and warn his uncle to do the same just as the screaming hordes of wild Comanches came running from all directions. But Charlie was a sure shot with his stick and he would always save his Uncle Robert — except sometimes he would save his Uncle Charles instead.

When he got tired of fighting Indians, he could always get up on his pony and become a Pony Express rider. Cousin Jim's father, William Fulkerson, a former Pony Express rider, had taught him how to ride, how to jump out of a saddle in a split second, and how to jump on a horse quick as lightning. But the best game of all – better than being an Indian fighter, better than being a Pony Express rider – was being a cowboy. Charlie herded his imaginary cows by the hour.

Often he didn't go to school, but instead went down to the wharfs along the Mississippi River. He loved the smell of the wet wooden docks and the sounds of the whistles blowing, the paddle wheels churning, the dock hands screaming orders, and the Negroes singing their old plantation songs as they hauled heavy bales of cotton. He loved the color, the activity, the hustle and bustle, and best of all, he loved listening to the men going out west.

Each time his father found out that Charlie was skipping school to spend his time on the wharf, he punished him. Afterward Charlie would stay in school for several days. He'd walk to the school at Oak Hill with his cousin Dan. The dogs in the neighborhood were always happy when Charlie was back in school. He would share his lunch with them, then fill his empty lunch pail with beeswax so he could model figures at school. He taught himself to make horses or buffalo or bears with his hands out of sight below the desk.

The summer that he was twelve, Charlie finally decided to run away, work on a farm outside of St. Louis, and earn enough money to pay his own way West. He talked his best friend, Archie Douglas, into coming with him, but one night was all Archie could take away from his home. When he returned, his mother convinced him to go and tell Mrs. Russell where Charlie was.

"Mrs. Russell, Ma'am," Archie hesitated, "my

ma says I should come over here and tell you that Charlie's okay since you're worried sick. He's just outside of town working on a farm to make enough to go out West."

"Charles," said Charlie's mother, "you'll have to go out to that farm and bring Charlie home."

"No, Mary Elizabeth. I'll not. I do indeed intend to visit the farm where he's working, but not to bring him home. I'm going to tell the farmer to work him all summer, to give him the hardest jobs he can think of, and when Charlie comes home we're going to act as if he hasn't been gone at all. Maybe he'll get some sense into his head and get down to his books and give up this nonsense about being a cowboy."

After working hard all summer, Charlie had only saved eleven dollars, which wouldn't take him very far west. At home his parents behaved as if he had never been gone.

The next couple of years came and went without Charlie doing any better in school. If anything he was spending more time at the docks on the Mississippi listening to the stories of adventurers from the West or to the dreams of those planning to join them.

"Mary Elizabeth," said Charlie's father, "we must do something about Charlie. He's fourteen and if we don't do something soon, it will be too late. I think a military school is the only solution. We've got to get him away from here where he can concentrate on his studies." Burlington Military School in New Jersey seemed the ideal solution.

But it was far from ideal from Charlie's point of view.

Later Charlie told me that he spent most of his time in the guard house at Burlington. He learned right away that if he drew a cartoon of one of his teachers, a fellow student would gladly do his homework in exchange for it. But somehow the cartoons always found their way into the hands of the teachers and Charlie found his way into the guardhouse. A semester was all that either Burlington or Charlie could stand.

When Charlie returned to St. Louis, he spent even more time at the docks as if to catch up. Then Charlie's pa ran into an old family friend on the streets of St. Louis. Pike Miller was in St. Louis on a short visit from his home in Montana. Talking with him, Charlie's folks decided to change their strategy.

"Charlie, your mother and I have decided to let you go out to Montana with our friend Pike Miller. He'll keep an eye on you in exchange for your helping him out on his sheep ranch."

Charlie was so excited that he didn't say that he had no desire to be a sheepherder. All he had ever wanted to be was a cowboy, not a caretaker of smelly muttonheads, but he was afraid to say anything lest his folks not let him go.

He and Pike Miller boarded the train in St. Louis for Ogden, Utah.

The Russells watched the train pull out of the

station and disappear down the track. "Mary, stop crying," said Charlie's pa. "Charlie will be back before school starts in the fall. He'll get this nonsense out of his system and settle down and this will turn out to be the best thing we've ever done for him."

What a trip! Outside of Ogden a group of Indians waved the train to a screeching halt. One of the more experienced passengers told Charlie that the railway had made an agreement with the Indians. In return for right of way they got free trips. And if there wasn't much else to do why not ride back and forth on the "big iron horse?"

From Ogden, Charlie and Pike took the stage coach to Helena. Charlie asked to ride on top with the driver.

As they bounced along, Charlie thought he had never seen mountains so high or so beautiful, nor a sky so big and blue. The sky stretched from one end of the earth to the other.

Charlie's folks had given him money for the trip plus some money for a horse when he got there.

"Charlie, I know your folks gave you money for a horse. You know nothing about horse flesh or how to deal. Give me the money and I'll go to the stables and make a deal for you," said Pike Miller.

Charlie reluctantly turned over his money. Later, when he saw what Pike Miller had spent it on, he was sick. He had dreamed of a pinto that would run like the wind but instead he saw Pike Miller leading two old brown wagon-pullers up the street. To add insult to injury, Pike had Charlie drive the wagon filled with supplies behind Charlie's two old broken down horses to the ranch.

When they got there, Charlie was tired and hungry and sore. He fell into his bunk. When he awoke, all he could hear was the constant irritating baa-baa-baa of smelly muttonheads.

At breakfast Pike told Charlie to take the sheep out to graze. "Now, Charlie, there is a big rock on the rise to the right of the meadow. You keep your eye on that rock. When the sun goes down behind it, you come in."

That's exactly what Charlie did. He took the sheep out. He found the rock. He sat down and took out some paper to do a little drawing. He kept his eye on the rock and as soon as the sun went behind it, he came in.

"Where's the sheep? Where's the sheep?" screamed Pike Miller, like a crazy man.

After that Charlie got all of the dirtiest, meanest jobs at Pike Miller's, and on a sheep ranch there are plenty of them.

In town one day he heard about a horse wrangler's job being offered at the stage coach relay station. He went to Pike and said, "I quit. I've had enough of all of these stinkin' sheep."

"I won't say I'll be sorry to see you go," said Pike. "Where'd you get a place?"

"There's a job at the stage coach station, wrangling horses," replied Charlie.

As he rode up to the station, he saw Pike Miller riding away. When he went in and applied, he wasn't surprised that he was turned down.

"Are you that ornery Russell kid that lost all them sheep?"

So Charlie was without a job, without money, and without anything to eat. All he had was two old brown wagon-pulling horses. He decided to go down by the stream and camp. He could ponder what he was going to do and the horses could graze. Charlie built a fire as he gazed into the flames he heard the sudden creak of a saddle behind him. He looked around and there sat a mountain man.

"What's you doin', kid?"

"I'm campin'," responded Charlie.

"I don't smell nothin' cookin'."

"I didn't say I was cookin', I said I was campin'." And before Charlie knew it, his whole story was spilling out, one word tumbling over the other faster and faster. He told the mountain man that all his life he had dreamed about being a cowboy, but it just so happened that the only friend his ma and pa had in Montana owned a sheep ranch.

The mountain man's name was Jake Hoover.

"Listen, kid, I know what it's like to be sixteen and without a job or money or even something to eat. When I first came out to Montana, I was full of dreams of finding a strike and making it rich in the gold fields. As a matter of fact, I really did find a strike, but I was young and gullible. I didn't know how to protect what was mine. Two city fellows slickered me out of my find. Now, I've got an elk steak that's far too big for me to eat by myself, so why don't you come over to my camp and we'll talk about it?"

Charlie went over to Jake Hoover's camp and they talked about it. Jake invited Charlie up to his cabin in the hills. Charlie accepted and they talked about it for two years.

Jake Hoover earned his living by hunting. He furnished fresh meat to the ranchers down in the valley who couldn't take time — or didn't want to take the time — to hunt. Charlie couldn't quite bring himself to raise a rifle, sight a beautiful wild creature, then pull the trigger. But once Jake had his kill, that was different, for the animal became Jake's living. To carry his share of the load, Charlie skinned and cleaned the animals. He saw how all the muscles lay.

In the evenings, Jake would tell Charlie stories of the West as it had been when he arrived. Jake was a great story teller and Charlie was a great listener, so Jake talked and Charlie drew pictures. If they didn't look right to Jake he'd make Charlie draw them over and over again.

After two years, Charlie decided to go back to St. Louis for a visit. He especially wanted to show off his soft shirt, red silk half-breed sash, high heeled boots and

Stetson hat.

The front door bell of the Russell home was answered by a longtime servant who hardly recognized this sunburned cowboy as the young master Charles.

Charlie sashayed into the front parlor.

"Howdy," he said in his best Montana style. The house was suddenly alive with activity. Everyone came rushing to welcome him home with hugs and laughter.

"You certainly have changed," said Charlie's brother Silas.

"Where did you get all those rings?" asked his sister Sue.

"It's good to have you home, son."

Suddenly, there was a hush as Charlie's mother came sweeping down the stairs. Tears streamed down her face.

"Oh, thank God you're finally home, Charlie. We thought you'd be home last year. I guess it just took longer than we thought it would for you to get the West out of your system. We all missed you so! But that's all right for it's behind us." She cried and held him again in a tight hug as if to make sure that this dream she had dreamt for two long years had really come true.

There was a long silence.

"Ma'am, I've come for a visit – just a visit – I wanted to see all of you and have you see how well the West agrees with me. I ain't ever going to get the West out of my system. Why, it's bigger and better than I ever dreamed." With that, Charlie started telling them what had happened to him since last they saw him. Even then, "that ornery Russell kid that lost all them sheep" could really tell a story and before they knew it, he had them all laughing.

The days flew by. Charlie wanted to see and be seen by all he remembered. He could not wait to get out to Hazel Dell and see his cousin Jim, as well as Colonel William Houston Fulkerson. From the second Jim saw Charlie, from the minute he first heard Charlie's stories of the West, he pleaded with his father to let him go with his cousin back to Montana.

Jim's pleading finally prevailed on the Colonel and he was allowed to accompany Charlie back to Montana. They hadn't been in Montana but a few short days when Jim was bitten by a tick and began running a high fever. Charlie got the doctor as fast as he could.

"There's only one thing to do with this high a fever and that's to bleed him and make a poultice for his eyes," said the doc.

"I can't see how losing blood could help anyone get better," said Charlie.

"Are you a doctor as well as a would-be artist, young man?"

Even in Jim's feverish state, he screamed out when the leeches bit into his flesh, but that was nothing to the terrible howl when the doctor put the poultice on his eyes.

"There must be something wrong," yelled

Charlie as he tried to wipe Jim's eyes.

"Well, it's not my fault. Different patients react differently to medication," the doctor said defensively as he left.

Charlie sat up all night with his cousin. In the morning, Jim rallied a little out of his feverish stupor and suddenly shrieked "Charlie, I can't see." The doctoring had blinded him. Charlie ran all the way to the telegraph office to send for the Colonel.

The Colonel and Cornelia arrived in Helena as quickly as they could, but there was nothing they could do. Charlie parted from them in shared grief.

He struck out for Jake Hoover's alone. But luck was with him. On his way, he ran into John Cabler with the 12 Z and V outfit, which was looking for a night wrangler for horses, and they hired Charlie on. Now Charlie could ride all night and draw all day. When the outfit got into town, Charlie would go into a shop or bar and ask to put a picture up in a window or on a wall. He might even buy a whole round of drinks with just one picture. Pretty soon, people were talking about the "cowboy artist."

In the winters, Charlie either shared a shack in town with some of his cowboy friends or stayed in the bunk house of one of the ranches. He often told me about the terrible winter of '86 when he was at the OH Bar ranch. There had had an early thaw and the snow had started to melt, then on Christmas Eve a hard freeze turned the freshly melted snow into a solid block of ice.

There was no way that a cow could paw through it for forage.

One evening as they all sat around the table in the bunk house playing cards the door burst open and a grizzly old cowpuncher stomped in, knocking snow off his boots.

"Hey, close that door before we all freeze to death," yelled one of the card players.

"Don't talk to me about freezing," said Ol' Joe as he pulled off his gloves and blew on his fingers. He stomped over to the fireplace. His salt and pepper beard, frozen stiff, began to thaw and melted ice ran down his cheeks and dripped off his chin.

"It's miserable out there. I've never seen it this bad. Why, you can stack up them frozen carcasses of dead cows just like cord wood. It's so bad some of those cows are calving early and those poor little babies don't have a chance. They're frozen before their little ol' tiny bodies hit the ground." The hardened old face glistened with either tears or melted snow.

"I've got to write a letter to Louis Kaufman and tell him how bad it is. He's part owner in this spread," sighed Jesse Phelps. "I don't know what to say."

Charlie pulled out a little piece of paper no bigger than a postcard and started to draw. He drew one lone cow huddled in the swirling snow with her ribs pushing out against her skin. He called it "Waiting For the Chinook" — the warm wind that blows in and melts the snow. He showed his little picture to Jesse.

Jesse said, "Heck, no. I don't need to send no letter, I'll just send this picture."

Pretty soon lots of cowboys had heard of that little picture, and they were all talking about Charlie Russell, the cowboy painter.

In '93 Charlie got to ride on the cattle train to Chicago. He was proud to be chosen for the job because it proved he was darn good at cowboying. On the way back he stopped off in St. Louis, as usual not missing a chance to be with his ma and pa, his brothers and sister Sue. While he was in St. Louis, he took some of his pictures to William Niedringhaus, who owned a big ranch out in Montana. Niedringhaus had made lots of money in the enameled pots and pans business. When he saw Charlie's pictures, he was more than willing to be relieved of some of that money in exchange for pictures that showed the Montana he remembered and loved. He offered Charlie a commission to paint him more pictures. When Charlie got back to Montana he decided to give up cowboying and paint full time.

But it didn't work out like Charlie planned. You see, every time Charlie picked up his brushes and started to paint seriously one of his cowboying friends would drop by. They all loved swapping tales with Charlie, so they'd invite him down to the Mint or the Silver Dollar to have a drink. Well, Charlie would clean his brushes and put them up. He'd go down to have a drink, for that was just the neighborly thing to do. And after a friend has bought you a drink, then you buy him one. Such a kind gesture can't go unheeded so he returns the courtesy and buys you a second drink. Pretty soon Charlie's hands were shaking. Doc Sweat told Charlie that "liquor and paint don't mix," and that he'd better get out of Great Falls and away from his good friends.

That was why Charlie came up to Cascade. And that's how we met, and began walking along the river in the late afternoons or early evenings. I told Charlie everything. When I told him about losing the Purdy Mare because I didn't have the twenty dollars, he took out his handerchief, wiped my eyes, gave me a kiss and surprised me by giving me one of his two horses, his favorite, Monte. When I told him about my ma's burying, he understood well for his ma had died just before we met. His grief and my grief were made easier.

Charlie told me all about Lollie Edgar. She was the daughter of a well-to-do St. Louis family. When her father bought a ranch in Montana and brought his family out from St. Louis, it seemed only natural for them to entertain the son of their dear friends, the Russells, from back home. The more Charlie was with Lollie, the more he was smitten by her charms. Before he knew it, he was completely captivated by her, and it soon became obvious that the feeling was mutual. The Edgars, instead of being delighted, were vehemently against any such a match. They realized that Charlie wasn't having a youthful fling at being a cowboy, but was fulfilling his life's ambition. They took their little girl back to St. Louis posthaste.

Charlie and Lollie wrote to each other and Charlie carried Lollie's letters inside his shirt, next to his heart, when he was out riding the range. He read and reread them by the glow of the campfire until he had them memorized.

Finally, unable to stand it, he decided to go to St. Louis and ask her to marry him. But when he arrived there, he found she was engaged to another man.

"Oh, that must have been like a knife to your heart," I said.

"Her folks had told her I wasn't good enough for her. That I was nothing but a cowboy," Charlie said.

"That's not true! I bet she wasn't good enough for you," I declared.

Charlie laughed.

I didn't feel lonely anymore. Fall suddenly became winter. We would bundle up against the cold wind and snow, and walk along the frozen river bed. When sunlight sparkled on the drifts of snow like countless miniature diamonds, we ran and played like children, chasing each other with snowballs. Then the river began to flow again. The snow banks grew smaller and smaller, and crocuses appeared. We continued to walk along the river holding hands and talking while bare limbs slowly dressed in their summer greenery. We would lean against the bridge railing, and look down into the waters to see our reflection looking back at us. We made a handsome couple despite the difference in our ages for Charlie was a fine figure of a man with broad shoulders and a straight back. Cowboying had given him strong lean muscles and he always wore a soft shirt, tight pants, half-breed sash, Stetson hat, high heel boots and rings on his fingers. In a crowd of a hundred cowboys, or even a thousand, he was the one you'd notice.

As if by magic the trees became even more radiant in gold, umber, red and orange. As we stood on the bridge our reflection was shattered by falling leaves. Summer became fall. It was on that very bridge that Charlie asked me to marry him.

"Oh, no, Charlie." I remembered what my ma told me about marrying too young. How she and my pa fought all the time and how he'd gone off and left her. Everyone told me not to marry Charlie for he had no ambition. That he drank. That he'd never amount to anything.

Everyone told Charlie not to marry me. There was too much difference in our ages. According to ol' Doc Sweat, my fainting spells betrayed a bad heart and I'd be gone in three years.

It didn't make sense, but Charlie begged me. Years later Charlie would do a little watercolor of his begging me with his arms open wide, and with that soft shirt on, and me running away. What the little watercolor didn't show was that afterward, I turned around and ran right back into those arms. As they held me tight, I said yes.

4

From Cascade to Great Falls

IT WAS THE PRETTIEST WEDDING YOU EVER SAW. I had a brand new blue dress that Ma Roberts helped me make and matching blue beads that Charlie gave me as a wedding gift. There were nine people at the wedding. We didn't go on a honeymoon. We couldn't afford that, for we had taken all the money Charlie had and fixed up our first home. It wasn't much. In fact, it was little more than a one-room shack. The Robertses owned it, and it was only a good stone's throw from their house. Charlie had saved up about seventy-five dollars and we bought some second-hand furniture and some paint. I painted everything — walls and furniture. Charlie helped, but he was used to painting with a much smaller brush.

That first year I wouldn't say we starved exactly. But there were times. One evening as we stood by the sink doing dishes, Charlie looking comical with a dish towel tied around his waist over his sash, he said, "Mame, I'm going back to cowboying. I've got to in order to make ends meet. We just can't live on what I take in paintin'."

"No, Charlie," I cried. "You're not going back to cowboying. You are an artist. Someday the whole country — no, the whole world — will know about Charlie Russell, the cowboy artist!" I stomped my foot.

My determination brought a chuckle to Charlie. "Well, Mame, if you believe in me that much, I guess I'll put off a little longer going back to cowboying."

I laid awake that night thinking. I knew the Robertses would share some of their food with us in exchange for chores I could do for them. Bob Thoroughman, an old cowboying friend of Charlie's, occasionally brought us by a chicken. I had learned a long time ago how to make a little go a long way and I knew we wouldn't starve. But I had to make a plan. As I lay there staring into the darkness, I knew that we had to leave Cascade. How was the whole world going to know of Charlie if we stayed in a little place like Cascade? We had to go where the people were, where the money was. In Great Falls, there were ten thousand people. We had to move to Great Falls. Once I made up my mind, I went right to sleep.

The next morning, I told Charlie.

"Mame, how can we afford to move to Great Falls when we can hardly afford to live in a free house and still eat?"

"Charlie, don't worry. You just go on painting and let me worry about how we can save up enough money to move to Great Falls."

I scrimped and I saved. I knew where every penny went. None slipped through my fingers.

One year later we moved to Great Falls. Before we left, I dropped by the *Great Falls Tribune* office. "I'd like to speak with the gentleman who writes *The Spray of the Falls*," I said to the man sitting at the first desk I saw, which was piled high with papers. He motioned with his head to a man at a desk in the back. I walked back to his desk. He was busy typing away.

"I'm Mrs. Charles Russell."

"Yes, ma'am." He looked up slowly, smiled, and stopped typing. "You're as pretty as everyone says you are."

"Why, thank you. I also want to thank you for the piece you wrote last year in the *Spray* before Charlie and I got married. I was especially flattered when you called me 'the popular Nancy Cooper.' I cut that article out, and I will always save it. People read your column before they read the headlines. And it's usually a lot more interestin'. I knew you would want to know that we are moving to Great Falls."

"Thank you, Mrs. Russell, for that information. I think Great Falls will be mighty lucky to have Charlie move here, and I think Charlie's mighty lucky to have a little lady as pretty and bright as you lookin' after his welfare."

I blushed, but I knew it would be in the next column of the *Spray*. I had been serious about everyone reading his column first. I was right. In the very next edition, the *Spray* said that Mr. and Mrs. Charles Russell were moving to Great Falls.

I cut that article out also and put it in my scrapbook.

We moved from one little house in Cascade to another little house in Great Falls at 1012 Seventh Avenue North. The only difference was that for this one on Seventh Avenue North, we had to pay rent.

I knew we had to raise the prices of Charlie's paintings. Some of his pictures hung at Charles Schatzlein's store in Butte. Because of the copper mines, Butte had Englishmen and Canadians coming in as mining engineers.They were paid big wages, and they loved Charlie's storytelling pictures.

One evening when Charles Schatzlein, or Dutch, as we called him, sat with us around the kitchen table, I said, "Dutch, I've been thinking. I believe we can get more for Charlie's pictures than we've been asking."

"Nancy, I think you're right," replied Dutch.

Charlie stammered, "I'd be embarrassed to ask too much. Why, everyone would think I'm trying to rob them."

"Charlie, I think you should let Nancy handle the business end. She has a better head for it than you do. Nancy, did you ever hear about Charlie's one, big business deal when he was cowboying?" asked Dutch.

I shook my head no.

"Well, then let me enlighten you," smiled Dutch as he leaned back in one of the kitchen chairs and began his tale.

"Back when Charlie was cowboying full-time, one of his friends came up to him and told Charlie he had to have a loan. He was desperate, for he had just learned from home that his brother was sick. Of course, Charlie, always having a soft heart for anyone in need, dug deep in his pocket and gave his cowboying friend all he had on him. The friend promised to pay him back as soon as he could. Well, there he was the very next day with money in hand. Saying he'd won at gambling and was going to split his winnings with Charlie.

"I thought you had a poor, sick brother. I don't want none of your winnings. You just give me back what I loaned you. I wouldn't have loaned it to you in the first place had I thought I was grubstakin' a gambler."

Charlie's cowboying friend took his winnings and gambled all that day and all that night. The next day he came back to Charlie and declared, "Oh, Charlie, I won. I won. I won. You won't believe it, but I won us a saloon. We are partners in a saloon. Now, how you gonna turn that down?"

Charlie couldn't. They invited all their friends to their Grand Opening. They told them that drinks were on the house. And their friends drunk them broke."

Dutch was laughing so hard he could hardly finish his story. Finally he said, "Come on, Charlie. Let Nancy handle the business and you handle the paintin'. I think she's right that you can get more for your pictures."

Charlie had been laughing too. He could always laugh at himself.

"I think you've proved your point. Okay, Mame, you take over the money end, and I'll take over the paintin' end," said Charlie as he gave me a wink.

And soon after that I found out something very strange — the dearer I made Charlie's pictures, the more people wanted them.

I was bound and determined to take every penny I could lay my hands on and buy us a house. I even knew exactly where it should be. There was only one street considered *the* street in Great Falls, and that was Fourth Avenue North. But no matter how hard I saved, I couldn't come up with enough for a lot on Fourth Avenue North.

"Where you been Mame?" Charlie asked.

"For a walk."

"It's bitter cold out there," said Charlie as he put down his brushes and took a long look. "Your eyes are shinin' and dancin', and your face is all aglow. What did you see out there?"

"Oh, Charlie," I said as I ran to him and hugged him. "I just saw our house on Fourth Avenue North in my mind's eye. It's a great big two-story white house with a big front porch. It's on the same block as the Albert Triggs."

"Mame, that's a vacant lot. I think the cold has done something to your brain," said Charlie.

"I know Charlie, but someday our house will sit there. Someday we'll live on the best street in Great Falls. Charlie, I want to live on the same block as the Triggs. The Triggs have been so good to me. They treat me like I'm somebody and don't hold it against me that I was a hired girl like some do. Margaret Trigg is the grandest lady I ever met, and Josephine is so smart, she's read everything. Remember when they took us to see Shakespeare's *Mid-Summer Night's Dream* at the Opera House? Josephine actually understood everything they said. I pretended I understood, but it didn't make sense to me.

"Mame, that's not your fault. That fella Shakespeare uses all those highfalutin words instead of jus' tellin' a good tale."

"But, Charlie, that's not the point. I want to understand. I want to be like them. I want to learn to talk and dress. And I *want* to live on the *best* street in town."

"I don't doubt you will. Mame. When you get something in your head, you just can't let go."

Charlie's pa came out to visit us in Great Falls. I wanted him to like me, and he did. He wasn't at all like Charlie. No, Papa Russell was quiet and reserved. You'd think he was a stern man until you got to know him. As Charlie would tell his stories about breaking an ornery bronc, or roping a wild longhorn, or running buffalo with the Bloods, Papa Russell's eyes would glow with love. He was so proud that Charlie could take these stories and put them on canvas. He also liked the way I was handling the business end.

"Papa Russell, I know that it would help for us to move. We need to be on *the best* street in Great Falls, which is Fourth Avenue North. Why, the Gibsons live on Fourth Avenue North and Fourth Street. All the important people in Great Falls live on Fourth Avenue North. Someday, Charlie is going to be the most important person in Great Falls. Someday not only everyone in Great Falls but everyone in Montana — no, everyone in the whole United States — will have heard of Charlie Russell as the great American artist. I've got to do everything I can to bring that about. One thing we've got to do is move to Fourth Avenue North."

"Nancy, you're not only pretty, but you're smart. Charlie needs someone like you behind him. Charlie's never been much of a pusher but I believe you have shove enough for both. I've been thinking about giving Charlie his inheritance from his mother and now might be as good of time as any."

"Oh, Papa Russell. Thank you, thank you, thank you," I squealed with delight.

I couldn't wait to tell the Triggs. They seemed to be just as excited as I was.

"Nancy, that's wonderful news," smiled Margaret Trigg. "I can't think of anyone I'd rather have as neighbors than you and Charlie. You will light up this whole street. Wait until Mr. Trigg hears. He'll be as thrilled as Josephine and I are. Of course, he'll want to spend every evening with Charlie and make a pest of himself. If he does, you just run him home."

"Oh, no, Mr. Trigg would never be a pest, and I'm planning on us visiting back and forth as much as we can," I said.

Josephine gave me a hug and said, "Nancy, that's wonderful. Why, we'll be so close. We'll be more like sisters than neighbors." I thought of my little half-sister Ella, whom I hadn't seen in six years. I wondered what she was like. Well, I had had no power to keep from losing her. But I did have the power to accept the sisterhood that Josephine was offering, and I knew that had I invented a perfect sister, she could be no better than Josephine. She was caring, intelligent, and loyal. I knew she would never let me down. Oh, she wasn't really pretty. In fact, she was rather plain. She had beautiful hair, but she kept it in a tight knot on the top of her head, which made her long neck look even longer and skinnier. She had big pretty eyes, but no one could ever see them because of her thick glasses. She taught school and looked the perfect part of the schoolmarm. Yet she had a wonderful wit and humor and a beautiful speaking voice with just a hint of her parent's English accent. There were good reasons that she had attracted William L. Ridgely, her constant suitor in a whirlwind romance in 1899.

Will Ridgely was the first man who paid attention to Josephine. He was charmed by her wit and grace — and it probably didn't hurt that her father, an English immigrant, had done well as owner of the Brunswick Saloon. The Triggs were the pillars of the community and the leaders of the Episcopal Church. Miss Josephine was loved and respected by every child who attended her classes and their families as well. It would be a distinct advantage to a young man trying to make his mark in Great Falls to marry Josephine Trigg. And since she was the Triggs's only child and the apple of her father's eye, it didn't seem right for her to leave her father's house so, after a brief honeymoon, William and Josephine Ridgely returned there to live — on Fourth Avenue North.

Even after the wedding everyone referred to her as "Miss Josephine."

It seemed to take forever for them to build our house, but by the end of summer it was finally finished. I had known what it would look like long before they started. It would be a two-story white house that any passerby could tell was the home of a man of importance. There was a big porch across the front where you could sit on a summer's evening and catch a cool breeze or watch the people go by or entertain your friends. There was a little parlor right behind the front door which opened into the side of the house. This could be a waiting room for the many clients who would visit

Charlie one day. There was a large living room adjoining an equally large dining room, where I planned to have many dinner parties. There was a downstairs bathroom with a pull chain commode and a beautiful porcelain bathtub with hot and cold running water set majestically on four eagle-claw feet. I had vowed long ago that when I had a home I would never have to pump water.

Next to the kitchen there was a small bedroom for the maid we would have some day. Upstairs we had another bathroom. This one didn't have a bathtub, just a sink and a commode. There were three large bedrooms, and a small room I called the trunk room or storage room. I had red-flocked wallpaper on the living room walls, and a floral paper with the same touch of red on the walls up the stairway. The furniture in the living room was covered in deep red velvet. We moved in in August and I invited friends and neighbors for an open house. I just happened by the *Great Falls Tribune*, and happened to drop in to see that nice man who wrote the *Spray of The Falls*, for I knew he would want to know for his column that the Russells were at home in their new house on Fourth Avenue North.

I thought I had everything I could wish for, but Charlie was painting in the dining room. He'd taken it over with his canvases, paints, and brushes. That wasn't all. He was always bringing in an Indian coup stick, or war bonnet, or moccasins, or a saddle, or blanket, to use in one of his paintings. Every time a tradesperson came in and noticed a painting of Charlie's he'd ask some fool question which of course started Charlie telling about the times he was cowboying, or about that winter he was living with the Bloods. The tradespeople so enjoyed Charlie's stories that they brought friends the next time to hear Charlie's stories and look at his paintings.

I knew this had to stop. He needed a studio. All important artists had studios. The problem was, Charlie liked painting in the dining room. He liked visiting with the tradespeople and enchanting them with his stories. I started talking to Charlie about how nice it would be for him to have a studio away from the interruptions of the house.

Finally, Charlie agreed on the condition that his studio would be like the log cabin he had shared with Jake Hoover. I couldn't get logs, but I got the next best thing — telephone poles. Our friend George Calvert began building the studio on the lot next to our house. When it was about three feet off the ground, one of the neighbors dropped by and came into the dining room where Charlie was painting.

"Charlie, what in the heck are you building with those telephone poles? I've never seen anything like it. It's the funniest looking corral I've ever seen."

Charlie didn't say anything, but I could see he was embarrassed. After the neighbor left, he said, "Mame, it may not be fittin' to have a telephone pole studio on Fourth Avenue North. The neighbors might not like it."

After that, Charlie wouldn't go near the studio

even though his good friend, George Calvert, was in charge of its construction. I went right on ahead with it — and kept my fingers crossed. The day it was finished, Albert Trigg came over and said, "Come on, Charlie, let's go see that studio. It looks mighty nice from the outside. I want you to show me the inside."

I held my breath.

When Charlie and Albert Trigg came back to the house after their tour of the studio, I knew that Charlie loved it.

The studio had a huge fireplace at one end and on Sunday mornings Charlie would invite his friends over. Charlie Beil, Horace Brewster, Young Boy, a Cree Indian, and others came to eat Charlie's bachelor bread, beans, and bacon. He'd tie a big, white flour sack on as an apron and when everything was ready he'd yell, "Come and get it." They would sit on their haunches eating, just like they used to do around the campfire. After the meal Charlie would always pull out his fixin's and roll his own cigarette. That was the signal for them to start telling the stories of their cowboying days. Some Sundays, Teddy Blue Abbot, who could tell about the terrible blizzard of '86 better than anyone, would come. Olaf Seltzer was a young man from Denmark who came as often as he could, for he couldn't get enough of the cowboying stories.

Olaf was like a sponge that soaked up everything he heard. He so wanted to be a cowboy, a man of the West, that he had immediately lost his accent. He met

Charlie at the thirty-third birthday party that some of Charlie's friends threw for him at the Mint Saloon. Olaf just happened to be there, but it was a night that would change his life. Charlie was in rare form. And when Charlie Russell told a story, a kind of magic spell was cast. Young and old alike were caught in it. Olaf Seltzer was. He wanted to be just like Charlie Russell. He had studied art in his homeland and now he decided he would devote himself to painting the life of the West, of the cowboy and the Indian. And who better to hear the stories from than Charlie Russell and his friends?

I didn't mind Charlie spending his Sunday mornings this way while the women were at church. As long as he remembered that the weekdays were for painting.

We planned to go back to St. Louis in 1903 to deliver some paintings for the St. Louis World's Fair, then we were to go on to New York City. I knew we had to have a large portfolio of paintings to make the kind of impression I wanted.

Charlie got up early every morning. I think it was a habit from his cowboying days. He always cooked his own breakfast and before going out to his studio he brought me a cup of hot water with lemon juice. Margaret Trigg had told me that this would help my digestive problems, which she thought caused my fainting spells. I'm not sure that it helped my problems, but it became our morning ritual. I could hear Charlie tromping up the stairs every morning carrying the cup of hot water carefully so as not to spill a drop. He'd hand it to me and tell me to drink it all down before it got cool or it wouldn't do any good, then he'd lean over and give me a hug and a kiss and go to his studio.

I knew I would have to get out of bed when I heard the back door slam. For if Charlie was out in the studio painting, then I must do my part and take care of the correspondence or contact the framers or write up an ad to put in the next Great Falls Directory. Charlie would paint all morning and then, just like clockwork, I would hear the back door open at twelve noon. I always had his lunch ready and he always ate it as though he were starved. After lunch he would lay down for a nap, then jump up, wash, and make sure his half-breed sash was just so and his Stetson hat was cocked at the right angle before he left the house.

As he left I would hold up two fingers. Charlie knew exactly what this meant. He was to have no more than two drinks. I had told Charlie over and over that I didn't mind his Sundays spent swapping cowboy tales in the studio but that I felt it was such a waste of time for him to go down to the Mint or the Silver Dollar every afternoon. I reminded him, time and again, that we would need a great number of paintings to take to show in St. Louis and New York if we were going to make an impression. I repeated Doc Sweat's adage that liquor and paint don't mix. But it seemed to make no difference what I said. Charlie was bound and determined to waste his afternoons with his friends. Usually he remembered my two-finger signal and when he came home, he would hold up two fingers to let me know that he had only had two drinks. But occasionally he would hold up three or four fingers.

Finally, by the fall of '03, we had enough paintings as well as enough money saved to make our trip. Before we left, I went to the best store in Great Falls and bought a beautiful blue wool outfit. The dress had a tight bodice that showed off my small waist and a long sweeping skirt. It had a blue velvet collar edged in cream-colored lace. There was a blue wool fitted coat to match that buttoned all the way down the front. It also had a blue velvet collar. I felt like Mrs.Rockefeller when I put on that suit.

"Mame, if you wear that outfit when you're showing my paintings, nobody's going to look at them," Charlie said when I modeled it for him.

We took the train to St. Louis. That first night, as I laid in the Pullman and listened to the clickety-clack of the wheels on the rails, memories of the trip out from Kentucky flooded me. I could almost feel the hard wooden bench, smell the soot and sweat and hear the babel of foreign tongues. I thought of my mama, that cold little house, and running to get the doctor. Tears stung my eyes.

"Mama," I said softly, "I'm on the train again, but this time I'm sleeping in a Pullman and I have a beautiful blue wool dress." Soon all I could hear was the sound of the wheels as I drifted off to sleep.

5

Back East To St. Louis

WHEN THE TRAIN PULLED INTO THE STATION in St. Louis, my stomach was tight with excitement. Charlie's pa was the only member of the Russell family I had ever met. I knew he liked me, but I wanted the rest of Charlie's family to like me too. I wanted Charlie's childhood friends to think he had made a good choice. I had my dark blonde hair piled high in a halo of curls. I was wearing my new blue dress and coat. I pulled a mirror from my purse and checked my face and hair for the thousandth time.

"Mame, you're just meetin' the folks," said Charlie, "not being presented to the King."

"I couldn't be more nervous if I were meeting the King of England," I replied.

As I came down the Pullman car steps, I caught sight of Charlie's pa and gave him a wave. All of Charlie's family were there, offering hugs and welcomes all around. Charlie's sister Sue took my arm and guided me through the crowded platform. She was talking a mile a minute.

"Oh, Nancy, I've so been looking forward to meeting you. I've heard such wonderful things about you from father. I had just about given up on Charlie's ever getting married, but I can see he was just waiting for the right girl to come along."

I was feeling more confident until we got into the Russells' fine carriage and rode down Lindell Boulevard. The expanse of gardens and mansions took my breath away. There had already been a frost so the maples and elms were in brilliant shades of red and gold.

I had never been in a city as big and beautiful as St. Louis. As we drove along, I could not keep my excitement to myself. I was filled with questions. We passed one mansion after another. I wanted to know who lived in each. I realized that the Russells were well acquainted with all the residents of Lindell Boulevard.

"I never dreamed there were houses like this. They are all so beautiful and grand," I said.

"If you think these houses are beautiful and grand, you simply must see the Faust House. Oh, Papa, have the driver make a little detour to One Portland Place so Nancy can see it."

An unusually large and majestic house appeared. Sue told me it was the Faust House, and that they had five stained glass windows made especially by Tiffany's and an organ that was three stories high and we were all going there for a dinner party a week from Saturday.

"Oh, you mean that I'm really going to get to see the inside of that beautiful house," I squealed.

"Of course. The minute they heard that Charlie was coming for a visit, they insisted you come with us to a dinner they are giving in honor of David R. Francis and his committee. He's the chairman of the St. Louis World's Fair. In fact, that's all you'll hear about while you're here. The one-hundred-year celebration of the Louisiana Purchase is all anyone can talk about. We're caught up in the fever too. It's highly contagious," laughed Sue.

The next few days proved Sue right. We went out to the fair grounds. As we wandered around, I couldn't believe my eyes. They were building a magnificent Fine Arts building at the top of a hill just behind Festival Hall. At the bottom of the hill they were digging out a lagoon. They were constructing three separate waterfalls to cascade down the hill from the Festival Hall into the lagoon. Each was to be lit with different colored electric lights. In fact, the whole World's Fair was going to be lit with thousands and thousands of electric lights. This would be the very first time such a magnificent use of electric light had ever been undertaken. It was unbelievable. The Fine Arts Museum looked like a prince's castle to me. They were building it out of a material called staff which could be molded into any shape, after which it would harden and take on the appearance of marble. It was a fairy tale. I knew Charlie must have a painting in that museum when the fair opened, for there would be people coming from all over the world to share in this magic. I was constantly seeing things that were hard for me to comprehend.

One day I rode on an elevator. I had never been in one before. I was with Sue. We entered an ornamental iron cage, with an iron door that closed behind us. With a jerk the cage suddenly started to ascend.

"Oops, there goes my stomach. I think it's gonna fall out," I cried.

There was dead silence in the elevator. Sue's face turned brilliantly red. When the elevator stopped she rushed out as if it were on fire. She didn't speak to me until we got home.

"Oh, Nancy how could you? Don't you know that *no* lady ever uses such a word as 'stomach'? It is considered an obscene word," cried Sue.

"Sue, what's an 'obscene' word?" I asked timidly.

"That is a word that is never, never used in the polite company of ladies and gentlemen. But what made it worse, Nancy, is that after you said *that word* , you looked so young and innocent. All the gentlemen turned and stared at me, and thought I had said *that word.* I've never been so embarrassed," said Sue.

"Oh, Sue, I'd never do anything to embarrass you. I've just never been any place as big as St. Louis — and I've never been on an elevator before. Besides, I thought my stomach *was* going to fall out." I was determined to make my point.

"Nancy, you're impossible," laughed Sue. "And it's just as impossible to stay angry with you." She walked over and put her arm around me.

I knew Sue liked me. She said that because I was so enthralled with everything I saw it was a joy to be my guide.

"Have you ever seen *Aida*, Nancy?" Sue asked me one day.

I shook my head no. I wasn't even sure what an Aida was.

"You must go to opening night at the Odeon Theater," she insisted. "Friday the twenty-seventh is the beginning of the season for the Choral Symphony Concerts. They're going to sing excerpts from *Aida*. There will be a chorus of three hundred voices. Oh, you can't miss it. Besides, everybody will be there."

"Well, you all can go hear all that caterwauling, but not me," said Charlie, who had just walked into the parlor. "I can't understand a word they are saying and if good ol' English isn't good enough for them, then I'll go some place I can understand."

The night of the opening I dressed in my new blue wool and accompanied Sue and her husband, Thomas G. Portis, to the theater. Sue was dressed in green taffeta and wore long white kid gloves. She had emerald and diamond earrings that matched her dress. You could hear the rustle of her full skirt as she walked. T.G. was dressed in full cut-away tails and white tie. He looked every inch the southern gentleman. When he talked, his soft accent revealed his Alabama background.

We sat up in the Russell box. I looked down at all those beautiful people and all those beautiful clothes, and I knew what money and power and influence could do. I knew that every safety deposit box in every bank in St. Louis was empty that night, for every jewel that was owned was glittering around throats, or on fingers, or wrists, or hanging from earlobes. I didn't care that I couldn't understand a word they sang. In fact, I didn't pay much attention to the stage, not even to the chorus of three hundred. I couldn't take my eyes off of the audience. I'd never seen so many silks and satins, ruffles and laces, beaded and spangled dresses, in my life. It was a whole sea of color and sparkle before me.

As we left the opera when it was over we discovered Charlie leaning up against the door.

"How was it? I bet your ears will hurt for a week. I had a lot more fun than you folks. I went to the Zoo building down Olive Street and got to see this fella with a swell act, Bosco, the Wild Man, eater of live snakes," laughed Charlie.

"Oh, Charlie, you're impossible! Won't you ever grow up?" Sue scolded with artificial disgust, for Charlie could never make Sue angry. She adored him.

While we were in St. Louis there was a big article in the newspaper about Charlie calling him "a well-known native western artist." "Native son makes good," it said, and quoted Charlie as saying he owed all of his success to his wife Nancy.

I read the article over and over. I loved the quote, and I was thrilled to see my name in print.

Someone else read that article.

"Mame," said Charlie, "I think you better sit down. I've got a letter here I think you'd better read."

"What is it, Charlie?" I asked.

"I think you better sit down," repeated Charlie.

"Don't be silly," I replied.

"It's from a J. A. Cooper at the Cooper-Finder Restaurant, across the river in Paxton, Illinois. He says he read that article, and he says he's your pa."

I felt as if I'd been hit. My head swam. I hadn't had a fainting spell in a long time.

"He says he wants to meet you," said Charlie.

I felt as if I were holding on with just my fingertips, and I didn't want to slip away. I didn't want to faint, so I sat down. Charlie handed me the letter. The first time I read it I couldn't separate the words or comprehend their meaning. Every word swam together before my eyes. All I could remember was that my ma had waited and waited for my pa to come back. Young as I had been then, I could still remember waking up at night at Grandpa Blue's and hearing my ma's muffled sobs. My pa had run off and left my ma — and me.

"I don't think I want to go across the river and meet him," I told Charlie.

"I think you should or you might always regret it," said Charlie.

"I'll think on it," I replied.

The next morning I told Charlie, "I'm going to write him a letter and say that we will come to Illinois next Monday to meet him. We're going to the Fausts' this Saturday, and I'm not going to let anything spoil that."

If I thought the outside of the Faust Mansion was beautiful and grand, it was nothing compared to the inside. When the Russells' carriage arrived, we were helped down the steps by a footman all dressed in polished knee-high black boots, a red jacket with a black velvet collar, and a white, stiffly starched shirt. I had never been helped from a carriage by anyone so elegantly dressed. Yet the footman didn't compare to the butler who opened the door. Father Russell pulled his invitation from his evening jacket's inside pocket and laid it on a silver tray the butler was carrying. T.G. Portis did likewise. Father Russell told the butler that his son Charles and his wife were accompanying him. In a loud and melodious voice the butler announced: "Mr. Charles Silas Russell, Mr. and Mrs. Charles Marion Russell, and Mr. and Mrs. T.G. Portis."

I saw a flash of anger cross T.G.'s face and I suddenly realized he didn't much care for Charlie's being announced before he was. Always the well-bred southern gentleman, he recovered quickly. I noticed that neither Charlie nor Sue were at all aware of the look on his face. They were both so busy greeting friends and acquaintances, and introducing me.

Before long there was a big crowd standing all around Charlie, who was telling stories of his cowboying days. He leaned back on his high-heeled boots with his thumbs caught in his red silk half-breed sash. Several rings glittered on his fingers. If a stranger had walked into that room, the first person to catch his eye would have been Charlie. And once Charlie started telling his stories, he drew people to him like a magnet. I stood there looking at Charlie, thinking how lucky I was to be in this gorgeous parlor and to have my Charlie the absolute center of attention.

"Well, my dear, you must be the adoring child bride I've heard so much about," said a gray-haired matron as she approached me. She wore a black velvet dress with layers of lace and little silk ruffles that made her already large frame seem much bigger. As she came gliding toward me like a battleship, the crowd opened up like the Red Sea had for Moses. When she reached me, I realized that she was a full head taller than me, so I was looking into her ample bosom. It made a perfect display counter for a large diamond and pearl necklace. I had never seen so many diamonds on one person before. I could hardly pull my eyes away and look up into her face.

"Oh, yes, ma'am," I stammered. I should have stopped there but I raced on, "Oh, I've never been in St. Louis before. I've never seen anything as big as St. Louis. I've never ridden in an elevator before." Everyone turned from Charlie and was looking at me. I felt my face get hot and I knew I was bright red.

Luckily, at that very moment, the butler announced dinner. I felt as if fate had stepped in to save me from saying something even more embarrassing. The whole group moved as one into the dining room where a long table was lit with hundreds of tall tapers in polished silver candlesticks. The flickering candlelight reflected on hundreds of crystal prisms that hung from the chandelier overhead. I started to sit down, but a strong firm hand restrained me.

"I think you'll find your place card down the table next to mine. May I introduce myself? I'm David R. Francis."

"Oh, yes, I've heard so much about you and your wonderful World's Fair. Charlie and I have been out to the fair grounds to look at the construction. I think it's the most wonderful thing I've ever seen. I bet there's never been anything ever like it." I could see Mr. Francis was pleased with my opinion of his fair.

One of the many servants held out a chair for me, and I slid into it. I noticed that there was a little white card in front of my place with my name on it. I looked up and down the long table and realized that everyone had a card showing them where to sit. What a wonderful idea. This way you could introduce people who would enjoy each other's company or get even with someone who had been nasty to you by seating him next to a terrible bore or arch enemy. I must remember this, I thought. Then I looked down and suddenly realized that there were more forks and spoons lined up on either side of every plate than I had ever seen. I panicked. Which one was I to use? I didn't want to embarrass Sue again as I had on the elevator. But much more important, I didn't want all these beautiful people to think me a fool. I kept my eyes on Mr. David R. Francis's hands as each dish was served. Whichever spoon or fork he picked up, I did likewise. I'm sure it was a wonderful dinner, but I can't remember what I ate. Mr. Francis did not seem to notice.

"Mrs. Russell," he said. "You must come back next year when the Fair opens. It will be a once-in-a-lifetime experience. President Theodore Roosevelt will throw a switch in Washington, D.C. and flags will unfurl, motors will start and thousands of electric lights will flash on here in St. Louis. There never has been anything like it before."

"Oh, we do plan to come back. Of course, it would be an even greater thrill for me if one of Charlie's paintings were hanging in the Fine Arts Pavilion. We've brought four of his paintings with us on this trip for the Fair's Hanging Committee to see. Since Charlie's a native of St. Louis, and this is the celebration of the anniversary of the Louisiana Purchase, I think it would only be fitting."

"I think you have a point. Let me get you the name of the director of The Palace of Fine Arts."

"Is it true that each state is going to have an exhibition?" I asked.

"Yes, indeed."

"Will the director of The Palace of Fine Arts have any say in those exhibits?"

"No. Each state is in charge of its own."

"Do you know if Montana is going to be represented?"

"Yes, they are."

"I think I should get in touch with the Montana World's Fair Committee when I get home. You know Charlie is the most famous artist in Montana. It seems only natural that they will want to show some of his pictures so that people from all over the world can know what a Montana sky, a Montana mountain, a Montana cowboy, or a Montana Indian truly look like."

"Mrs. Russell, I think Charlie Russell is a most fortunate man to have such a pretty young wife who also is such a business manager," Mr. David R. Francis replied.

His kind words gave my spirits a lift. And he hadn't even noticed me staring at his hands. I was very pleased with myself until I went back to the sitting room after dinner. The men were all collecting in the library, and the women were all going back in the sitting room. Just as I entered I heard the voice of the gray-haired, diamond-and-pearls-on-black-velvet say, "She's pretty enough but did you notice she didn't even know what a place card was? And, my dear, she didn't know a soup spoon from a teaspoon. She actually had to watch David Francis to know which fork and spoon to use. Her manners are appalling, her grammar is atrocious, and her clothes are amusing."

I backed out of the door before anyone could see me. As I hurried down the hallway I said half aloud, "I can learn how to talk. I can learn how to dress — and I can sure learn which fork and spoon to use."

Monday came before I was ready for it. When I had written that letter to J. A. Cooper, it seemed a long way off. With Charlie by my side, we took the Russells' fine carriage and followed the road that crossed the river by bridge into Illinois.

When I first saw J. A. Cooper, I was surprised how little alike we were. I had large blue eyes and honey blonde hair. I tended to be a little bit plump. He was dark-haired and dark eyed, lean and wiry. But he had the same energy and drive I did.

"Oh, Nancy girl, it's sure good to see you. And who would have thought that my little girl would grow up and do so well for herself by marrying a famous artist? Why, your name and everything was in the newspaper. You sure done good," said J. A. Cooper.

I wanted to like him. I even wanted to love him. I yearned for a family. I remembered all those days, weeks, and months I had been alone after Ma died and Ella left. Loneliness is a terrible thing. Charlie and I had so much and he had so little. I knew we could make room for him in our lives.

"I know we'll get on right well," said Charlie. "But I can't quite call you 'pa' since I'm halfway between your age and Mame's, so I guess I'll just call you 'Coop.'"

I could tell Charlie had made another friend, but then everyone loved Charlie. He always knew just what to say to make people feel good about themselves.

"Well, I can call you 'pa,' and I'm going to," I said as I gave him a hug.

We spent the rest of the afternoon visiting. I told him we planned to go on to New York, but would be back in St. Louis the next year to see the World's Fair. That the HangingCommittee had selected Charlie's painting, *Pirates of the Plains*, to hang in the Main Hall Exhibit, so we'd definitely be back to see it. I promised I'd write between now and then.

"Mame, you did the right thing going over to see your pa," Charlie said on the way back to St. Louis.

"I know, Charlie, and I'm glad you *made* me go. It would not have been right to leave without seeing him. He is so lonely. We have had over twenty years of not knowing each other. Now we have a lifetime to know each other."

May 3d 1907

Friend Sid for fere
you will worry about me
I am droping you a line.
I intended leaving here seven
weeks ago but I cant brake
away from Rockyfeller an his
bunch every time I try an make
a git-away he invites me up
to have crackers an milk
with ~~with~~ him he shure hates
to see me leave John sends
~~sends~~ his regards to the
bunch an wanted me to
remember him to Piano Jim
an W A Clark
with best wishes to friends
your friend C M Russell

6

New York City

IF YOU THINK ST. LOUIS IS BIG — you should see New York City! Everyone was hustling and bustling about. "They all look like ants rushing in and out of an anthill. I wonder what they all do? I wonder where they all live? I wonder why Manhattan Island doesn't sink with all these tall buildings?"

I said all this half to Charlie and half to myself as we waited for a hack at the train station. I wanted to ride in one of those new taxi cabs. I thought nothing would be more exciting than to ride up Fifth Avenue in an automobile.

"I don't want to ride in no skunk wagon," Charlie said. "Good ol' horse power is good enough for me."

So we took a hack to our hotel, the Park View. I don't know where the hotel got its name. There was no park. When we entered our room, there was one little window and the only view was a brick wall blackened with layers of soot. The window pane was streaked with the same soot. Charlie raised the window and leaned out to get a breath of fresh air, then reeled back in and held his nose.

"Pew! That smells worse than any cow shed I've ever been in. When I looked down, it looked like a black hole in the earth and smelled like something's been dead there for a week. Mame, when can we go home? There we can get a breath of fresh air and look at the beautiful heavens and mountains that good ol' Mother Nature gave us."

"Oh, Charlie, you're just homesick. Pretty soon you'll be caught up in all the excitement and you won't have time to look at that dirty brick wall and think about Montana. The sooner everyone sees your paintings, the sooner you'll be famous and everyone will be talking about 'Charlie Russell, the Cowboy Artist.' I can't wait. Now, the first thing we have to do is rent a gallery and hang your pictures up. Oh, Charlie, isn't this wonderful? We're really in New York City and soon everyone will know about you," I said as I threw my arms around him and gave him a big hug.

My enthusiasm rubbed off and Charlie said he'd give me a hand unpacking. But the room was so small that there was space for only one of us to squeeze between the bed and the dresser.

"Charlie, you just sit on the bed and talk to me while I put everything up. It will be faster that way.

Then we can go out and rent you a gallery."

I had hoped we'd be able to rent a gallery near John Marchand's studio. He was a friend who had been in Montana and had suggested we come to New York where the contracts were. He said a good living could be made by illustrating books and magazines. We went to his studio and tried to rent a gallery in his neighborhood. I hadn't realized how expensive it would be. Finally I had to settle for a small, dark basement gallery. I didn't want Charlie to see my disappointment.

"Charlie, this is only our first show in New York City. After everyone sees your paintings and loves them and buys them we'll move to a better gallery. We'll rent a gallery that's full of sunlight to show off your pictures better."

Hardly anybody came. Pretty soon we ran out of money.

"Charlie, when John Marchand was out in Montana, you were sure good to him. You took him under your wing and showed him around. I think it's time for him to return the favor. I'm sure he wouldn't mind. And, Charlie, I think there would be plenty of room for you to set up your pictures in his studio. Lots of people would have the chance to see them, for there's always lots of people going in and out." I suggested this with a sweet smile.

Charlie knew how disappointed I was that we had to give up our basement gallery. He also knew I wasn't ready to go back to Montana. I hadn't done what

I came to do. While John Marchand took Charlie around I began knocking on doors. I'd knock on doors of editors, publishers, gallery owners, calendar printers, with a group of Charlie's pictures under my arm. I knocked on doors. I knocked on doors and I knocked on doors. And, you know, I found out something very strange. It didn't hurt being a pretty woman. Doors open for a pretty woman. Once you get inside you can get that contract.

If anybody tried anything, I would open my eyes wide. I would bat my eyelids. I would smile sweetly and say, "Oh my, I would never have expected this from you." I would look shocked and hurt. The flustered offender would be first embarrassed and then protective. In order to make amends, he'd offer me a contract maybe for the illustration of a book or maybe a magazine article.

While I was knocking on doors, taking Charlie's pictures around and getting contracts, Charlie was holed-up in our room. Charlie hated New York. The noise hurt his head, the rushing around made him tired, the crowds gave him a closed-in feeling, and he was terrified of getting lost. He had no mountain, waterfall, or crooked tree to guide by. One day he did get lost and he wandered around in circles for hours until luck brought him back in sight of the Park View's striped awning. I had returned home exhausted from my day's travels and was half-sick with worry when Charlie finally showed up.

"Where have you been?" I almost screamed.

"I got lost. This city's too big. Mame, when are we going home?"

"Charlie, we're not going home until we do what we came to do. Here I am out trudging around the streets of New York until my feet hurt so I don't think I can take another step. I'm carrying your big, heavy pictures until I think my arm will fall off. And you just sit here holed up in this room."

"What will I do? I can't stand those noisy crowded streets. I can't understand what half those folks are sayin'. Let's go home."

"Give up?" Now, I was screaming. "No! We've come too far."

There was silence.

"Now, Charlie," I said in my calmest, sweetest voice. "You are a great artist. Don't waste your time and talent sitting here homesick. I heard that Frederic Remington is getting hundreds and hundreds of dollars for his bronzes. I know you can mold better. Why not do something that we could have cast while we are here in New York? The greatest foundry of all, I hear, is right here in New York."

Charlie took out a big ball of beeswax. He was never without his beeswax. He was always fashioning bears or deer, coyotes, or antelope. Often he would fashion these lifelike creatures out of wax with his hand in his pocket. When he brought the little animal out for view, it amazed everyone. It seemed impossible to transform a blob of wax into a perfect animal inside a pocket. No matter how many times I saw Charlie do it, it was always hard for me to believe. Charlie's hands moved quickly and the ball of beeswax began to take form. As I went around making contacts, Charlie worked on his model. It kept him from being bored, and I was pleased he was doing something. "How'd you like that, Mame?" asked Charlie one day as he showed me a figure of a cowboy on a horse. The cowboy was riding into town after a long trail drive ready to whoop it up. His gun was aimed skyward to let the town know he was coming. Charlie called it *Smokin' Up*. Anyone looking at it could feel the sheer joy of that cowboy.

"Charlie, it's wonderful!" I touched it lovingly. I turned it all around and studied it from every angle. This was indeed better than anything Remington had ever done.

We had twenty-six castings made. But after Charlie had finished with *Smokin' Up*, he returned again to his misery. I went to visit John Marchand, who had offered to take Charlie around and introduce him to some editors and publishers.

"John, Charlie needs to get out of that hotel room. He needs to be with men, so he can swap stories. I'd really appreciate it if you could sort of take him under your wing. Charlie won't get out on his own." To my delight, John talked Charlie into going with him one evening to the Player's Club. At first Charlie was a little shy, for this was a whole group of strangers. But they all wanted to know who this fellow was in his soft shirt, tight pants, red silk sash, Stetson, and boots.

"Why, that's Charlie Russell, the cowboy artist from Montana," said Will Rogers. The minute he recognized Charlie he rushed over to give him a slap on the back. They had met on the train coming to New York and from the very first shared an easy friendship that grew with the years.

"What are you doin' here?" asked Will.

When Charlie turned around his face lit up. "What are you doin' here?" asked Charlie.

"Why, I'm trying to sell a few jokes and I expect you're trying to sell a few paintin's. I hope you're having better luck in New York City than me."

Pretty soon the two were no longer at the Player's Club; they were swapping stories back on the open range. Everyone crowded around to listen. You couldn't have lasso'd that audience any tighter with a rope. No one wanted to miss a word.

After that evening, Charlie started visiting John Marchand's studio. As people came in, he told them the story behind each of his paintings. Charlie was a master. Pretty soon folks were coming just to listen.

One day a gentleman came in all dressed up. He stared at one of Charlie's paintings a long time. Charlie went over and explained the painting. The stranger said he was a lawyer, but had always yearned to be a cowboy out West. He asked Charlie what he wanted for the painting. Before Charlie could say a word, I spoke up.

"Five hundred dollars," I said. Charlie turned white. The lawyer fella turned on his heel as if to leave, but he didn't. He walked over to a desk, pulled out a check book, and wrote out a check for five hundred dollars.

After he took the painting and left, Charlie turned to me and said, "Mame, now that we sold a painting, can we go home?"

"Sure, Charlie," I replied.

But before we left New York City, I bought myself a fur coat and Charlie a Prince Albert overcoat. The words I heard in St.Louis were still burning in my ears — that my grammar was atrocious and my clothes were amusing. I knew I could learn how to dress.

When we got home Charlie was so restless he was no help at all in unpacking. I knew what was wrong with him. He was dying to go to the Silver Dollar and the Mint Saloon and see his friends.

"All right, Charlie, go. You're no help to me here. But remember, just two," I said as I held up two fingers. Charlie was out the door like lightning.

Down at the Silver Dollar he told all his friends that he didn't like New York City.

"Why, Charlie?" asked one old-timer.

"I don't ever want to live anywhere where you're nobody. And you're nobody in New York City unless you're a millionaire. I always want to live where everybody is somebody."

Everybody nodded in agreement.

"But boys, that ain't the worst of it. In New York City the bartenders won't even drink out of the same bottle with you — how do you know you won't be poisoned?"

The old-timers shook their heads in amazement.

"And they give you a little slip of paper and you have to walk clean over to a cash register to pay — and you walk yourself plumb sober," said Charlie.

Everyone chuckled.

"Boy, it's good to have you back, Charlie."

While Charlie was down at the Silver Dollar and the Mint, I was unpacking. As I brushed and hung our clothes, stored the suitcases and carried Charlie's brushes, paints, and canvases to the studio, I was thinking about our next trip to New York City. I knew that next time we would sell more than one painting.

7

The World's Fair

"Oh, Nancy, you are going to love it. Everything you can imagine is there and some things you couldn't imagine because they've never been seen before. You can unpack tomorrow. We must not lose a minute going to the fair." said Sue. "Have you ever had an ice cream cone? No. Have you ever had iced tea? No. Have you ever had a hot dog? No. Because they've never existed before."

Sue was asking and answering her own questions. And although we were tired from our journey, we were so caught up in her eagerness for us to see these magical sights and taste these heretofore unknowns that our fatigue vanished.

"Oh, yes," I said. "The unpacking can surely wait. Lead on to the unbelievable and unknown." I laughed as I put my hat back on. We had just arrived in St. Louis.

We had lived up to our word and returned in the fall of 1904 to see the St. Louis World's Fair. Everyone in that city had caught "Fair Fever." They couldn't visit it often enough, and it was easy to see why. My grandest dreams of what the fair would be when construction was finished and the exhibits were in place didn't come even close. The eight huge palaces that housed the exhibits were more magnificent than anyone could possibly have imagined. They resembled huge marble palaces fit for some foreign potentates.

We took the streetcar to the entrance at Lindell Boulevard and DeBaliveve and walked up the Plaza of St. Louis, the largest of all the avenues.

"Why are you so quiet, Nancy?" asked Sue.

"I can't believe my eyes," I whispered. I was awe-struck. "I am sure this avenue is at least twelve city lots wide."

"Oh, it is and just wait until you get to the lagoon at the end."

As we walked down the avenue, on our right was a statue of DeSoto and on our left one of Joliet. They were much bigger than life-size. The Louisiana Purchase Monument was a shaft one hundred feet high and topped with a statue of Peace holding a globe representing the world. It was held up by four statues representing North, South, East, and West.

Although it was early fall, it was a warm and bright day. Women were still carrying parasols or wearing large straw hats for shade. The lagoon was filled with boats gliding through the shimmering water. Each was powered by a man standing at the back of it with a long pole. They were singing but I couldn't understand their songs.

"Sue, what are they singing?" I asked.

"Oh, they're from Venice. They were brought here just for the fair," Sue answered.

Some of the boats were shaped like swans, some had serpents heads, and others were mermaids. Water cascaded down the hill from the Festival Hall into the lagoon like molten crystal.

"Sue, the water is so clear, and last summer it was so muddy."

"The fair fathers realized that they couldn't have muddy water coming down the cascades. How would people see the changing colored lights at night? Isn't it strange? For years people have been complaining that the water in St. Louis was too thick to drink and too thin to plow. But it wasn't for drinking that the water supply was clarified. It was for the effect that the colored lights would have on the waters tumbling down the three cascades. Wait until dark when they turn on the colored lights. You'll see it was well worth it."

We walked up the hill to Festival Hall. Of all the beautiful palaces, it was the crowning jewel. Sue rushed us inside because we were just in time to hear Charles Galloway play the organ.

"The dome here is larger than the dome of St. Peter's, and it is entirely covered with gold leaf," bragged Sue. "The organ is the largest in the world. Before they finished setting the pipes in place they brought in a Shetland pony and let him walk inside the largest pipe of the organ. The pipe was that big."

When we got into the auditorium, not one of the thirty-five hundred seats was empty. It sounded like a great swarm of bees. With the first note from the organ, a hush fell over the crowd. Music flooded the domed hall. Although I had never heard any music like this before, I was secretly pleased that there weren't any chairs, for I could not wait to see more of the fair. We quickly slipped out.

Sue took us to the Palace of Manufacturers where there were goods for sale from all over the world.

"Do you know there are nine miles of aisles in this building?" asked Sue. "Of course, we can't see everything in here today, so let's go to the Palace of Varied Industry, then to the Palace of Education and Social Economy. There are whole schools there from kindergarten to the highest level of universities.

"I never did take to schools much," said Charlie. "I think I'll pass that one."

"Oh, Charlie," said Sue. "You'll find it fascinating, for it's not just classrooms, but there are whole schools for the blind, the mute, and the deaf, and teachers from all over the world. But if you're not interested we can go to the Palace of Liberal Arts where there's an entire printing press so that you can watch them print the weekly *Fair Magazine*, and an entire hospital that has doctors and nurses and tiny real babies in incubators. Would you prefer to go to the Palace of Transportation and see the trains arriving every minute from St. Louis through the sixty-foot high door or see the one hundred and forty automobiles that were driven here under their own power from Boston, New York, Chicago, and Philadelphia?" Sue asked.

"Sue, I'm tired just listening to you," said Charlie. "I think I'd like to go some place and sit."

"We can go to either the Italian Restaurant in the West Pavilion or the German Restaurant in the East. The German overlooks an exact copy of the famous Charlottenburg Castle, located right outside of Berlin."

"Oh, let's go to the German," I said. I had never seen a real castle.

Not one of the twenty-five hundred seats at the German Restaurant was empty. We had to wait for a table, but it was worth the wait for we had a wonderful view of the Charlottenburg Castle.

"If I lived to be a hundred and came to the fair every day, I couldn't see it all. But I'm going to see everything I can while I'm here in St. Louis," I told Sue.

"You've caught Fair Fever, and you haven't even seen it at night with all the lights on. After we eat our supper we'll go to the Palace of Electricity. There you can talk into a machine that will record your voice on a thin wire and play it back to you."

I almost gobbled down my delicious plump German sausages served with hot sauerkraut. I couldn't wait to visit the Palace of Electricity, for I loved new inventions. When we entered the Palace of Electricity, who should we bump into but David R. Francis himself.

"Oh, Mr. Francis, your fair is simply magnificent. I've never seen anything like it, and we've only seen a very small part."

"Why, Mrs. Russell, how very nice to see you again, and I'm so pleased you could come to our fair. Have you seen it lit at night?"

"No, but I just can't wait for it to get dark today. Everyone says it will be the most breathtaking sight I've ever seen," I replied.

"Well, then I have someone I want to introduce you to. Please come with me and meet Mr. Thomas Edison."

"Mr. Edison, this is really an honor. I know somewhere I read that the discovery of fire changed mankind forever, but I think your discovery of electricity will have a far larger effect." He took my hand. "I would really love to have you show me how I can talk into your machine and have my voice recorded on a thin cord of metal and then have it played back."

"I'd be delighted, Mrs. Russell." Mr. Edison led me over to his recorder. "Now, just speak up into this cone-shaped instrument."

I yelled. "I love the St. Louis World's Fair." Mr. Edison played my words back. They were high pitched and the sound crackled, but they were my words. It was hard to believe.

Charlie didn't seem to be interested in the recording, nor was he interested in standing in line for a turn to talk on the telephone to someone in Chicago, Springfield or Kansas City. Charlie was always scared by new things. He seemed to feel that the world was moving too fast for him, or maybe that Mother Nature whom he loved so well was being intruded upon.

It was dark when we left the Palace of Electricity. As we walked outside suddenly the lights came on. The Palaces, the Cascades, the Ferris Wheel at the pike, the three-hundred-foot wireless tower with its elevator were suddenly outlined with thousands of glowing lights. We just stood and stared. Even Charlie was struck by the beauty of the fair under the electric lights.

"Oh, I'm coming back tomorrow, and I'm going to ride that elevator up to the top of the wireless tower so I can get a view of the entire fair."

"Not with me," laughed Sue.

"I promise, cròss my heart, I won't say stomach." I told her. "Then I'm going to ride the Ferris Wheel. I can't wait.

"You'd have to hog-tie me to get me on that contraption," said Charlie.

"That's all right, Charlie, you don't have to ride it, but nothing is going to keep me off," I said.

We took the streetcar home, dropped into bed and were half-asleep before our heads hit the pillows.

I woke up early the next morning. Charlie was already up. I practically flew down the stairs, for I couldn't wait to return to the fair and ride the Ferris Wheel, or Observation Wheel, as some called it.

"You're up bright and early," smiled Sue.

"I couldn't sleep. I was too excited about riding the Ferris Wheel and seeing more of the fair," I said.

"I thought if we left early, maybe we would beat some of the crowds."

"It's always crowded," said Charlie's pa. He had decided not to go to the office that day, but to come with Charlie, Sue and me to the fair.

He was right. Even the streetcar was crowded. This time we went straight to the pike and to the Ferris Wheel. There was a long line waiting to pay fifty cents each to take a ride on the Ferris Wheel. It was not like anything I had ever seen. There were thirty-six cars and each car held sixty people. Just as eager as I was to ride, Charlie was equally determined not to put one foot aboard it.

"Come on, Charles, I want to show you an exact duplicate of the Tyrolean Alps. There's a waterfall in the Alps that flows into a lake. Near the lake is an inn where the best food at the fair is served. And there's a young cowboy there who twirls his rope and spins his stories for the folks while they eat. He's been asking when you were coming," said Charlie's pa.

"You mean gum-chewing Bill Rogers is here?" Charlie's face suddenly brightened and a smile spread across it.

"We'll meet you at the St. Louis Inn in the

Tyrolean Alps," said Charlie's pa. "You know where it is, Sue." With that, the men were gone.

The line for the ride moved forward. Finally it was our turn. As I stepped into the car, I was suddenly frightened. Maybe this wasn't a good idea. The car quickly filled. The door was closed. I panicked. I wanted out. With a jerk the car lifted off the ground and started up. I closed my eyes and couldn't open them. I was terrified. When we reached the top the car jerked to a stop and swung in the breeze.

"Do you know they rent out these cars for private dinner parties? They've even rented them for small wedding receptions," Sue said, trying to keep me from being so scared.

I opened my eyes and looked out, then I looked at the ground below. I quickly shut my eyes.

"From here you can see the elephants sliding down the slide into a little pool at Hagenbeck's Circus. Oh, and you can see the reenactment of the Boer War. Look at all those horsemen charging," said Sue.

I opened my eyes and indeed you could see the elephants. You could also see people riding camels. A miniature train was going around the outskirts of the fair, whistle blowing, bell ringing, as it stopped to let people on and off. There were Chinese all dressed up in their silks, little black hats and pigtails, running and pulling rickshaws. I could see the Tyrolean Alps mountain tops rising up in the distance. I wasn't frightened any longer. I wanted to see everything from the Ferris wheel as if I were a bird viewing the Fair. My view didn't last long, for with another lurch the car started its downward ride. The next time we started upward I kept my eyes wide open, for I didn't want to miss a thing.

Our Ferris Wheel ride was over too quickly for me. I really wanted to ride again. What better way could I possibly get an overview of everything going on at the fair? But I didn't want to stand in that long line again; besides, I wanted to see things up close that I had seen from my seat in the heavens and I knew Charlie would get a big kick out of watching the animals at Hagenbeck's Circus.

"Sue, let's go over to meet Charlie at that St. Louis Inn in that Alps place," I said.

"I was talking to a man who had just returned from the real Tyrolean Alps, when he came to the fair. He thought his eyes were deceiving him, especially when he saw the men walking around in their short leather pants, yodeling. He really thought he was back again in the Alps with all the little chalets with their funny roofs and gables. He had to pinch himself to make sure he was in St. Louis," Sue said as we walked along the pike toward the Alps.

You couldn't miss them, for their peaks reached up into the sky and truly looked snow-covered. I had never been in the Alps, but I had to pinch myself, for I certainly couldn't believe it. I was used to the mountains in Montana, but I couldn't for the life of me figure out how they could create mountains on the flat land of Missouri for the fair, or build the waterfall splashing down the side of the mountains.

When we got to the St. Louis Inn, it took us a few minutes to spot Charlie, for the tables were crowded. He and his pa were sitting at a table talking to Will Rogers.

"Oh, Charlie, you should have ridden on the Ferris Wheel with me. It was wonderful. I could see the whole fair and everything that's going on, the elephants sliding down a slide, the gondolas on the lagoon, the rickshaws racing around. I could even see them fighting the Boer War." I clapped my hands in excitement.

"Charlie, you ought to see those fellas reenacting the Boer War. Why, they charge at each other, shoot each other off their horses, and bite the dust. Then when it's all over, they pick themselves up, pat each other on the back, walk out arm in arm, and come back later in the day to do it all over again," said Will Rogers.

"Oh, Will, it is so nice to see you again. We heard you were amazing everyone at the fair with your rope tricks," I said.

"Mame, there isn't a man alive that can handle a rope like Bill Rogers," said Charlie. "He's been showing these folks from all over the world that he can do anything but pick his teeth with rope. 'Course, he's been tellin' them a few good jokes, too."

"Well, Charlie, I've got to go back on now. I entertain 'em while they eat. That way they stay longer and order more food."

Charlie, his pa, Sue and I sat for a while watching Will perform. When he twirled his rope, it seemed to become a part of his body. He was one with it. I looked around the room. There were people there from everywhere, and even those who didn't understand English were enjoying his rope tricks and his jokes. There were Japanese, Chinese, Germans, French.

After a while, I said, "Come on, Charlie. I want to show you something that I know you will enjoy."

"Not that blame wheel."

"Oh, no!" I said as I took him by the hand and led him to Hagenbeck's Animal Circus. The elephants were still sliding down the slide and splashing into the pool, then climbing out as fast as their huge bulky bodies could and hurrying back to the slide.

"They're like children at play. But I've never seen children at play having as much fun." We were leaning up against a fence that separated us from all the wild animals of the circus. A coyote came up to the fence and stared at Charlie, and I think it would have licked his hand had Charlie offered it.

"I think he's a might lonesome for his friends back home and I think he knows I am, too." said Charlie.

After we left the animal circus we walked on down the pike, taking in the sights.

"Charlie, from the Ferris Wheel I could see a whole village of huts off the ground on poles and I could also see a whole bunch of tepees. Sue says there is an encampment of Indians here. There also are different kinds of natives from all over the world. There are little pygmies, and giants from Argentina. Let's go see them. I want to see everything."

Charlie felt right at home with the Sioux and enjoyed talking sign with all the Indians, no matter what tribe.

Sue and Charlie's pa had left the fair early and returned home. But I wanted to see it lit again under those thousands of little light bulbs. I wanted again to see the heavens lit up by fireworks that closed each day's activities at the fair. When we got home Charlie was telling Sue about the Igorots from the Philippines. I think Charlie was really impressed by them, for they were such handsome, well-muscled people. And believe me, you could really tell because they wore so few clothes.

"It's a good thing this fall is warm or those Igorots would freeze," I said to Sue.

"I think they are terrible! Do you know that they are dog-eaters? The pound has agreed to supply them with twenty dogs a week. It just makes me sick. We women got together and signed a petition to bring a stop to it, but Judge William H. Taft said the pound had every right to supply them with dogs. They say that families that live near the fair have put their dogs under lock and key to keep pets from being dinner for those awful dog-eaters." Sue's eyes were ablaze.

I never really liked looking at the Philippine village after that, but there was so much more to see at the fair. I went back time and again. Often, I would go to the Palace of Fine Arts to see Charlie's painting. Also, to see if anyone in the throng of crowds that passed through the exhibit wanted any information about the artist, and to be helpful if someone wanted to purchase a Charles Russell painting. It never hurt to mix business with pleasure.

Time passed so quickly that I was astonished to realize that the fair's closing date, December first, was quickly approaching.

"Oh, Charlie, I don't want to see the fair close. It's the most exciting sight I've ever seen. I tried to see it all, but I don't think anyone could ever see it all. Why do they have to take it all down? Do you know they are going to destroy all of those magnificent palaces? Do you know they are going to blow up that fabulous Ferris Wheel? I think it's a shame," I said, my voice trembling.

We were all out at the fair closing night. We watched at midnight as David R. Francis pressed a plunger. The beautiful lights went off, the color stopped shimmering behind the cascades, the wireless tower went black, the Ferris Wheel was lost in darkness. Suddenly fireworks lit the sky spelling the word "Farewell," then another burst "Good-bye" and a band started playing *Auld Lang Syne* .

"Mame," Charlie said. "You're crying."

8

Helping Charlie

"Charlie, isn't it exciting to be back in New York City? It's so alive. Everyone seems to have something important to do."

"You don't count important here unless you're a millionaire. I'd rather be in Great Falls where everybody is somebody," replied Charlie.

"I know, Charlie, but we have some important work to do here before we go home. I know you've been gone a long time and you're homesick. I also know we are going to sell a lot more than one painting this trip. I know which doors to knock on this time."

I was right. We did sell a lot more than one painting. What was more important, I made some very good contacts with the people who really counted, the people with influence and power who could give Charlie contracts for illustrating books and magazine stories.

When we got back to Great Falls, I hired a maid. My time was too valuable for helping Charlie to be spent cooking, doing dishes, or cleaning. I kept up all of Charlie's business correspondence.

Charlie still rose before daylight and made his own breakfast, then went into his studio to paint. This was the time when I could sit down at my desk and take care of the accounts. Charlie had no head for money. Always, as regular as clockwork, he would come in at twelve noon ready for lunch. After lunch, he napped. When he woke up, he put on his Stetson and headed out the front door. I knew where he was going and I couldn't help but be angry, for Charlie was fast becoming a renowned artist.

"Charlie, it is an absolute waste of time for you to go down to the Mint or the Silver Dollar. Your friends can't afford your work. You could get so much more done here in your studio. Just think of the beautiful picture you could paint."

"But the fellas are awaitin' for me. The pictures will get done."

"Don't you have more than two drinks, Charlie Russell. You know how your hand shakes when you've had too much," I said as I held up a two-finger signal.

Charlie nodded and held up two fingers.

He'd come home about five o'clock and he'd always hold up as many fingers as he'd had drinks. If it were more than two, I couldn't help clenching my teeth. Charlie knew I was angry so he would hold his hands out to prove that they weren't shaking. Then he'd take my hands in his and give them a squeeze.

"Mame, I know how hard you work to make me a success, but I just can't give up visitin' with my friends. It's like the milk of life to me." Then he'd give me a hug.

You just couldn't stay mad at Charlie very long.

In the evenings, Albert Trigg often came to visit with Charlie or we would have Albert and Margaret and Josephine for dinner. I would make it a special occasion and dress up. I wanted to show how much I had learned about fashion since my first trip back East. I would also have Charlie make place cards for everyone. I was even more determined to have place cards when we had large dinner parties. We entertained often. Charlie loved having friends around, and they loved being with him. And who knew, with the right invitation list there might be someone who would want to buy a picture.

He would draw wonderful little pictures on the place cards and often Josephine would print the names, for her printing was precise and neat. Her face would brighten up like a child's when I asked her for the favor.

"Oh, no, Nancy, it would never be too much trouble to print on Charlie's cards," Josephine always replied. As she sat at the big oak table in the living room, painstakingly printing the names of our dinner guests, her plain features took on a glow and she was almost pretty.

One day when she was sitting at the table, absorbed in printing the text of a poem that Charlie had illustrated beautifully with watercolor, Charlie came in and leaned over her shoulder. He gave it a pat and said, "Miss Josey, I sure wish I could print half as good as you. Why, your printin' is a thing of beauty."

Josephine blushed right down to her toes. "Charlie, how can you say that? You're a famous artist. I can't even draw a straight line," said Josephine.

When Charlie left, I said, "Why Josephine, I think you have a crush on Charlie."

"Oh, Nancy, don't be silly! Charlie's your husband and you're my dearest friend. You know everyone loves Charlie." Josephine turned an even darker shade of red.

I didn't have many close friends in Great Falls. Everyone was Charlie's friend; I had lots of acquaintances. I was too busy running our business affairs to spend time giving teas and those who belonged to the Great Falls social club, The Maids and The Matrons, and considered themselves the upper, upper crust could never quite forget that I had been a serving girl at the Roberts's when I met Charlie. And Charlie's cowboying friends down at the Mint or the Silver Dollar could never quite forgive me for taking him away from them and 'chaining him to an easel.' Occasionally when my name was left off a guest list for one of The Maids and The Matrons teas it hurt. I would find myself crying when I read about the party in the newspaper, always in the upper left hand column of the society page, the sacred space reserved for Maids and Matrons functions.

"That's all right," I said to the newspaper I was

holding in my hand after I had read about one such party. "Someday we will be so famous you won't dare leave me off your guest list."

I wasn't aware of how far Charlie's reputation had spread, but people knew about him even as far away as California, where every word written about us was eagerly consumed by bright blue eyes that I hadn't looked into for years. I wasn't aware until the morning I received a telegram that read "Arriving Great Falls 3:30 Wednesday afternoon by train. Your sister, Ella."

I rushed out to the studio where Charlie was busily painting and burst in on him. "Oh, Charlie, listen to this," I said breathlessly. He knew it was important for I tried never to interrupt him while he was painting. He put down his brush and stared at my flushed face.

"What is it, Mame? You look like you're about to pop with good news," Charlie said with a laugh.

"Ella's coming. My sister, Ella, is coming tomorrow. She's arriving by train at 3:30. Isn't that wonderful? I haven't seen her or heard from her in years. I wonder if I'll even recognize her. Oh, I must get everything ready for her visit. I wonder how long she can stay. I can't wait to see her," I said as I rushed out of the studio and ran to the house to begin preparations.

The next afternoon, Charlie and I stood on the platform at the train station. I gazed down the tracks searching for the first puff of smoke and listening for the sound of the whistle signaling the oncoming train.

"How do I look? Do I look all right? Do you

think Ella will recognize me? You know I was only sixteen the last time she saw me, and she was hardly more than a baby. She was only six. I wish I had worn my blue wool. Mama always said I looked my best in blue," I rattled on as I paced back and forth on the station platform.

"You look beautiful, Mame. Calm down or you're goin' to walk a path in the boards," Charlie said, looking down at the wooden platform.

Just then we heard the whistle and caught sight of smoke. I reached over and took Charlie's hand. He gave my hand a squeeze. The train chugged to a stop and passengers began climbing off. I searched their faces one by one. Then suddenly Ella was climbing down the train's stairs and standing on the platform.

Her tattered clothes were too tight or maybe she was too big. One of her buttons had popped and a roll of fat was protruding just above her waistline. She was clutching a worn carpetbag that had pieces of clothing spilling out at the top. She looked around. When her gaze rested on me, she started walking toward me. I ran to her and threw my arms around her.

"Oh, Ella, it's been so long. I was afraid I wouldn't recognize you," I said as I searched her face. There was no mistaking those bright blue eyes. They were Ma's eyes, and there was no mistaking the chestnut curls.

"I recognized Charlie Russell, the famous artist, from pictures of him I've seen in the newspapers. I figured you had to be Mamie," Ella replied.

"Welcome to Great Falls," Charlie said with a grin as he took the carpetbag from her and led the way to the buggy. Charlie put Ella's bag in the back seat and helped her in, then helped me into the front seat next to him.

The trip home was in dead silence. After all those years, I couldn't think of anything to say. When we got home, I showed Ella upstairs to the guest bedroom. I went downstairs and waited for her.

"I'm goin' to leave you two girls to talk," said Charlie as he walked out of the front door. "You've got lots of catching up to do."

I waited for Ella. Finally she came down the stairs and stood in the doorway of the living room.

"Come in and sit down. As Charlie says, we have a lot of catching up to do," I said as I patted the place on the sofa next to me.

"Do you have anything to eat? I'm hungry," Ella said.

"It's only a couple of hours until dinner," I answered.

"I'm hungry. Rich folks like you sure have got something to eat," Ella replied.

"Well, let's go into the kitchen, and I'll see what I can find. I think there is some freshly baked bread, and I'm sure some jam," I said.

When we got to the kitchen, Ella spied a chocolate cake I had baked for dinner.

"How about some of that cake?" Ella said as she sat down at the kitchen table and pointed toward the cake.

"That's for dinner," I apologized.

"I'm not goin' to eat it all," Ella said.

I cut her a piece and sat it in front of her and watched her gobble it down. Afterward, she demanded another. After three pieces and two glasses of milk, she stared at me and said, "I guess you know from my telegram that my pa's dead."

I nodded.

"Before he died he told me to come here. He'd kept up with you in the newspapers. He showed me every article he read about you and your famous husband. He said you were so lucky. He never did find any silver in Idaho. He married again just after Ma died and ended up on a chicken ranch in Boise — a smelly, stinkin' chicken ranch. He heard that California was the land of milk and honey. All he had to do was get a grubstake, get out there and life would be sweet. Just as we got out to California he took sick and died. But he said before he died I should come here, and you would take care of me. Because he had taken you in when you didn't have a home. He said you were able to give me a good education since you have so much, and I am your only sister."

I looked at her. There was something about her manner that reminded me of someone. Suddenly I knew who it was. Cousin Thom. It was the way she held her head, the way she talked.

"You're right, Ella. You are my only sister, and I will see to it that you receive an education," I said.

"I'm goin' to be a famous writer, you know. I want to go to the university and take a course in writing, and I'll become rich and famous. You won't be the only one in the family to get your name in the newspapers," Ella said as she licked the chocolate icing off her pudgy fingers.

"I said I'll see to it that you will get an education. I didn't say I would send you to the university. I am willing to send you to secretarial school right here in Great Falls. There is always a need for good secretaries and with a diploma from secretarial school, you can always get a good job," I said matter-of-factly.

Ella stared at me in disbelief. Her mouth dropped open. She got red in the face. "How can you treat me like this?" she said. "I'm your only sister. What would Ma say? I bet she's rolling in her grave."

"You can either go to secretarial school in Great Falls or not. It's your choice," I said calmly.

"Nancy, you are as bossy as ever. You never changed," Ella cried. She jumped up from the table, ran up the stairs, and slammed her bedroom door.

I went to the foot of the stairs and called up, "We are going to serve supper at six-thirty. The Triggs, who are our best friends, are coming. I expect you downstairs by six-fifteen."

Ella reluctantly came down the stairs at six-fifteen. She had changed her dress for one as ill-fitting and shabby as the one she had worn on the train. She pouted all through dinner, answering Josephine's and Margaret's polite questions with grunts. The only time she brightened was when the chocolate cake was served. Immediately after supper, she went upstairs.

Charlie, Margaret and Albert Trigg went into the parlor. Josephine and I cleared the table and took the dishes into the kitchen.

"I'm sure Ella is tired after her long trip," Josephine said.

"Oh, she's just mad that I won't send her to the university, so she can become a famous writer. I told her I would send her to secretarial school. There's a lot more demand for secretaries than there is for writers. She needs to learn a trade so she can support herself," I said.

"It's hard for someone to let a dream die. That's why she's angry. I'm sure it's not with you. I'm sure she's grateful that you have opened your home and heart to her and let her stay here, and are willing to send her to school. Nancy, you are so good," Josephine said as she took the last dish off of the table.

"Oh, Josephine," I said. "Ella may be my sister by flesh and blood, but you are more a sister to me."

Josephine put down the dish and with sudden tears in her eyes came over and hugged me. "I've never had a sister, but if I have one it's you, Nancy."

The next morning I was sitting at my desk going over the accounts when I looked up and saw the cook carrying a breakfast tray up the stairs. By the time I caught up with her, she was halfway up.

"What's this?" I demanded.

"It's breakfast for Miss Ella. She said she was going to have breakfast in bed every morning and I was to bring it to her," stammered Cook.

"I'll take it," I said as I grabbed the tray.

I knocked on the door, then entered.

"Oh, I thought it was the maid bringing me my breakfast," Ella said as she sat up in bed.

I put the tray down carefully on her lap and said, "I want you to enjoy it because this is the last breakfast in bed you'll have."

"What good is it to have servants if they don't wait on you?" Ella demanded.

"You better get something very straight. You are welcome to stay here. I'll be glad to pay your tuition for secretarial school. I will be glad to feed you and clothe you, but no one will wait on you. Everyone here pulls his own weight. You will help out in the kitchen. You will help around the house. Have I made myself clear?" I asked. I turned on my heel and went out the door and down the stairs. Later that morning I was in the parlor showing a prospective buyer from back East several of Charlie's watercolors when Ella came down the stairs. She came into the parlor and interrupted our conversation.

"I'm Ella Allen, Mrs. Russell's only sister. Can you believe she won't send me to the university, but is making me go to secretarial school?"

I coughed and motioned with my head for her to leave. She ignored me.

"Not only that, but I can't even have breakfast in bed. What's the good of having a maid?" Ella rambled on.

The prospective buyer turned red and stammered, "I can see this is not a good time to look at these watercolors. I'll be going. Maybe another time, Mrs. Russell." He left as quickly as he could get out the front door.

"Ella," I said as I stepped toward her. "Don't you ever do that again." I suppose she could read the absolute fury in my eyes for she stepped back.

"There are two rules that you are never to forget. One, you are never to interrupt Charlie while he is painting, and two, you are never ever to interrupt me while I am selling one of Charlie's paintings.

"If you do, I will pack you up and you will be on the next train back to California. Now, I suggest you go out into the kitchen and see if you can help Cook," I said through clenched teeth.

Ella rushed out of the parlor past Josephine, into the kitchen.

"I didn't hear you come in," I said. "Did you hear what I said?"

"Yes," Josephine said. "You mustn't be too hard on her. You can tell she's had a hard life, and you two have been apart for many, many years. It will take time."

Josephine was right. It did take time. I wouldn't say we became loving sisters, but we developed a mutual acceptance. Ella lived with us and went to secretarial school. Upon graduation, she got a job with the *Tribune* as a secretary. We got along better after the Triggs introduced Ella to Frank Ironsides, a fellow Englishman. Ella was captivated by his English accent. She even reduced a bit and improved her grooming when they began to keep company. After they were married Ella put on such English airs that Charlie always referred to her as "Mrs. Stonehenge." But one thing she never did again was interrupt me when I had a prospective buyer.

Reverend Newell Dwight Hillis was one client I am glad Ella did not alienate. One afternoon when I answered the door, there he stood, a powerfully built man in a clerical collar.

"Mrs. Russell, I'm Reverend Hillis. I'm at the Park Hotel while in town for a lecture and I have seen a picture of your husband's at the bar there. I would very much like to discuss a one-man show in Brooklyn, New York."

"Won't you please come in," I beamed.

"Your husband is a genius," Reverend Hillis said as he entered the sitting room.

Being in full agreement, I knew that I was going to like this man. Brooklyn, New York, I thought.

"Mr. Russell is working in his studio this morning, but you and I can talk. Where are you planning to have this show?" I asked.

"At our church, The Plymouth Church of the Pilgrims," he replied.

My smile faded. "Having it in a church, it seems to me, would limit the number of people who would come. Isn't there a gallery or a museum that would be more suitable?"

"Quite to the contrary, our church is the center of activity for the whole community. Forgive me if I sound immodest, but some consider The Plymouth Church of the Pilgrims to be the most important church in America. Henry Ward Beecher was pastor there. We will invite not only our members but all the influential people of Brooklyn to see this exhibition. And, of course, gentlemen of the press."

I had no idea who Henry Ward Beecher was, but I knew this was a man who had spent his life learning to cultivate an audience, and that I could learn from him. Of all the ministers in New York, he was the one in Great Falls on a lecture circuit. There must be a reason.

"We would be delighted to come to Brooklyn to your Plymouth Church for a one-man show," I said, extending my hand.

Reverend Hillis took my hand in his large, strong one and gave it a firm shake.

"Won't you come meet Charlie?" I asked.

"Lead the way, my dear, for I have waited with great anticipation for that very event. Not every day has one the fortuitous opportunity of meeting America's most famous western artist." Reverend Hillis boomed as if from a pulpit.

I led the way. Charlie was absorbed in painting a cowboy on a bucking bronc. The cowboy was hanging on by the reins for dear life and his legs were squeezing against the horse's twisting and turning body. There was plenty of daylight between him and his saddle.

"Charles, this is Reverend Hillis of the Plymouth Church in Brooklyn, New York. He wants us to have a one-man show there. I told him we would be delighted."

Charlie put down his brush and pulled out his tobacco pouch to roll a cigarette. After he had lit it, he asked, "I can't see why a church would want to show a bunch of cowboys getting knocked off horses."

"Oh, Mr. Russell, your paintings are far more than that. They are true poetry in motion. The beauty of God's nature leaps from your canvases. Man's courage and vulnerability cry out to the viewer. As I told your wife, you are indeed a genius."

Charlie grinned and turned a little red. "No, I'm just a cowboy with a paint brush, but we have a deal. I do the painting and Mame here does the business, so if she said we'd be there, we will."

"Fine, fine, Mr. Russell," Reverend Hillis said as he pumped Charlie's hand. "Tell me now about the painting you're working on, if it isn't an imposition."

"Well, that was a bad one. He was wild and mean. They'd tried to break him before, even tried to break him the Indian way in a river. He had a real reputation, and lots of cowboys who thought they were good had tried . . ."

I slipped out of the studio as Charlie began his story. Reverend Hillis sat in rapt attention. It was hours before he left and Charlie came into the house.

I spent a year putting that show together, but it was well worth it. Critics loved it. Afterward we were invited to have many one-man shows, including one at the Alaska-Yukon-Pacific Exposition in Seattle. But the most important invitation came in 1911 from the Folsom Galleries at 396 Fifth Avenue, New York City.

"Oh, Charlie, this is the big break we've been working for," I said when I put down the letter.

"I must go to New York early to be sure that invitations go to the right people. The paintings must be hung to their best advantage. We have to work with the lighting. And I may want to change a frame or two. Someone from the *New York Times* must interview you before the show opens. Isn't Bill Hart in a play on Broadway right now? I bet he knows someone at the *Times*. And I know Will Rogers will help us. We've got to make the most of this."

"Whoa, girl. You're makin' me tired just listenin' to all we've got to do," Charlie moaned.

"Charlie, you just paint. We are going to need some large pieces for this show. I want the Folsom Galleries' walls covered from ceiling to floor with Charles Marion Russell paintings."

Charlie shook his head slowly as he walked to his studio. Sometimes my enthusiasm bewildered him but I had learned that planning and preparation were essential. I still remembered the little basement gallery we rented on our first trip to New York. I was so thrilled to hang Charlie's paintings. But nobody came. That was never going to happen again.

We went to New York early with lots of paintings. Although Charlie didn't outwardly show concern, I knew he, too, felt the importance of this venture. I had made out a list of people to be invited to the opening, among them our friends Bill Hart and Will Rogers. They would add excitement and glamour to the opening. Patrons would love it. I planned to hang the show myself, for I knew what paintings worked well in combination and which needed more light to reveal their subtle changes of color.

"Charlie, I'm going to the gallery," I said, early in the morning of our first day in New York. "There's so much that needs to be done. Will you be all right?"

Charlie still didn't like New York. He still preferred his hotel room to the crowded streets.

"I hear Ed Borein got himself a place up on Fifty-seventh Street. That's where all the boys hang out. They say Ed makes a great pot of chili and there's almost always one on the fire. I think I'll just mosey on up that way and see if ol' Bill Hart or Bill Rogers might be there. It will be good to see those fellows again," said Charlie.

"If they are, please, Charlie, have them ring up. I need to speak with them about the opening."

Later that day, as I returned to our hotel room, the telephone was ringing.

"Hello," I said.

"Nancy, this is Bill Hart. It sure is good to see Charlie again. New York will be a much better place now that you both are here. Charlie said you needed me."

My exhaustion vanished. "Oh, Bill, it is wonderful to hear your voice. I never come to New York without thinking of you and how you took Charlie and me to see the ocean for the first time on our first trip here. I still remember putting my foot in the Atlantic with Charlie holding one of my hands and you the other. I must have been very loud," I laughed.

"And what a sight you made, dancing in the waves with your blonde curls blowing in the wind," Bill chuckled.

"That was fine. It will be so good to see you again. You know Charlie is having a one-man show at the Folsom Galleries. Now you must mark your calendar for April twelfth, for you must come to the opening. It would mean so much to both Charlie and me to have you there."

"Of course, I'll be there. I wouldn't miss it. Is there anything else I could do?" asked Bill.

"Now that you mention it, Bill," I said, "Do you know anyone at the *New York Times*? You know how powerful that paper is. Well, it would do all kinds of good if I could arrange for Charlie to have an interview with one of their reporters before the show opened."

"I've got some connections. I'll see what I can do," Bill said as he hung up.

I laid down on my bed, closed my eyes and smiled. The next morning a reporter from the *New York Times* rang up requesting an interview with Charlie.

"Mr. Russell has a very demanding schedule, but I'm sure we could make time. How would two o'clock tomorrow afternoon suit you?

Charlie always wanted his lunch right at noon, then he'd lie down for an hour's nap. At two, I knew he'd be awake and refreshed.

I changed my clothes three times before the young reporter arrived, and retouched my makeup twice. I had learned long ago that comeliness was useful. I wanted the interview to appear in the Sunday paper, which more people read than any other edition.

When there was a knock at the door, I opened it with my best smile, and a young reporter — actually he wasn't but a year or so younger than I was — smiled back. I showed him into the parlor, for we had a suite this time, and excused myself to get Charlie. When I went into the bedroom, Charlie was lying on the bed staring at the ceiling.

"He's here. Charlie, let me straighten your tie," I said as I brushed cigarette ash from on his shoulder.

"Mr. Russell, it is an honor to meet you. I asked for this assignment, for I have long been a fan of your work. The way you can capture the courage in a cowboy's eyes on a bucking bronc, or the sadness in the features of an old Indian, or the beauty and the danger of a buffalo herd stampeding, is enormously admirable!"

Charlie relaxed visibly.

"Tell me," said the young reporter as he pulled out a pencil and pad. "How long were you actually a cowboy? When did you go to Montana? I've heard you lived with the Bloods. Is that true? I've also heard that Mrs. Russell acts as your business agent. It's hard to believe that anyone so young and pretty could have a good head for business. I want to know all about you." He poised his pencil to write.

"Well—" Charlie said, "I was almost sixteen when I left St. Louis for Montana."

Soon Charlie was into his story of the early days and the reporter was hanging on his every word, sometimes laughing so hard that he forgot about writing in his pad.

After several hours he suddenly looked at his watch. He jumped up because he was late for another appointment.

"I can't believe that time has flown by so fast. It really was wonderful to meet you, Mr. Russell, and you, too, Mrs. Russell. I must run now. I'd really love to stay. I could listen to Mr. Russell all day."

"If you need any further information, please

don't hesitate to contact us," I said as I showed him out. "Oh, by the way, don't you think this would make a perfect piece for your Sunday edition, the Sunday or so before Charlie's big show opens at the Folsom Galleries?"

"I think so, Mrs. Russell, but I don't make those decisions, my editor does," he replied.

"But you might suggest it," I said as I opened the door for him.

I didn't know whether they would print one sentence, one paragraph or one column of the interview. I could hardly wait. But it wasn't one sentence, nor one paragraph, nor one column. It was almost a full page and Charlie's picture was right in the center of it. And it was in the Sunday edition, March nineteenth, 1911.

"Oh, Charlie, this is wonderful!" I said as I hugged the paper to me, after I had reread the article. "Look at this headline — 'Cowboy Vividly Paints the Passing Life of the Plains.' Let me read you part of the first paragraph. 'Kid Russell or to be formal, "Charlie" Russell, or to be ridiculously formal Charles M. Russell, cowpuncher that was, painter and sculptor that is, has come to town from Montana for his first one-man exhibition. He has brought with him a score of the paintings and bronze groups of Indians and cowboys and wolves and buffaloes that are making him famous. Also he has brought along plenty of brawn and sinew and the indescribable gait of the man who lives in the saddle.'" I paused.

"Go on, Mame," Charlie said with obvious enjoyment.

"Charlie, how can anyone resist coming to your opening? They'll come not only to see your paintings but to meet you. Listen to this last paragraph— 'Somebody once wrote to Andy Adams, author of *The Log of a Cowboy*, asking exactly how cowpunchers dressed in the early eighties. 'Ask Charlie Russell,' Adams replied. 'If he painted a naked cowpuncher swimming across a river, you'd know it was a cowpuncher.''' I put the paper down and hugged Charlie. "We'll have a huge crowd. I couldn't have written it better myself. We couldn't afford to take out a whole page of advertising in the *New York Times*, but here it is in the Sunday edition."

I wasn't a bit surprised on April twelfth when the Folsom Galleries were packed for Charlie's opening. Everyone who was anyone showed up. That night when we returned to our hotel suite I was still so excited I couldn't contain myself.

"Charlie, we have arrived. We have arrived." I talked on and on about the opening, wanting to relive every moment. Charlie was exhausted. He undressed and went to bed, but I was too excited to sleep. I wanted to savor the taste of that night. Finally, I crept into bed and cuddled next to Charlie's sleeping form, thinking that life had never been so sweet.

9

Life in Great Falls

I THOUGHT THE MONTANA STATE LEGISLATURE would come, hat in hand, and beg Charlie to paint the mural they were planning for the State Capitol. But oh no, they were going to have a competition. They had set up a selection committee. There was only one man alive who could possibly paint that mural; that was Charlie Russell. There was only one man who could paint a Montana sky, or a Montana mountain, or a Montana Indian, and that was Charlie Russell. Charlie wanted to do it.

"Charlie, you have to go after that job. You're the only one who can possibly do it right," I urged.

"I don't know, Mame. I've never painted a mural before. I'm not sure I can do it," he said.

"It's just a big, big painting. Why, it would be an insult if they gave it to any other artist. Who else has had a one-man show at the Folsom Galleries? I can't believe they could consider anyone other than you, Charlie, but most of all I can't believe you would hesitate one minute about entering. If you want something you have to go after it." My voice rose.

There was a minute of silence.

"I know, Mame," Charlie said just above a whisper.

I went to Charlie, who was sitting in the big chair in the living room, and sat down on the floor beside him. I pressed my cheek against his knee. In a soft voice, I said, "Isn't your good friend, Frank Bird Linderman, the Deputy Secretary of State, on that selection committee? You've told me many times how you both came out to Montana as boys, and what a steadfast friend he is."

Charlie stroked my hair gently.

He got the job. Many people think it's the best thing he ever did. Everyone in Great Falls seemed to share in the pride of Charlie's success. As his fame spread, all the important people who came to Great Falls wanted to meet Charlie Russell, the cowboy artist. If they expected to find rubes here, they were greatly surprised. Because of the copper mines, many of the founding fathers of Great Falls were engineers with degrees from prestigious schools in the East. Their wives were graduates of the best finishing schools. Professors from Ivy League schools always seemed eager to come to Montana to give a lecture and even more eager to sit in our parlor afterward to have tea and visit with Charlie.

On one such occasion a visiting professor of English literature was expounding on the beauty of Keats's verse. I sat listening intensely, trying to memorize some of his beautiful phrases. I had just poured us all some tea, and was holding my cup with my little finger carefully curled. Charlie was concentrating on eating cookies. When the cookies disappeared, there was nothing left to hold Charlie's interest. He stood up.

"I think I'll go in and take a bath," Charlie said. "You know it's Saturday night."

The professor blushed. I blushed. Charlie stood up, stretched, started out of the room, then turned and said, "Even if I do clog up all the sewers in Great Falls."

"Oh, Mrs. Russell, I must be going," stuttered the professor, apparently unused to being abruptly ignored.

"I'm sorry," I apologized. "It's just unless you're talking about cowboys, Indians, horses, the land . . ." I shook my head.

After he left I went storming upstairs. I could hear Charlie singing at the top of his lungs in the bathtub in the bathroom downstairs. He had a couple of favorite songs that he used to sing to the cattle. When the singing finally stopped I knew he was on his way upstairs. I was sitting at the dresser brushing my hair when he came into the bedroom. He caught my eye in the mirror. Through clenched teeth I said, "Charlie, how could you?"

"I've never been so bored. If I'd stayed there another ten minutes, I'd been sound asleep and snorin'. I bet that fella don't know the front end of a horse from its rear, and he probably wears lace on his B.V.D's."

Still everyone of note came to see us when they came to Great Falls. Often we had house guests, especially artists. Then Charlie wasn't bored. If he loved talking about cowboying, he also loved talking about painting. Bill Krieghoff, the portrait painter, came to Great Falls and, of course, he stayed with us. One morning at breakfast I looked up and caught him staring at me.

"Mrs. Russell, do you know you have an extraordinarily beautiful face?" He didn't wait for me to answer. "But it's not your beauty I want to capture, it's your vitality. It's that energy radiates from you."

"You flatter me," I blushed.

"See, you're blushing. That's what I want to paint — the girl-like quality of a successful business woman. It's a dichotomy. What a challenge. I just can't decide if I want to paint you in hat and gloves — the way you look when you enter a New York office — or in a simple frock with your hair falling softly on your shoulders as you look this morning."

It ended that Bill painted two portraits — one of each. In one I was dressed in black silk embroidered with pink and red silk roses, carried a black velvet muff, and wore a black hat with pink and red tulle and a black feather. Bill said I looked every inch the grand lady.

Then he painted me in a soft green voile dress looking at a vase in which I was about to arrange some fresh-cut flowers. Bill and Charlie liked the one with the green dress. I preferred the black silk.

Phil Goodwin also stayed with us. In fact, Phil was visiting the summer we put in the fireplace mantel at our Lake McDonald lodge.

Years before, Charlie had found a spot next to the lake where he could escape every summer. He'd take his gear and go camping. I had gone with him several times, and I knew why he loved it so. It was perhaps the most beautiful spot on earth. The first time I saw it I could only whisper, for I was so awed by the reflection of the snow-capped mountains in the crystal surface of the lake.

"Charlie if ever we can afford it, we are going to build a place here and come every summer. A view like this could renew one's soul," I said as I closed my eyes and crossed my heart to make a promise.

The promise came true in 1906. In 1907, we built our summer home and christened it "Bull Head Lodge" after Charlie's famous emblem. It just so happened that's when Phil Goodwin was visiting. He and Charlie made a big to-do over the christening.

"I think we ought to break a bottle of champagne on it, like they do for a ship on a maiden voyage," suggested Phil.

"Seems like a waste to me," answered Charlie. They were working on the fireplace, sketching elk and deer into the wet cement and having more fun than little boys playing with mud pies. As Phil sketched, he would stand back proudly and observe his handiwork.

"You know, that doesn't look half-bad," said Phil when they finished.

"It's beautiful. What a great mantel. There's not another like it in the whole world," I said with delight.

"It's a fittin' mantel for our lodge," said Charlie.

The woods around the lake were full of wild animals. Charlie put salt licks out for the deer. By the end of that summer they were not afraid to come right down in front of Bull Head Lodge to get a drink from the lake. Charlie sketched them often. They would lift their heads when they heard him and stand quite still as if posing just for him. Maybe they knew his drawings would make them immortal.

Each summer at Lake McDonald seemed better than the one before. Charlie would paint and not waste his afternoons at the Mint or the Silver Dollar. But he still loved visiting with his friends. It seemed talking to his friends was the prime to his pump. Solitude was not good for Charlie's work.

We always had lots of friends and family visiting us at Lake McDonald. Charlie's father and his stepmother Florence came, as did Charlie's nephew, Austin, and niece, Isabel, and my pa. Of course the Triggs were frequent visitors. There were many more. We had to devise a way from the very beginning to screen off the sleeping areas when we had a full house. Charlie made a screen with muslin panels. Since many of our early guests were artists, they would draw on the muslin and then sign the panel. It became a tradition for each visitor to sign. The screens became a wonderful record of our good times.

There was the big tourist center at Lake McDonald Lodge across the lake from our Bull Head Lodge. Since John Lewis had built it, everyone called it Lewis House. I loved taking our house guests there for dinner. We would take them in one of the two large passenger boats that ran up and down the lake. I dressed for dinner. Charlie wore his half-breed sash, boots, Stetson, and of course, the rings. We would land at Lewis House dock and make our way up the short path to the lodge, entering the enormous two-story lobby. There was a balcony around the lobby held up by posts made of huge tree trunks stripped of bark and polished to a high gloss. A large man could barely put his arms around them.

An enormous rock fireplace was always lit in the evenings, for even in summer the night air held a chill. The glow of firelight reflected on the highly polished columns, providing a grand setting for dinner. As we entered they would ring the chimes and announce that "The Charles Russell party has arrived."

Every head would turn. Lake McDonald was a popular vacation spot for people from all over the country. One never knew who might be staying at Lewis

House and might be interested in buying a Charlie Russell painting. I had the manager of Lewis House hang Charlie's paintings around the walls of the lobby.

After dinner, guests would inevitably approach Charlie, introduce themselves, and tell him how much they admired his work. Then they would ask Charlie to tell them the stories behind the paintings. Within a minute or two, Charlie would have them completely captivated. Seldom did a summer pass that we didn't sell some of the paintings hanging in the lobby.

"Nancy, I thought you built this place on Lake McDonald to get away, to have a vacation," said Josephine on one of her visits to the lake.

"Of course, we are away. But wouldn't it be silly not to sell a painting if someone wanted to buy it? How could I possibly say 'wait until fall'?" I answered. "And don't I sleep in late here?"

"It's so cold here in the early morning that anyone would hate to leave the warm covers," Josephine laughed.

I knew she wasn't criticizing me. She was just making a statement. But didn't she realize that those visitors from back East staying at Lewis House might not have another opportunity to see Charlie's paintings and to meet him? We should take advantage of every opportunity, vacation or not.

In the fall we'd return to Great Falls for the snows come early in Montana. I always had a pang of regret when we closed up Bull Head Lodge and left beautiful Lake McDonald.

"I'm going to miss this place until next summer, Charlie," I always said.

"There's somethin' special here," he'd reply.

But it never took us long to get back into the Great Falls routine.

I was busy, but when the women of the Episcopal Church came to me and asked me to head up their money-raising project, I agreed. After they left, I flew out to the studio to tell Charlie.

"Guess what?" I asked excitedly. "Oh, you'll never ever guess! I'll have to tell you. The women of the Episcopal Church came to *me* and asked *me* to head up their fund-raising. You know what that means. It's a great honor. I think what we need to do is to put on an opera. I'll never forget that opera I saw in St. Louis. I wonder what opera company I can get to come to Great Falls?" I flew out of the studio and ran back to the house before Charlie had time to answer. There was so much to do.

At this time, Charlie's nephew Austin was staying with us. He had been visiting us at Lake McDonald that summer. When it came time to leave, he asked if he could come to Great Falls with us rather than return to St. Louis. It was time for him to go into the family business, but he prefered to stay out West where the excitement and adventure was. He loved being around his Uncle Charlie, whom he idolized. We were delighted to have him for he was pleasant company and always willing to help out.

I decided that the opera we were going to give was *Little Almond Eyes*, the story of a young Oriental girl. In order to make the money-making project a success, I needed some help.

"I need you and Austin to make me hundreds and hundreds of little yellow paper figures. I want to hang them on the lapels of every man, woman, and child in Great Falls. Every time anyone sees one of these figures he will be reminded of the opera," I told Charlie as I pushed him and Austin out of the house toward the studio.

Austin enthusiastically joined the project. He would jump up early in the morning, race out to the studio and spend most of the day there. After several days I decided to visit the studio and check on the progress of the paper figures.

"Where are all of the yellow paper figures I need to promote the opera?" I asked.

"Here they are, Mame," Charlie said as he proudly displayed a few Chinese figures.

Each was different. There was the Chinese laundry man from Utica, his wife, and each of his children, all beautifully painted on the yellow paper. There were other Chinese portraits staring up at me from the row of paper figures that Charlie had laid out for my inspection.

"No, this won't do. You don't understand. I want hundreds of these. I want one for *every man*, *woman, and child* in Great Falls," I scolded.

Austin and Charlie looked crestfallen, especially Austin. He thought I would be proud of the meticulous care he had taken with his figures.

"Now, don't put on so much detail. Don't you understand? I'm going to use these figures to advertise the opera. I want hundreds of people to come because I won't be satisfied with making the same amount as they made last year. I am determined to make twice as much." I left the studio.

"It looks like your Aunt Nancy has her mind made up and once her mind is set there's no turnin' back," said Charlie to Austin. "We both best get busy."

We didn't make twice as much as they had the year before. We made *four* times as much. I took the leftover money across the river and gave it to the Cree Indians. Every time I saw them my heart ached. They were so poor. They had migrated into Montana from Canada and the government wouldn't do anything for them because they were Canadian Indians. The Canadian government would do nothing for them because they were living in the United States. People in Great Falls ignored them too, and acted as if then they would go away. But how can you ignore starvation? Those poor little children half-naked in the cold with their rib bones sticking out above swollen, empty bellies. I knew the Cree Indians desperately needed the extra money I had made on the Church fund-raising project, so I took it upon myself to go across the river and give it to their chief.

I thought the members of the church would praise my money-raising efforts. I certainly thought they would understand my giving the extra profit to the Cree Indians. The first Sunday after our successful opera, I took very special care in my grooming, changing clothes three or four times because I wanted to look my very best. I took extra care with my makeup and combed my hair into curls to frame my face. I wore a broad-brimmed, black hat trimmed with black lace and a white ostrich plume I had bought in New York. I knew that the minister would recognize me from the pulpit and compliment me on the job I had done as chairman of the money-making project. If I were asked to stand I had already chosen the words I would say. I checked myself one last time in the mirror.

But the minister didn't say a word about my efforts from the pulpit. All he did was to shake my hand as I left the church, smile and almost whisper, "Thank you, Mrs. Russell." As I hurried out one of the ladies of the women's association grasped me by the shoulders and swung me around to face her.

"Mrs. Russell,' she hissed, "I wouldn't have worked so hard if I'd known you were going to give that money to those dirty savages." Then she wheeled and stormed away before I had a chance to respond.

I was so mad I stomped home. I stomped out to Charlie's studio and interrupted his regular Sunday morning get-together. Charlie was standing by the big stone fireplace stirring a pot of beans. I could smell the bacon frying and the bachelor's bread baking. Charlie had the flour sack tucked in his sash and his sleeves were rolled up. He took his Sunday morning cooking very seriously. Every head turned when I came in.

"Do you know what one of those mean-mouthed women of the church said to me? 'I wouldn't have worked so hard if I'd known you were going to give that money to those dirty savages.'"

"Well, Mame, you know maybe she's never been cold, maybe she's never been hungry, maybe she's never lived in a tent," Charlie explained.

"Of all people in the world, I thought that you, Charles Marion Russell, would take my side. You love the Indians. How often have you told me about the time you lived with the Bloods?" I said.

"Mrs. Russell, you know Charlie don't find fault with nobody. As he always says, you need to walk in that fella's moccasins. And I bet he's right. I bet that lady at the church never has been cold or hungry. She didn't mean any harm in what she said to you. Why, everybody in town knows how hard you worked. I never saw so many little yellow paper figures hanging off of so many people," said one of Charlie's friends.

My hurt pride was salved a little, for I knew he was right. Charlie always thought the best of people. I left the studio to go back to the house. Charlie turned back to his pot of beans and the hum of conversation started up again.

10

Going Abroad

"REMEMBER THE TIME you lived with the Bloods in Canada?" I asked Charlie. "Remember what they wore, their tepees, their horses?"

"Why?" Charlie asked back.

"I think you should draw those Indians and the Canadian Rockies. And those Royal Mounties with their beautiful red jackets and polished buttons. We can take them when we go to Calgary for the Stampede and your one-man show. There must be royalty at Calgary. If we can make a big enough splash in Canada, the ripples might travel all the way to England." I sat at my vanity, brushing my hair until it shone.

Charlie was sitting in a big chair pulling off his boots. He looked up and said, "I ain't lost nothing in England."

"You are beginning to be known back East. That's important. But to be really famous you must be known in England. If we handle everything just right, this trip to Calgary will open the doors to England. Please, Charlie, take my advice." I got up and gave Charlie a hug.

"I don't know why you're so fired up to go to England, but it couldn't hurt to paint those Canadian scenes. It's beautiful country."

I was right. There was royalty at the Stampede, the Duke and Duchess of Connaught and Sir Henry Mill Pellat. Sir Henry bought five of Charlie's paintings. So I wasn't surprised when we received an invitation in 1914 to exhibit Charlie's paintings at the Dore Gallery on Bond Street in London, England.

England!

I had been at parties for years where people talked about England. It seemed that everyone had traveled abroad. Now I, too, was going *abroad.* We took the train to New York, stopping in St. Louis to see Charlie's family. Sue insisted on giving us a big dinner party.

"Yes, it's true," I said at dinner, "we're on our way to London, England."

"You must shop at Harrods. You've never seen such a store!"

"You must go to Westminster Abbey."

"You must see the Tower of London."

"Take the boat trip to Greenwich."

Everyone was talking at once.

"Oh, I'll have to write this all down. I'll never remember." I laughed. I looked around the table. Only one couple kept quiet, their eyes on their soup plates. They had not been abroad.

After everyone had left, Sue, T. G., Charlie, and I went into the sitting room.

"Don't you think everyone had a good time?" asked Sue. "I know they were glad to see you two again."

"Sue, it was beautiful. The food was delicious. If everyone had as good a time as Chas and I did your party was a huge success," I replied.

"When did you start calling Charlie 'Chas'?" Sue asked.

"When Mame decided that my status had gone up as a painter, 'cause I was invited to show at the Dore Gallery. 'Course, she still calls me Charlie when it's just us, but when she's talkin' to other folks it's now Chas," Charlie replied.

"Well, Chas or Charlie or whatever Nancy wants to call you, I bet you will take London by storm," said Sue.

"Oh, Sue, I wish you and T.G. were coming with us. I can't wait to board that big luxury cruise liner in New York and sail all the way across the ocean to the other side of the world. "

The liner was all I ever dreamed and more. As we climbed the gangplank, I held on tightly to the rail, for it was a much bigger ship than I had imagined. We were shown to our handsome stateroom.

"Come on, Charlie. Let's go back outside and

watch the ship pull away," I said, taking his hand and pulling him with me. The sounds of people calling good-bye and the answering calls of bon voyage mingled with the toots of tug boat horns as the ship slowly pulled away from the dock.

"We are really on our way to England, to the Dore Gallery," I sighed. New York City slowly disappear over the horizon.

But Charlie spent much of his time leaning over the rail 'feeding the fishes,' as he called it. He'd been tossed and turned on many a bucking bronco, but nothing had ever turned his stomach like the rolling movement of the ship at sea. When he wasn't by the rail he was lying down in the cabin.

"If you take a walk with me around the promenade deck and get some fresh air, you'll feel better. If you must lie down, why don't you lie in one of the deck chairs? The people on this trip are so interesting. There's a lot of money walking around on that promenade deck. We just might get a commission or two on our way to London," I said as I tried to coax Charlie up on deck. I loved walking around the deck studying the passengers with their beautiful clothes, furs, and jewels. I knew they could buy a Charlie Russell painting. Perhaps they needed to know that a famous artist was aboard. I stopped by to see the ship's doctor.

"I'm Mrs. Charles Russell. My husband has been quite seasick. I would like something for him."

"Of course, ma'am. That name sounds familiar.

Isn't he a painter of sorts?" said the doctor as he poured out some green medicine into a small bottle.

"He is *the* Charles Marion Russell, America's most famous artist of western subjects, and we are on our way to London, England, for a one-man show at the Dore Gallery on New Bond Street," I said, taking the medicine from his hand and putting it in my purse.

That evening we received an invitation from the captain of the ship to join him at his table.

"Please Charlie, oh, please. I've never eaten at a captain's table. Take the medicine I brought. I know it will make you feel better. You know how you love to visit with people. You've hardly seen anyone on this trip. I think dinner at the captain's table will do you good," I pleaded.

"I feel like I swallowed a bull-whip snake, and he just won't stop thrashin' around," said Charlie.

"Well, take the medicine and see if you don't feel better."

Charlie did, and he did feel better. That evening we sat at the captain's table. Everyone wanted to know who was the broad-shouldered man in the soft shirt, tight pants, red silk sash, and high-heeled boots. Soon Charlie was telling them his cowboying stories. The bull-whip snake was forgotten.

When we arrived at Southhampton, it was rainy and gray. I had gone out on deck early because I wanted to catch first sight of the English coast when it appeared upon the horizon. I couldn't see anything because of the fog, but as we got closer I could hear the fog horns at the lighthouse, the bells ringing, the tossing buoys, and the screeching of the sea gulls as they dove through the air toward the wake of our boat looking for garbage thrown overboard by the ship's cooks.

The fog and drizzle continued on our whole trip by boat train to London. But it couldn't dampen my spirits. We took a taxi to our hotel, the Warwick, where we had a suite.

"Let's not unpack. Let's go straight to the Dore Gallery. I can't wait to see London." I danced around the room.

"Mame, you're just like a little kid waiting for ol' Santa to come," said Charlie.

"Santa never brought me anything as good as a trip to London. I can't wait to see the sights," I said as I took Charlie's hand and led him out of our suite.

Charlie was caught up in my excitement.

"Shall I hail us a cab?" Charlie asked.

"Oh, no, let's walk a ways first," I said. "Do you know that Queen Elizabeth may have walked on these very same stones, or maybe Henry the VIII?"

"I hope they could do it a smart better than me." said Charlie, for his high-heeled boots were made for a Montana saddle, not for rain-slick cobblestones. The rain had stopped, the fog had cleared and the sun was trying to shine. The high-pitched tile roofs with their hundreds of chimneys shone in the sunlight.

"Charlie, it's beautiful," I exclaimed.

"It don't hold a candle to a Montana sky," said Charlie.

I ignored his remark. "I think the sun's shining is a good omen for our trip," I said as we heard the chimes of Big Ben announcing the hour. "Even Big Ben is welcoming us. Charlie, we're going to take London by storm," I declared.

We did. The critics loved Charlie's work. The English were fascinated by the scenes of cowboys and captivated by the mystique of the Indians. Even the Queen Mother came to view Charlie's show. I spent the whole day before her visit practicing my curtsy.

"Mame, aren't you even coming to bed?" asked Charlie.

"Not until I get this curtsy right."

"You'll be so tired you'll fall over from lack of sleep," said Charlie.

I knew that when I met the Queen Mother I wouldn't be tired or sleepy no matter how late I stayed up. I wanted to savor every minute of that meeting — to memorize it, so I could relive it time and again.

The whole trip to England was like a dream — a dream come true. Not only was Charlie's show a success, not only did I get to meet the Queen Mother, but Lord and Lady Ramsey gave a party in Charlie's honor.

"Nancy, you've changed clothes three times, combed your hair twice, and spent as much time painting your face as I do a picture. If you don't get ready, we're going to miss our own party. Lord Ramsey's carriage has been waiting for us for an hour. It's a ways out to his place," Charlie said.

"Charlie, don't rush me. The more you rush me, the further behind I get and all of my fingers become thumbs. I want to look elegant tonight," I said as I finally put the finishing touches on my hair.

"You look beautiful. Why, you'll put all those other ladies to shame," Charlie said as we left our suite at the Warwick.

"The women in the Episcopal Church would be green with envy," I said as I got into Lord Ramsey's carriage for our long ride to his manor house.

It was a fairy tale come true. There was a castle with many turrets reaching up into the heavens. There was a long circular drive with a reflecting pond in the center where water lilies bloomed in profusion. When our carriage stopped at the mammoth front door, it was opened by a servant who wore white stockings, satin knee pants, a velvet jacket, and a ruffled shirt.

"He has silver buckles on his shoes," I whispered to Charlie.

"He looks old enough to have played marbles with Oliver Cromwell," Charlie whispered back.

As we entered the enormous front hall, Charlie said, "This they could use as a skatin' rink."

"Shhh," I said as Lord and Lady Ramsey came to greet us. Lord Ramsey bowed low and took my hand and kissed it. I blushed. I don't know why. I wanted to look as if I belonged. I wanted to do everything that lords and ladies do — but I couldn't help it. I couldn't get used to having my hand kissed.

"Welcome to England and to our home. We are delighted to have such distinguished visitors. We were quite taken by your show at the Dore Gallery," Lord Ramsey said as he guided us around the room introducing us to his other guests, all of whom seemed to have titles. After our introduction, Lord Ramsey suggested we view his family's collection of art.

"We have some good examples of Sir Joshua Reynolds, Gainsborough, a Turner or two, but mostly there are portraits of my ancestors," Lord Ramsey said as he started the guided tour.

We went from one "skatin' rink" as Charlie put it, to another. There were paintings hung in enormously ornate gold leaf frames from ceiling to floor. Most were of stern-looking people in silks and satins, and ruffles and lace. If children accompanied them, they were equally unsmiling. Occasionally, there was a family dog in the picture, but even the dogs looked as if they never wagged their tails.

Every now and again, there was a piece of armor on the wall, or a battle ax or sword. There were several knights' full suits of armor.

"I don't see how a fella wearing one of those suits had any chance of gettin' up if he fell off his horse," said Charlie.

Quickly I asked about one of the ornate shields.

"That belonged to one of my ancestors. It bears

the family crest. That very same shield saved his life when he was fighting in the Crusades," Lord Ramsey explained.

I knew very little about the Crusades. There were lots of things I hadn't had a chance to learn about in that little one-room school house back in Kentucky. I knew I would go home and read up on the Crusades, so the next time I came to England and ever met anyone whose ancestors had fought in them at least I would know what they were.

One room opened onto another with more stern portraits. I could tell that Charlie was bored. Had they been portraits of Teddy Blue, Charlie Bird, Young Boy or Buffalo Robe, he would have been enthralled. We were saved by the bell as another costumed servant walked from room to room striking a gong to announce that dinner was served.

Lord Ramsey took my arm to lead me into the dining room. I motioned to Charlie to do the same for Lady Ramsey.

Lord Ramsey led me through the dining room door to my high- backed embroidered chair at the long polished table gleaming under the light of countless candles and heavily laden with ornate silver. After I was seated I looked back at the doorway just in time to see Charlie and Lady Ramsey on the threshold. They couldn't both enter the dining room at the same time for she was what Charlie called "Norman built." As Charlie stepped back to let her through, there was a terrible ripping sound. Charlie's high-heeled boot was on her train. He jumped off, as he would say, "fast as a cat on a hot griddle," and Lady Ramsey proceeded to her place at the end of the table. I was mortified.

"Mr. Russell, Sir Henry Mill Pellat tells me that you actually wintered with the Bloods in Canada in your early days in Montana, and that's where you learned to be so very perceptive of their ways. I'm sure we would all be fascinated to hear about your stay. It's obviously had a great influence on your work. And you know, we English seem to be enticed by stories of your noble savages," said Lord Ramsey.

"Well, it was the winter of '88. I ran into Sleeping Thunder. I could sign a little and he could sign so we could talk pretty good. He liked the way I could make a little bear out of a piece of beeswax. He thought I had pretty good medicine, so he ups and invites me to winter with his folks. I didn't have any better offer that winter so I ups and accepts. It was a good winter except they ran out of salt. They wanted me to stay on when spring came and maybe if they'd had some salt, I would have." Charlie started telling about that winter, and as always he had a captive audience. As course after course was served, his stories got better and better and all the guests seemed disappointed when the evening was over.

"Charlie, I thought I would die when I heard Lady Ramsey's train rip," I said as we were riding back in the carriage. "And I couldn't believe how everyone acted as if they hadn't heard it. The English are *so very* civilized. And they dearly loved your stories," I said.

"Those lords and ladies are right friendly folks," Charlie said. He had really enjoyed himself.

"Charlie, while we're so close, let's go to Paris," I said. "I've always, always wanted to see Paris. Everyone says it's just a short boat ride from here."

The ride across the channel was more than a little choppy and Charlie was more than a little seasick. But Paris was worth it. It was more beautiful than I had imagined, with its wide boulevards and fountains. We saw Notre Dame, surely the most beautiful church ever built. Charlie was interested in the gargoyles. He thought that it was pretty clever of those Frenchmen to use those strange ugly faces as waterspouts.

The Eiffel Tower was taller, the Seine clearer, and the Louvre bigger than I expected. Everything was better as far as I was concerned. I was in Paris, France, and I wanted to see all the sights. Charlie was homesick and wanted to go home.

I literally dragged Charlie to the Louvre. I wasn't going to leave Paris without seeing the *Mona Lisa*. I had heard all about that painting from those guests at Sue's party. We found it. As Charlie and I stood in front of it, I read from the brochure that the *Mona Lisa* was "famous for her mysterious smile."

"I bet it's mysterious because you can't see it at all," said Charlie.

"It's so small. I expected a great huge painting. This is the only thing in Paris that is not bigger or better than I thought," I said.

"Now that you can tell everybody you've seen the Mona Lisa, the Eiffel Tower and Notre Dame, can we go home?" asked Charlie.

"Not just yet. Lord Ramsey's friend hasn't gotten in touch with us yet. I know Lord Ramsey wrote him."

When we returned to our hotel from the Louvre, there was a note awaiting us from Lord Ramsey's friend.

"Charlie, it's an invitation to dinner. I would love to tell those Episcopal ladies that I was entertained not only by royalty in England, but also by royalty in France."

There were even more silver and candles, more courses of food, more flowers, and livery servants. Toward the end of dinner, the Marquis told Charlie that since we were so close, we absolutely must go to Rome. He insisted that the most beautiful and magnificent art in the whole world was in Rome.

"Only in Rome can you see Michelangelo's Sistine Chapel. If you go to Rome, you might *even* see the Pope," the Marquis said.

"I wouldn't go to Rome if I could see Jesus Christ himself," answered Charlie.

There was dead silence. Then the Marquis began to chuckle. "Touché, Mr. Russell."

"Chas is just homesick," I answered.

We took the next boat home.

II

Jack

WHEN WE GOT BACK TO GREAT FALLS, I made sure a reporter from the newspaper had the opportunity of interviewing Charlie about our trip. I also made sure he was made aware that the Queen Mother had come to Charlie's show. When I read the article I wondered what other eyes in Great Falls were reading the same article.

"I think I'll invite a few of the ladies from the Episcopal Church over for a proper English tea. You know the English truly have a fine idea there. There really is nothing nicer than tea in the afternoon," I told Charlie that evening as we sat in the parlor after supper. I was reading my favorite article in the newspaper.

"If I stayed in England six more months, I'd come back a roaring democrat. 'Course havin' them in for tea, you could lay it on them 'bout meetin' up with the Queen Mother and Lord and Lady Ramsey. You sure were taken by that royalty, Mame," Charlie said.

"Don't tell me you weren't just a little bit impressed?" I asked.

"Everyone's the same under all that glitter. Mother Nature is the same to us all," answered Charlie.

"Well, the ladies at my tea party will be impressed. And I'm going to see to it that newspapers all over the country get the information that we had a successful show. Charlie, you have a national following. We've been out of the country for quite a while, and we have to let friends know we're back — and that you are back to work. First thing in the morning, I'm going to write all our dealers and all the galleries that handle your work. I need to buy some more of these papers to cut out this article and slip a copy into each letter."

We received more invitations to have shows than we could possibly handle. We received inquiries from patrons who had one or more of Charlie's paintings and were interested in buying yet another. I was pushing Charlie to paint more. I went out to his studio with a letter from Dr. Phillip Cole.

Charlie was sitting in his studio. His back was turned to his neglected easel. At his feet sat five or six boys from the neighborhood. Charlie had taken down an Indian war bonnet that usually hung on the wall. He had put it on his head and had used his brush and oils to smear strokes of red paint across his cheeks and down his nose.

"And War Scars, though bleeding from his wounds, slayed his enemy and scalped him," Charlie said as he held up an imaginary scalp and gave a chilling victory war cry.

"Boys, what are you doing here?" They all jumped at the sound of my voice. "Haven't I told you a hundred times, you are *not* to bother Mr. Russell while he is painting," I said.

"Oh, they're not bothering me. I was just tellin'em the story of *War Scars at Medicine Whip*." Charlie said sheepishly. He knew I wouldn't tolerate his work being disturbed by a bunch of boys who should be home doing their chores.

"Now, I want you boys to go home immediately," I said in a voice that left no doubt about my sincerity.

"Yes, ma'am," they all muttered as they got up and left.

Charlie sat for a time, then he got up and put the war bonnet back up. He took his handkerchief out and wiped his face. "Mame, I love havin' those little ones around, watchin' their eyes dance as I tell them my stories. We've been lucky in about everything. In fact luckier than I ever dreamed — but we ain't been lucky enough to have a kid of our own," he said almost to himself.

There was silence.

"Luck has nothing to do with it. We have worked. We have struggled. We have planned. This success just didn't happen. We don't have time for a baby," I replied just above a whisper.

I turned and left the studio. Charlie turned back to his painting.

But he wouldn't let the subject go.

"I miss Austin around here. I even miss her highness, Mrs. Stonehenge. A house needs to have young people around. It needs children. And we aren't gettin' any younger."

"Charlie, we have some really big shows this year. There's the Folsom in New York, then on to Gumps in San Francisco. The Panama-Pacific International Exposition is being held at the same time as your show. Can you imagine what this can mean to your career? There will be people from all over the world. Then we will end the year with a big show in Chicago at the Thurber. All of our time, energies and efforts have to concentrate on these shows. The more famous you become, the more people expect, and the more I have to do," I said.

The shows were more successful than I had dreamed. But Charlie didn't like Chicago; he never really liked big cities. He told his friends at the Mint, "If I owned a summer home in Chicago and a winter home in hell, I'd spend my summers in my winter home." Of course, it got a big laugh.

One thing Charlie took very seriously was wanting to have a child around. And as if fate were answering his deepest longings, Joe DeYong came into our family.

Joe was an Indian boy, not yet twenty. He had been born in Missouri and his family had moved to Indian Territory when he was very young. He had come all the way from Oklahoma to Great Falls just to meet his idol, Charlie Russell, for he dreamed of being an artist. He was very shy, partially because he was deaf and partially because of his Indian background. When he was with Charlie, he became a different person. Charlie could sign, so they could talk, and Charlie's true love for the Indians gave Joe a sense of security and self-worth. Joe wasn't used to this from a white man; from his idol, it was almost too great a gift. Joe and Charlie would work for hours on end in Charlie's studio. Joe always referred to Charlie as "The Chief" and called me "Wise Woman."

When Joe showed Charlie his work, Charlie would tell him in sign language what he thought of it. At first, Charlie was very kind, but as he got to know Joe better he would kid him a little. Charlie could tell Joe stories in sign and at the end of a very funny one, Joe would laugh until he cried. He adored Charlie. And I couldn't help but adore Joe for he brought Charlie such joy.

Joe and I became good friends since Charlie had long ago taught me to sign. But even Charlie's and my friendship couldn't keep Joe from being deeply homesick for his mother. After he became deaf from an illness as a young boy, Joe was cut off from most people; therefore, he and his mother had a special closeness.

"What's wrong?" I signed to Joe one day when I caught him sitting on the front porch looking out at the sunset with tears running down his face. "I miss my mother," he signed back. "I wonder how many sunsets she has left? I love the Chief. I love you, but I love my mother more."

"We love you, too," I signed.

"She's getting old. Maybe I should go back to Oklahoma."

"No, Joe, she should come out here. Wouldn't you like that? I know the Chief and I would."

Joe's tears stopped. His eyes sparkled and he broke into a big grin.

I was expecting an ancient Indian woman, but Joe's mother was just a few years older than me. She was short and almost as round as she was tall. She had the same sweetness and shyness that Joe had. Before long she worshipped Charlie with the same devotion too. She was always fluttering around trying to take care of Joe. "Just like a banty hen taking care of her chick," Charlie said, and it stuck. From then on, she was known as Banty.

I thought our household was full. Joe wanted nothing more than to sit and paint with Charlie out in the studio, and Banty wanted, in every way, to let us know how grateful she was for what we were doing for her son. Charlie's paintings were selling better than ever.

But Charlie couldn't still his longing for a child.

"Mame, I'm fifty-two and you're thirty-eight. I guess we're past time to have a baby of our own. Haven't you missed having a little one?"

"Charlie, there's so much to do. You know we have another big show in Chicago. The last was so successful."

"But what if a baby came along, a beautiful baby who needed a home, who could bring joy and happiness into our lives? What would you say?" Charlie asked.

"Well, I guess we'd have to see if that happened," I answered.

"It just so happens that Dr. Hawkes called. A friend of his, another doctor, knows this young girl who's about to have a baby and wants to know if we might be interested in adopting it."

I was stunned. Charlie was really serious.

"I'll have to think about it, Charlie," I said.

We didn't discuss the adoption for weeks, but I knew Charlie hadn't forgotten it. He had made up his mind on the adoption thing. Finally, he brought it up one evening as we sat in the parlor. I had been expecting him to broach the subject again.

"You know that girl I told you about? It's just about her time. Have you been thinking on it?" Charlie asked.

"I have. I know how much you want a child around the house. And you're right — we aren't going to get any younger. If we are ever going to adopt a baby, now's the time. So if that's what you want, Charlie, it's okay with me."

"Yeppeeiiii!" yelled Charlie as he stood up and did a little dance.

"But you must understand we'll have to hire a nurse," I reminded him.

"Joe and Banty and I can take care of the little tyke when you're busy," Charlie said.

"Charlie, your time is too valuable painting, and I'm so busy and gone so much setting up shows and keeping up with our business. The only way we can have a baby around here is to have a nursemaid."

"Whatever you say. I sure hope it's a pretty little girl. Since there's so much difference in our ages, I think you ought to have a daughter. I know you'd love having a daughter, for a mother and daughter are always so close. You know they say a son is a son until he finds himself a wife, and a daughter's a daughter all of her life. Think how much fun you'd have dressin' her up and showin' her off as she grows up, teachin' her to cook and so forth." Charlie's face glowed.

"I hope it's a boy," I said. "Every man needs a son."

The baby was a boy. We went to the hospital to see him. He was beautiful. The day we brought him home from the hospital, everyone was waiting on the porch for us: Joe, Banty, Josephine, Margaret and Albert Trigg and the new nursemaid we had hired. Charlie was holding the baby, for I was driving our new car. Charlie never did learn to drive. I always thought he felt that learning to drive would be the ultimate disloyalty to his beloved horses.

Charlie could not wait to show everyone the baby.

"Oh, he's beautiful," said Josephine. "May I hold him?" Charlie handed him to her as if he were made of glass. Josephine cooed and spoke baby language as if he could understand. I saw tears in her eyes and knew she was thinking of the baby she had borne years before when she was married to Ridgley. The baby, a little girl, had only lived for a few days. Sometimes a tragedy can bring two people closer together and sometimes it drives an irreversible wedge between them. The Ridgley baby's death destroyed Josephine and William's marriage. It was a subject no one ever talked about.

Banty couldn't wait to get her hands on the baby. Reluctantly, Josephine handed him over.

After everyone had had a chance to hold him, we went inside. Charlie sat down in the big chair in the living room holding the baby.

"It really is time we all got back to work," I said as I took the baby out of Charlie's arms and gave him to the nurse. "Charlie, you need to be in your studio. We have a deadline to meet for the Chicago show. And I have a million things to catch up on. I've still got to write a brochure for that show."

Charlie and Joe went out to the studio. Banty followed the nurse upstairs. Margaret and Albert left for home. Josephine lingered.

"Nancy, you are so lucky to have a baby in the house. Enjoy every minute of it," she said as she left.

Josephine came every day to see the baby. Nothing seemed to give her as much joy as holding him, rocking him, and singing him lullabies.

"When are you going to have him baptized?" she asked one day.

"Not until after the Chicago show. I'll be gone. Charlie is staying here to catch up with his work. We've never had so many commissions." I said.

"Have you finally decided what to name him?" Josephine asked.

"Charlie wants to call him Childe, but I'm insisting on Jack. And for his middle name Cooper, which was my maiden name. Charlie agrees that Jack Cooper Russell has a mighty fine ring to it."

"When are you going to tell him he is adopted?" Josephine asked.

"When he is old enough to understand," I answered.

"I think the sooner the better. Children understand a lot more than we give them credit for," she said. "And when are you going to tell him about his mother?"

"Never! And I want you to promise me on your word of honor you never ever will either," I said.

"She was a beautiful young girl who made a mistake."

"I will not have Jack have that stigma. And what would people think? No, Jack is never to know he is illegitimate. Never," I resolved.

"I think you are wrong. It couldn't hurt Jack. He had nothing to do with it. It's always better to tell the whole truth. When he's older and asks you about his mother what will you tell him?"

"I'll handle that when the time comes," I replied. "Now, help me plan his baptism. I want it to be the most elegant baptism they have ever had at the Episcopal Church. I'll buy his baptismal gown in Chicago. I want it to be creamy-colored silk with lots of lace."

When I was in Chicago for Charlie's show, I spent hours looking for Jack's baptismal gown. I finally found one that was exactly as I had pictured — candleglow silk with antique lace imported from Ireland. I spent almost as much time shopping for my own costume. It was a heavy silk brocade suit of a darker shade of cream matching my hair color. The suit had a standup mink collar which framed my face.

We made a handsome picture as we stood with the priest on that December day in 1916 for Jack's baptism. I had chosen our wedding anniversary, September ninth, to put on Jack's baptismal records as his birth date. I didn't want to use his real birthday — it might give him a clue to his mother. I knew I didn't want him ever to find out about that girl. As I stood in the nave of the Episcopal Church, I didn't give it a thought. All I could think about was how perfectly everything was going, just as I planned.

It had been snowing the day before, but it

stopped during the night and that morning the sun shone brightly and the fresh snow sparkled in the sunlight. The church was full. Jack, looking beautiful in his baptismal gown, slept in Charlie's arms. The priest was dressed in his finest robes. Everything was perfect until the preacher reached for Jack to dip water on his head for the baptism. Jack woke up. When the water touched his head he started to cry, then the cry became a scream. He screamed and screamed. The congregation first tittered and then laughed. I was so embarrassed. I thought the baptism would never end, the priest would never shut up and Jack would never be quiet.

Jack was still screaming when we got home. We had invited several friends who attended the baptism to come for tea. Among those invited, of course, were the Triggs. Josephine immediately took Jack and began rocking him. His screaming stopped. His eyes closed as if a curtain had fallen, and he was asleep. She gently carried him upstairs and put him in his bed.

"Thank heavens. I was getting a splitting headache. How could we possibly have tea and cakes with all that screaming? Jack practically ruined his baptism," I told Josephine when she returned to the parlor.

"Why, he's just a baby. You sound as if he planned to misbehave," Josephine said in a shocked voice.

"I've spent hours and hours planning this — shopping until my feet hurt, all over Chicago, for his baptismal gown; planning, with cook, what cakes to make for the tea; sending out the invitations; making arrangements for my father to be here. I could have put a show on in New York, or London for that matter, in the amount of time I put into this baptism," I said.

"It was a beautiful baptism. And no one but you was upset with Jack's crying. He's just a baby. You can't expect him to be perfect. Now come on, Nancy, your guests are arriving. Let's have tea and some of those delicious cakes," Josephine said.

Charlie was already meeting our friends at the front door and showing them into the dining room where the table was laden with tea cakes. I went in to start pouring tea and soon the sleeping baby upstairs was forgotten.

When Jack was only a few months old, in the spring of '17, Albert Trigg had a small accident. He cut his hand. No one thought anything of it. It wasn't even a bad cut. Four days later, he was dead from blood poisoning. Josephine was distraught. Margaret was inconsolable. I took care of all of the arrangements. I called the undertaker, the church, and bought the lots at the cemetery. While I was at Highland Cemetery, I bought lots for Charlie and me right next to the Triggs. I felt this was only fitting since we had been more like family than friends. After Albert Trigg's burial, Josephine came to see me.

"Mama and I can never thank you enough for taking care of everything for us. Oh, Nancy, you are so strong. I don't know what we would do without you.

And I can't tell you how touched our hearts were when we learned that you had the lots next to ours at Highland. What a dear friend you are," Josephine said as she gave me a hug. "I loved Papa so, and I miss him so," she said as she sat down and started to cry again.

"We all do. Charlie has been grieving his loss. They were so close. Charlie says it helps the hurt to play with Jack. Charlie says you can't think of the dead when a baby is cooing and gurgling at you. I bet it would help you, too," I said.

As Jack grew older, he grew even more handsome. Charlie loved to walk up and down the street with Jack in the carriage Charlie's friends had given him. They'd even had a silver bull head skull —Charlie's emblem — put on the front of the carriage. Everyone would stop and tell Charlie what beautiful baby Jack was. As if he knew he were being discussed, Jack would bestow upon them one of his dazzling smiles.

But Jack was just as quick to scream and throw a temper tantrum. Maybe it was Charlie's age, maybe it was because he had waited so long for a son or maybe it was because he couldn't stand to see Jack cry that Charlie spoiled him so. Of course, I was gone frequently, but I never went any place without bringing Jack home a beautiful present. I'd even shop for him when I didn't have time to shop for myself. When he was two, I bought him the most beautiful white rabbit overcoat with a white rabbit hat to match. He looked gorgeous with his dark eyes and dark hair. I think he knew he was beautiful in that coat and hat and he loved to wear them. I was going to make sure that Jack had everything I never had when I was growing up on that farm in far-off Kentucky.

The more I was gone, the more time Josephine spent with Jack. She brought home books from the library where she was now working and would come to our house in the evenings and on weekends to read to him. The minute he saw her, he would come running with outstretched arms screaming, "Nomee, Nomee," for he couldn't say Josephine. Josephine would sit in the rocker. Jack would scramble into her lap, and she would read to him.

"You've grown so big while we've been gone," I told Jack when we returned from a trip," Jack stretched as tall as he could on his almost three-year-old frame. "And you're more handsome every day." I hugged him. "Now, run along and play. I've got a pile of mail to go through."

"But I want to stay with you, Mama," Jack said as he clung to my legs.

"Later, Jack, I must see the mail now. You understand," I said as Jack turned and went outside.

Josephine was standing in the doorway. "You really should make time for him. He missed you so."

"Jack has everything a child could possibly need. I spend a fortune on his clothes. Charlie spoils him rotten. You've read him every child's book in the library. What do you mean?" I was a little miffed at Josephine.

"He has everything but a mother," she said softly.

12

Traveling

"OH, CHARLIE, IT'S COME," I said as I raced into the studio at our lodge at Lake McDonald. "I can tell from the Canadian postmark. I bet you it's an invitation to have the exhibit at Saskatoon. I'm right! I'm right!" I said as I tore open the letter and read its contents. "We're invited to have a one-man show at the university while the Prince of Wales is there for an official inspection in September. His Royal Highness, the Prince of Wales, I can't believe it. Charlie, did you hear me?" I asked.

Charlie turned from a watercolor he was working on. "I don't know if I can go. I promised Frank Linderman I'd illustrate his new book," Charlie said as he studied the half-finished piece in front of him.

"You can't be serious. How could anyone turn down this invitation? Do you realize who will be there? Don't you understand what this can do for your career?"

I was absolutely bewildered. "You go visit Frank at Goose Bay and explain. I'm sure he will understand."

Charlie went to Goose Bay. When he returned, I asked what Frank had said.

"I didn't have the nerve to tell him. It's only July. Maybe I can get them done before we go to Canada," Charlie said.

"You can't work on his illustrations. You have got to work on the Saskatoon show. This is a once-in-a-lifetime opportunity. The Prince of Wales will someday be King of England. Frank is your good friend; he will want you to take advantage of this opportunity; he will want what is best for you. Now, let's get busy on the show," I said.

Charlie worked feverishly. He was caught up in my excitement. The rest of the summer vanished and before we knew it, we were on the train to Canada.

"As long as I live, I will never forget this day. September nineteenth, 1919. A red letter day. When the Prince of Wales becomes the King of England, I will tell everyone the day, place and time I met him. Did you know it was two-thirty? Isn't he good looking? I think it was his uniform with all the gold braid and medals that made him look more like Prince Charming than the Prince of Wales," I said as I looked out the window of our hotel in Saskatoon.

I turned from the window. Charlie was reading a letter. "Charlie, have you heard one word I was saying?"

"It's from Frank Linderman. He says he has to have all of the watercolors and pen and ink sketches immediately so his book can make the Christmas sales. They aren't all done," Charlie said.

"Well, you will just have to write him in the morning and tell him you will have them in a month, that you had other work you had to get out on time. And if that doesn't suit him, then he can get another artist. Of course, I know he won't. I know that Scribner's only wanted his *Indian Old Man Stories* because you said you would illustrate it," I said as I started getting undressed.

I had wanted to relive every single minute of that day with Charlie, but now I couldn't. I wanted to share with Charlie a plan I had put into operation that very day. I had met with a Mr. George Lane, a Mr. Burns and Mr. Cross who were going to head up a committee to buy a painting of Charlie's and present it to the Prince of Wales during his official visit. Just think of the headlines — "Prince of Wales Receives Russell Painting." Our trip to Canada was everything I dreamed it would be. When we got home, Charlie got busy on the Linderman watercolors and sketches. He received another letter. He read it aloud to me. "Friend Chas," he began. "Have a telegram from Scribner's saying that book would now have to go over for a year, as it's too late to make a change. I wish you would send me back all my manuscript of all tales and Indian stories. I note that you said there was work you had to get out on time. You had my stories since last March and wrote me that you had started on pictures last May. I guess I don't count. If you ONLY had guts enough to have told me you wouldn't do my stuff I'd have been thankful to you, for now I shall have to wait another year, but not on you.

Yours, Frank."

"Isn't that just like Frank Linderman? Doesn't he know how lucky he is to have Charles Russell illustrating his book? Well, you just send him back his manuscript. You have far more important work to do," I said as I angrily grabbed the letter from Charlie's hands and reread it for myself. I couldn't believe my eyes.

"Now, Mamie, don't get all fired excited. Frank's had it rough lately. He had that big fire up at Goose Bay when ever'thing burned but the house. I think when the last tall pine fell, it sort of broke his heart. Then you got to remember that gal, Jeannette Rankin, who beat him when he ran for Congress. It can hurt a man down deep to lose an election. All he's got is his books, and he's got two girls in college.

"I've already written him a note and told him that I was sorry he got snuffy, and I knew he'd been up against a string of bad luck. I sent him four watercolors plus four sketches and told him they weren't worth a damn to me and he could have them," Charlie said with a note of hurt in his voice.

"You what? I can't believe it. No one gets illustrations for free. Everyone pays. They either buy them or we get them back. You know that, Charlie. Didn't we agree a long time ago that I would take care of the business end and you would take care of the painting end? Frank Bird Linderman has taken advantage of your friendship."

Frank didn't change illustrators. Charlie finished the rest of the illustrations and the book was published in 1920. But the relationship between the Lindermans and the Russells was strained. It bothered Charlie. It hurt him to have anyone out of sorts. I did what I could to convince him that Frank should be grateful.

When the spring of '21 came and passed and Frank didn't ask Charlie up to Goose Bay for a visit, Charlie was visibly hurt. Then came the fall of '21, and still no invitation. Charlie was crushed. I decided to take matters into my own hands.

I found out from mutual friends, Ed and Lucille Borein, that the Lindermans had rented a house in Santa Barbara. They were staying right across the boulevard from the beach. I decided to rent the house next door. I knew that no one could be around Charlie Russell long without loving him. You just couldn't stay mad at Charlie. I was betting on it.

Since '19, we had been spending our winters in California. The Montana cold made Charlie's joints ache. I had never liked the terrible winters. Besides, California was *the* place to be in the winter. The millionaires from back East had discovered the sunny skies, palm trees, and blue ocean. People like the Wrigleys had built huge homes in Pasadena. Hollywood, with its movies, was creating a wealth of its own. If I thought that royalty was something in Europe, it was nothing compared to the American royalty that had just been born, born to be worshipped. Film stars were the kings and queens of Hollywood. California also had its barons, rich oil barons. We already had friends in California — Will and Betty Rogers, Bill Hart, Harry and Ollie Carey, Ed and Lucille Borein. California was the perfect place for the winter.

Santa Barbara was a small California beach town with a definite Spanish flavor, as its name suggested. It was also a town that warmly welcomed artists and writers. The townspeople made something of heroes or celebrities of them. The Lindermans had arrived there in October of '22. We didn't get to Santa Barbara until November.

I remember the day we arrived. One of the first things we did was go next door and call on the Lindermans. They seemed surprised to see us and at first were very stiff. We visited with them as if nothing had ever gone awry. Charlie began reminiscing about some of the good times he and Frank had had together. You could practically observe the thaw. We visited for several hours. The Linderman girls, Wilda, Verne, and Norma, had warmed up to Charlie and were laughing at his stories although they were still very cool toward me.

Finally Charlie said, "Boy, you ought to see how little Jack has grown, just like a weed. By the way, where is Jack?"

"I don't know. I presume next door with the maid," I answered as I got up to go check on him. When I got to our house, I found the maid unpacking. She thought Jack had gone with us to the Lindermans.

We looked everywhere for Jack. All of the Lindermans helped us. We broke up in search parties. Some went down the boulevard, others along the beach. Where would a six-year-old go? Finally, Charlie found him at the round-house having the time of his life. An engineer had let him sit on his lap while he turned the engine around.

Finally, I saw Charlie coming up the street carrying Jack piggyback on his shoulder. I was furious. How dare he go off like that and scare us all to death.

"I should blister your bottom, young man. How could you?" I said.

"Aw, come on, Mame, don't be mad at him. Why, he's only six. He didn't mean any harm. He's not hurt. That's all that counts. We should have a party, a celebration welcoming home the prodigal son," Charlie said as he picked Jack up off his shoulders and set him down.

"Charlie, you must not spoil the boy so. He really deserves a spanking, but I'll let it go this time. Jack, you go in with the maid. We are going out to dinner with the Lindermans."

We went to a little cantina in Santa Barbara that had marvelous Mexican food. Charlie loved chili, the hotter the better. Before the evening was out, Charlie and Frank were laughing and telling each other stories just like the old times. Mrs. Linderman and her daughters, however, were never again friendly toward me. But I didn't have time to worry about that.

There was a constant round of social events. There were fabulous dinner parties with movie stars. Every hostess wanted Charles Marion Russell, the famous cowboy artist, to attend. They knew that once Charlie accepted, their party was assured of success because Charlie always lived up to his reputation as a great story teller, and he dearly loved telling the stories of his cowboying days. Charlie and I worked out an act; Charlie would tell a wonderful story in sign language and I would interpret it for our listeners. It was always the hit of the evening.

Occasionally Charlie's stories were a little off color, and I would blush and say, "Oh, I can't say that." Our audience loved it. Of course, then we would receive more invitations and with each one came the opportunity to meet someone who might want to buy a painting.

One of our favorite hosts was Charles Lummis. His house, with its large rooms and high-beamed ceilings, was the setting for wonderful dinner parties. He and Mrs. Lummis would invite fifty to seventy guests to their annual March Hare Party. At one such party, I looked across the crowded room and the back of a head caught my eye. There was something familiar about its shape and about those chestnut curls. She must have felt my unwavering stare because she turned to look at me. I recognized the blue eyes instantly and began pushing my way through the crowd.

"Ella, it's so good to see you," I said, throwing my arms around her. "You look absolutely wonderful. California must agree with you."

"Nancy, haven't you heard? Frank and I are divorced. I came to this party because I knew you and Charlie would be here. I wanted to say goodbye. I'm leaving for Alaska."

"You can't do that. We've just found each other again."

"I'm too old to be told what to do, Nancy," she said, smiling. "The farther away I get the better chance I have of finding my own dream. I hear that Alaska is the land of opportunity, especially for a single woman."

"But when will we see each other again? Why not stay here? What better place is there than California? There are plenty of publishers here, and the movies too. We could make you a future here."

"Nannie, you never change – always trying to run everyone's life. But maybe I don't change either. I need to start over in a new place. I know there's something better owed to me out there."

We talked on for a while as the party hummed around us. When the evening ended, we said goodbye and soon after Ella left for Alaska. She certainly could be stubborn.

That special evening was not the only one we

spent with Charles Lummis, a colorful character who always wore Navaho clothes — white pants, a velvet shirt, high-top Navaho buckskin shoes with silver buttons, and turquoise and silver jewelry. Charlie and Charlie Lummis made a pair when they stood together. Although Lummis was short, no taller than Charlie's shoulder, his style was expansive. He had walked to California, all the way from the Midwest, stopping to stay with the Navahos. That visit made an indelible mark on him just as Charlie's winter with the Bloods in '88 had changed him forever. No wonder they got along so well.

Lummis was a publisher and used lots of cowboy drawings in his publications. He was the first to buy and publish Ed Borein illustrations, so Ed was often at his parties.

After Ed married Lucille in '21, she was there too, although had she stayed home, she wouldn't have been missed. No one could understand why Ed, who had waited so long, married someone like Lucille. He was so warm and personable. He especially enjoyed telling Lummis about the time he cowboyed in Arizona, which of course would lead into Lummis's favorite subject, the Navahos. Lucille always looked bored, which certainly didn't help Ed sell his work.

Charlie loved to go to the movie studio with Will Rogers. Often he would run into old cowboy friends from Montana who had ridden into Hollywood to play as extras. Will introduced Charlie to Tom Mix, who'd come from Oklahoma as Will had.

It didn't make any difference if a man had herded in Montana, California, Arizona, Texas, Colorado, or Oklahoma. Once a man "had rode," a common bond was established between him and his brethren of the saddle. It was a fraternity, a brotherhood; and to be initiated, a man had to have ridden line in the freezing rain or choked on dust on a hot August day as he rode drag, or squatted on his heels around a campfire at daybreak while he washed down hardtack with hot coffee. Once a cowboy, always a cowboy at heart, no matter where a man went or what job he took. He could change into a business suit, live in New York and be chauffeured around in a big limousine, but deep inside, he was still a cowboy. Such was Malcolm Mackay.

Malcolm S. Mackay hadn't grown up in the West, far from it. He was the son of a wealthy New Yorker banker. He had been born in New Jersey and as a teenager had worked in his father's firm. In 1899, at the age of eighteen, he spent the summer in North Dakota and was bitten by the bug of the West. By 1901 he discovered Montana and it was love at first sight. He joined with Charlie Wright to form the Rosebud Land and Cattle Company. When Wright moved to Red Lodge to start a purebred Hereford ranch, Mackay stayed on at Rosebud. He increased both the size of the land and the number of cattle and would have been content to spend the rest of his days riding herd on Lazy L-branded cattle. But fate stepped in. He was notified that he was desperately needed back at his father's firm. When family duty called he had to answer although he left a part of him forever at Rosebud.

When the Mackays came to the Folsom Galleries to view our big show in 1911, he and Charlie became fast friends. They were kindred souls. They both belonged to the brotherhood. Malcolm bought a wonderful painting at that show, *Indian Hunter's Return*. It was the first of many. Each time we went to New York, we would go out to Tenafly, New Jersey to visit the Mackays.

By 1921 they had so many of Charlie's paintings they decided to convert a large room in their home into a special place to house them. It was. The interior resembled a log cabin. There was a large, arched fireplace at one end, with a rough-hewed log as its mantel. They waited for our annual trip to New York to have the dedication.

As always when we were in New York, they would send their chauffeur-driven limousine to take us to Tenafly. On the day of the dedication we packed a suitcase to take with us. We put in Charlie's Indian clothes and paint for his face. Charlie was determined to make this a dedication no one would ever forget, and he loved dressing up like an Indian. I packed my long white buckskin squaw dress. When the hotel desk called to inform us that Mr. Mackay's man was in the lobby waiting for us, we took the elevator to the lobby, and there he was in his gray livery with polished high black boots, a shining billed hat under his arm. He was standing as if at attention. When we stepped out of the elevator, he took the suitcase with our Indian costumes and ushered us through the lobby.

Every head turned. He opened the door of the hotel, then the door to the long black Cadillac. Malcolm Mackay was sitting in the spacious back seat. He had been at his office that day and would ride with us to Tenafly. The George Washington bridge had not been built yet, so we took the ferry. As soon as the whistles sounded and the boat pushed off, Charlie and Mr. Mackay got out of the car and walked up to the front of the boat to lean against the rail and look out at the river. I sat in the plush interior of the car and dreamed of someday having a chauffeur. Malcolm Mackay didn't seem to be aware that people stared as we drove by. I guess if you are accustomed to having a chauffeur, you don't get a thrill out of being driven by one.

The ferry finally arrived at the other side. When Charlie and Malcolm Mackay were settled back in the back seat, the chauffeur started the car. The Mackay's home was a world away from New York City, not just across the river. They had over four hundred acres of rolling countryside dotted with old oak trees and ancient maples. The long drive twisted and turned up to the big house. The house, built by Italian masons, had taken more than two years to complete at the end of the war and was rumored to have cost over two hundred and fifty thousand dollars which, in 1918, was more than a tidy sum. No wonder it resembled a castle. I was always thrilled to be invited to the Mackays and this was a very special day. Mrs. Mackay, rather than the butler, came to the door to greet us. She was followed by the Mackay children, Bud, Bill, Pete and Mary Ellen. They, too, were all excited about the ceremonies and couldn't wait to see Charlie again.

"Here's Charlie," Bud called out the minute the chauffeur stopped the car.

"Mr. Russell to you, Bud," admonished his mother, who was always very proper.

"Mr. and Mrs. Russell, welcome. We have been waiting for you. You would think we were dedicating a major building rather than one room with all of our excitement," Mrs. Mackay said.

"Well, it is a major dedication," I replied.

"Just wait until you see our get-ups," Charlie said.

I don't know who had more fun, Charlie or Malcolm Mackay. They burned into the log walls every single brand that either of them could remember from Montana, then Charlie burned his name and symbol into the mantel. Charlie, dressed as a Medicine Man, sat Indian fashion on the floor and gave the dedication speech in sign language. I interpreted, dressed in my white buckskin and moccasins. The long fringes on the sleeves rippled as I moved my arms. There were little bells and shells attached to the fringe hanging from my shoulders, and I knew the effect of their sound added to my speech. It was all very theatrical.

No spot could have received a more impressive dedication. They wanted Charlie to draw in the wet cement around the fireplace as he had at our Bull Head Lodge, but he declined, saying it was too easy to make a mistake and he didn't want to ruin another man's hearth. Instead, he promised to send them a poster to put over the mantel.

After the dedication Charlie and Mackay went outside and walked to the corral. Mackay kept twenty-five acres for his horses. Charlie had changed into his soft shirt, tight pants, and high-heeled boots. Mackay also wore boots and western clothes, for it was a ritual that every time Charlie came to visit they would mount up and rope the few cows Mackay kept on the place for that purpose. Maybe if they half-closed their eyes, they saw the snow-capped peaks of Montana against vast stretches of the deep blue and believed they were boys again, roping wild-eyed Longhorns rather than the fat, slow New Jersey cows who were used to their game.

After they had worn out their little-used throwing arms they came in for dinner. The Mackay's dining room table seated twenty but the table was set for only us and the family that evening. I had changed into formal clothes because Mrs. Mackay dressed for dinner.

"It's a shame that you're not wearing your beautiful Indian dress, Mrs. Russell," said Malcolm Mackay.

"Mame makes quite a hit as my interpreter. You ought to see the way she wows them out in California," replied Charlie. "In fact, Douglas Fairbanks thought she was pretty enough to be in pictures."

"Do you know Douglas Fairbanks?" asked Mrs. Mackay. "Is he as handsome in person as he is on the screen?"

No matter who you were, you weren't immune to being star-dazed by America's screen idol.

"Oh, he is much more handsome in person. Chas met him at the studio when he was all dressed up as one of the three musketeers. Chas came home and wrote him a letter and illustrated it with a drawing of him in his costume. Later, when we were all at the same dinner party, he came over to tell Chas how much he enjoyed the letter. He has the most wonderful smile and the whitest teeth I think I've ever seen."

"Was Mary Pickford with him?" asked Mrs. Mackay.

"She was. She is so little — I bet not over five feet — that she looks like a young girl," I said.

"Do you spend much time in California?" Mackay asked.

"We've been spending our winters there since 1919. You know how rough the winters can be in Montana. Of course, we spend our summers at our Lake McDonald lodge. Then we make at least one trip a year here to the East coast, plus the shows in places like Chicago, Minneapolis and Denver."

"I don't know how you do it. Mrs. Russell, you really are quite amazing," said Mr. Mackay.

"What do you do with Jack?" asked Mrs. Mackay.

"We take him with us to California, and he loves Lake McDonald. Of course, New York is no place for a child and our time is fully committed when we are having a show, so we leave him in Great Falls. We have a housekeeper, then there's Joe DeYong's mother, Banty, and Josephine Trigg. Jack calls her Aunt Nomee for he couldn't say Josephine when he was learning to talk. She's read him so many books that I don't doubt he'll be reading by the time he goes to school. He's an unusually bright child and extremely handsome. I'm already looking for a special suit for him to wear when he starts school. You know I always bring him a present," I said.

Changing the subject, I said, "I've heard, Mr. Mackay, that you have built your very own golf course. How wonderful it must be."

"Charlie calls it my cow pasture pool table," Mr. Mackay said with a laugh.

I looked across the table and noticed that Charlie was eating with the wrong fork. I tapped at the correct fork in my place setting. Charlie was too busy eating to see my signal. I coughed and tapped again. Charlie ignored me. There were numerous forks and spoons lined up in either direction from our plates. I had learned which was the correct choice for each dish.

When we were in the chauffeur-driven limousine going back to our hotel, I asked, "Why didn't you see my signal? I was tapping on the correct fork, and you just ignored it."

"Mame, food tastes just as good with one fork as it does with another," Charlie answered. "Besides, Malcolm Mackay doesn't have us up so he can watch our table manners. He has us so we can rope some cows and talk about the ol' days. He likes and understands what I paint. When we get home, the first thing I'm going to do is paint him a picture for over his mantel."

"That's a very astute move, since he's one of our best customers," I said.

I didn't find Jack the suit I wanted for him on that trip to New York, but I did before he started school. It was a beautiful black velvet suit with short pants, a jacket with brass buttons and a silk shirt with a bow at the neck. He looked like a picture out of a fashion magazine when he left for school his first day.

"Oh, Jack, I never saw a little boy so beautiful. You look just like a little Lord Fauntleroy.

"Is that good, Mama?" he asked

"That's wonderful," I replied.

When Jack came trudging home that day, he was a mess. His bow was gone. His jacket sleeve was torn. His nose was bleeding.

"Jack, what in the world did you do to your beautiful suit?"

"I got into a fight."

"Oh, how could you?" I asked. "How could you ruin your beautiful suit?"

"They called me a sissy," Jack replied. "I told

them I weren't no sissy. I was a cowboy just like my dad. They told me Charlie Russell wasn't my dad, that I was adopted, that I was an adopted sissy."

"That's no reason for you to fight. That's no reason for you to get hurt. That's no reason for you to ruin your beautiful suit," I said as I put a wet cloth to his bleeding nose.

"What does adopted mean?" Jack asked.

"It means you are very special, that of all the babies in the world we picked you. We chose to have you as our son," I said.

"Then they were right. You aren't my real mama. Dad's not my real dad. I guess the reason you leave me so much is because I'm adopted," Jack said.

"You know that's not true. You know how important it is for us to be at the shows. Painting is the way your father makes a living and selling those paintings is what I do. You know that, and you know without that you'd starve. We all would. Your father is a very important, famous artist, but that didn't just happen. It's taken years and years of work, long before you were born," I said.

"Where was I born? Who were my real folks?" Jack asked.

"Your father died before you were born. He was a hero. He had left to go to Europe to fight in the war even before the United States got involved. He gave his life so others might be free. Your mother had several other children and couldn't afford another in a home without a husband. She heard how much Charlie Russell loved children, and she knew we would give you a wonderful home, so she let us adopt you. Now go upstairs and take off your suit."

As Jack disappeared up the stairs, I turned to face Josephine.

"I heard Jack had been in a fight at school. Is he all right?"

"Oh, yes. His nose has stopped bleeding, but I doubt his suit will ever be the same," I replied.

"I also heard what you told him. Nancy, I don't think you should lie to him," Josephine said. "It's hard enough on him with you gone so much. If he finds out the truth, he's really going to feel betrayed."

"Not you, too," I really had had enough. "You know everything I do is for his own good."

"I think I'll go upstairs and see how he is doing," Josephine said.

13

Crisscrossing the Continent

We were crisscrossing the continent on a regular basis. Charlie's work was in great demand. Dr. Phillip Cole of Forest Hills, Long Island, New York, was becoming one of Charlie's major collectors. Although he was trained at Columbia Medical School, he didn't practice medicine. He had an auto parts manufacturing business in Brooklyn, which he inherited from his father after he returned from World War I. Since Dr. Cole had grown up in Montana and had in fact practiced medicine in Helena before the war, he had a deep yearning for the West. Luckily for us, he had given up his medical practice in Helena for that would have never afforded him the money necessary to build his collection.

His collecting began with his wedding gift from his father. It was a large oil of a buffalo hunt by Charlie.

I think Mrs. Cole was always a little disappointed in her father-in-law's idea of a perfect wedding present. She was from Montana too, but she resented her husband's fascination with western art. People in the East of her status could prove that they had taste if they collected French Impressionists. That was the standard set by Mrs. Potter Palmer of Chicago and who should know better than she what real art was?

Mrs. Cole often found fault. Charlie painted Dr. Cole a magnificent hunt scene, *Running Buffalo*, depicting an epic event that took place when the Archduke of Prussia went on a special hunt with Buffalo Bill. On the canvas, the herd is running desperately, being chased by Buffalo Bill and Archduke Alexis. In the foreground is a young buffalo calf with wide, terrified eyes looking as if he expected to be trampled momentarily. Mrs. Cole thought it was distasteful to have the frightened calf in the foreground. She felt it would bother any sensitive person. She especially didn't like the open mouth of the mother buffalo, whose tongue hung out wet with saliva. She thought that was crude. She instructed Charlie to paint out the buffalo calf and close the mouth of its mother. She had Dr. Cole return the picture.

"Charlie, you are going to have to fix this painting so Mrs. Cole doesn't think it's crude," I said to Charlie as I looked at the returned painting on the easel in his studio.

"It's not crude. That's the way a herd of buffalo look when they're running for their lives," Charlie replied as he looked at the painting.

"It's a wonderfully realistic painting, Charlie, but wouldn't it be just as realistic if you painted out the calf and closed its mother's mouth? Dr. Cole has been one of our best customers, and he loves your work. If he doesn't spend his money on your work, he'll spend it on Remington's or Charles Schreyvogel's, or Joseph Sharp's. He's a rich man, and I want him as our patron, not theirs."

"I'll paint out the baby, but that mama's mouth stays open and foamin' 'cause that's the way it is," said Charlie.

I returned the painting. Mrs. Cole liked it much better and found it not so crude.

Charlie did have a crude painting that I found very distasteful. I tried every way in the world to buy the painting back. I offered many, many times what Sid Willis had paid for it, but I had no success. Every time one of Charlie's old-time cowboy friends had a little too much to drink, he would come by to chew the fat with Charlie because he missed seeing him at the Mint. By 1908 Charlie had given up drinking. He did it for me and also because, deep down, he wanted to be a great painter and he knew he couldn't if he kept on drinking. Some of his friends thought I kept Charlie's nose to the grindstone. They would always say they had just been to the Mint to see Charlie's masterpiece, *The Joy of Life*, and it was worth every penny of the two bits it cost. They knew this would irritate me.

After one such caller, I laid down the law. "You have got to get SidWillis to let me buy that back. If you ask him, I know he will. It's embarrassing for an artist of your status to have a painting like that on display. It's embarrassing to have them snickering when they say they have just seen your *best* work. All they have to do is put a quarter into that infernal machine at the Mint Saloon and have the flap of that tent raise and reveal what — a beautiful scene of Indian life? No! — A cowboy copulating with an Indian girl," I said angrily.

"My, now, that's an awful big word for what comes naturally. That paintin' don't do no harm. It just brings back fond memories of times long gone," Charlie replied.

"Sometimes doing what comes naturally can bring on a great deal of embarrassment and trouble. Look at our good friend Bill Hart," I said.

The papers were filled with stories of his sensational divorce proceedings. The last time we were in California and at Ollie and Harry Carey's ranch in Saugus, I had asked Ollie about it. We always went up to their ranch when we were in California for Charlie loved to ride and rope and of course, exchange cowboy stories with the hands there.

"What's all this I read in the papers about Bill Hart?" I asked Ollie.

"I guess there's no fool like an old fool. He asked for it. I remember when he first met Wendy Westover. We were all on location. I must admit she was a beautiful young thing and her head was turned that a big star like Bill Hart noticed her. He'd send his limousine over to her bungalow to pick her up for dinner.

"I guess while the cat's away, the mice will play. There was lovely Jane Novack in New York buying the trousseau for her wedding to Bill. And back home Bill was knocking up Wendy. When Wendy's dad found out his little girl was going to be a mama, he confronted Bill and threatened to ruin him. He was a newspaper man from San Francisco, and said he would spread it through all the papers. America's cowboy hero would be disgraced.

"I think they might have had a chance for happiness had Bill not taken her home after he married her. Either that, or made his sister Mary move out, which he would never have done. But Mary wasn't going to let this slip of a girl come in and take over. Mary had been the hostess in that home too long. I think Bill was genuinely excited about the baby and thrilled about being a father, but that wasn't enough to hold the marriage together. It didn't last six months before Wendy moved out. After their son was born she sued for divorce and I guess she decided to get all she could. What Bill had been trying all along to avoid was bad publicity. It can destroy a public figure. What he got was headlines that he'd beat her," Ollie explained.

"I can't believe that. The Bill Hart we know would never beat a woman," I protested.

"Well, this fight's been going on for months now. Who knows when it will be settled? It's too bad that the little guy, Bill's boy, will be caught in the middle. Speaking of little guys, how's Jack doing? Last time he was up here he had really grown," Ollie asked.

"Sometimes I don't know what I'm going to do with Jack. We've given him everything a child could want. I even gave him the chance to take piano lessons. I always wanted to play the piano, but I never had the opportunity to learn. I asked Alice Calvert, who graduated from one of the best conservatories in the United States, to give Jack lessons as a special favor to us.

"Well, you won't believe what he did. At his last lesson, Alice left the room to answer the phone and she talked for a while. Jack was supposed to be practicing his scales. When she got back, Jack had taken out his pen knife and carved his initials into her beautiful piano. She told him she would never give him another lesson, of course, then she called me.

"When Jack got home, I could hardly control my anger. I told him how lucky he was to be able to take piano lessons. Now he had just thrown that opportunity away. Alice Calvert would never take him back as a student. He said he didn't care. Well, I was getting ready to give him a spanking when JoeDeYong came to his aid and convinced me it was better to make him write five hundred times, 'I will not carve my initials in the piano'."

"What did Charlie do?" Ollie asked.

"Nothing. Charlie can never bring himself to discipline Jack. He's so crazy about him," I explained.

"I know what you mean. I think when an older man has a son, he tends to spoil him," she said. "Look at Harry. He'd give Dobie anything. He even gave Dobie a goat."

"I know. That's the one Charlie made a model of as a gift for Dobie. Remember? He told Dobie, 'don't ever let anyone ever get your goat,'" I said.

"The children all love Charlie. They love it when he puts them on his lap after dinner, takes a left-over loaf of bread and digs out the center to use for modeling little creatures. And they're fascinated by his stories.," Ollie said.

I knew she was right. Children loved Charlie because he was an overgrown kid himself. If I didn't shoo away the children from his studio from time to time, he would never get anything done, and it was hard for him to keep up with the demand as it was.

His rheumatism flared up. For several weeks, he was laid up and he couldn't even make it down the stairs of our house in Great Falls. I knew a decision had to be made. We needed a home in California. We were spending more and more time there and that was where the money was.

The ideal place was Pasadena. I had had the idea tucked away in the back of my mind for several years; in fact, I bought a double lot on Michigan Boulevard. I had let my father build a house on one lot and now the time had come for us to build one on the other. I was afraid Charlie wouldn't like it and I was trying to think of the best way to approach him. Much to my surprise, he thought it was a great idea. He was tired of renting a different place every winter, and even Charlie knew that the Montana winters were too severe for him.

We still spent our summers at Bull Head Lodge on Lake McDonald. By now we had quite a complex there, for we had a guest house as well as a studio for Charlie. There was always so much to do at Lake McDonald, especially when we had guests, which was most of the time. I knew I needed help. I needed two strong hands to pitch in, for Charlie wasn't as robust as he used to be and I certainly couldn't do everything. Of course, I always brought a maid with us from Great Falls but she couldn't do the heavy work.

Fate heard my plea. We were invited to dinner at the John Lewises. When we arrived, I noticed a young man in his thirties chopping wood. I noticed how strong he was. John Lewis asked him to row over to Apgar and pick up the other dinner guests. I could not miss the easy way he pushed the heavy boat into the lake and how effortlessly he guided it through the water.

"What's your hired man's name?" I asked.

"It's Ted – Ted Taylor," Mrs. Lewis answered.

"Are you pleased with him?" I asked.

"He's a good worker, strong as an ox. Of course, he and his brothers have a little wild reputation because of the way they tear around these mountain trails on their motorcycles, and they do like a nip or two of whiskey. Rumor has it they have a way with women. I guess it's their good looks — that dark wavy hair and those dark eyes. But we've been very pleased with Ted," answered Mrs. Lewis.

We had a very pleasant dinner. The next day, I happened to bump into Ted Taylor at the general store in Apgar where he was picking up groceries for the Lewises.

"Pardon me. I'm Mrs. Charles Russell. I saw you yesterday at the Lewises."

"Yes, ma'am. I know. Everyone knows who you are," Ted said as he flashed me a big smile.

"I wanted to talk to you about coming to work for us. Whatever the Lewises are paying you, I'll pay you more. I'm in desperate need of help. Mr. Russell is not as strong as he once was, and he needs to concentrate all of his energy on his paintings."

"Oh, I'd be honored to work for the famous Charlie Russell. Here let me help you, Mrs. Russell, with your groceries. I'll take the Lewises their groceries and quit, then I'll be right over to Bull Head. Anything I can do to be of service, all you have to do is ask," Ted said as he picked up both my heavy box of groceries and the Lewis's. He loaded our groceries into the back seat of my Cadillac.

"Whew, that sure is a beautiful car!" he exclaimed.

"Do you know how to drive?" I asked.

"I sure do. Even got myself a license," Ted answered.

"It's almost too good to be true. I've always wanted a chauffeur. I hate driving these mountain trails. One of your duties will be to drive Mr. Russell and myself. Mr. Russell doesn't drive. It's hard enough to get him just to ride in a car. He'd still much prefer to be on the back of a horse."

Ted's smile got even bigger. "Oh, Mrs. Russell, I'd sure like that. I can't wait to get my hands on that beautiful steering wheel. I'll be over to Bull Head Lodge before you know it," Ted said.

He almost beat me there.

"I'm good to my word. Here I am ready to do anything for you, Mrs. Russell. Mrs. Lewis wasn't mad about me quitting on the spot when I told her I was going to work for you. She knew you and Mr. Russell needed help."

"Mrs. Lewis knows Mr. Russell has not been well and needs to devote his time and energy to his painting. I'm sure she's pleased to know you quit to help us out. Think of the places you will go and the people you will have an opportunity to meet when you drive us to California," I said.

"You mean you're going to let me work for you after you leave Bull Head? You mean you're going to let me drive you to California where I can meet all them movie stars?" Ted exclaimed.

"Of course," I answered. "If you work hard and

are reliable and responsible."

"This is the luckiest day of my life. I'll do anything you want. You'll see. I'll make myself indispensable," Ted promised.

"That's a big word for a country boy," I said.

"I'm not a boy. I'm thirty-six years old, and I bet there's a lot about me that would surprise you," Ted said.

There was. Ted anticipated my every wish, and there was nothing too big or small for him to do for me. Jack took to Ted immediately. Ted was right. By the end of the summer, he had made himself indispensable. After we closed up Bull Head Lodge, Ted drove us back to Great Falls.

It was a good thing Ted was with us. Charlie's rheumatism flared up again. This time Ted could help Charlie up and down the stairs. Even with Ted's help, some days it was too painful. Charlie was looking tired. I looked at him one day and realized that he looked old. The growth around his neck was more visible. Doctor Edwin said it was a goiter and needed to come out, but Charlie wouldn't hear of it. While we were in Great Falls, I had my dressmaker make Charlie some new shirts with much wider necks so when they were buttoned and Charlie had on his string tie, the bulge underneath was camouflaged. But I couldn't camouflage Charlie's wheezing and coughing, nor the jowls that he was acquiring in his once-lean face. He was past sixty but until recently he had looked ten years younger.

I had planned a show in Duluth, but E.G. Furmon of the Biltmore Salon in Los Angeles contacted me to say that Ed Doheny wanted to meet with us to discuss the possibility of Charlie painting two panels to hang in his study. Ed Doheny was a California oil baron who had seen Charlie's show at the Biltmore. I knew that this would be as important as the mural for the State Capital, and I also knew that Ed Doheny would pay a lot more than the State of Montana. Mr. Furman was making the arrangements with the Dohenys for us to get together and I could postpone the show in Dulúth until later. It was much more important to get the Doheny job.

Charlie and I took the train to California and met with the Dohenys. We got the job. When we returned to Great Falls, I told Charlie I would go alone to make the arrangements for the Duluth show. Charlie would stay close to his easel and paint the watercolor sketches for the Dohenys' approval before he began the big oil panels, which were promised by the end of the year.

"I'll take care of the Duluth show and then I'll go on to St. Paul. You finish the sketches. I know Ted and Cook will take good care of you and Jack. And I'm sure Josephine will check on you both every day. She says there are lots of new books at the library that she's dying to bring to Jack." I kissed Charlie and boarded the train.

When I returned, I was amazed and pleased to

see how well Charlie looked. His watercolor drawings were finished, and they were wonderful. I telegraphed Mrs. Doheny on December fifteenth to inquire whether they were going to be in Los Angeles during the next two weeks. They were, so we packed up and Ted drove us to California.

The Doheny house at Eight Chester Place was all bedecked for Christmas and even more beautiful than I remembered it. Ted drove us up to the front door, which wore a big green wreath and a red satin bow. Christmas decorations seemed strange in California when it was seventy-five degrees. Ted, dressed in a chauffeur's hat and a black suit, hurried around to open my door and help me out of the car, then he helped Charlie. Ted loved California. And I could see by his appreciative look that he was not disappointed in the Doheny house.

A butler let us in and showed us to the drawing room where Mr. and Mrs. Doheny were waiting. As we entered, they both came to greet us. They were a handsome couple. Mr. Doheny, a tall man with steel gray hair, was impeccably dressed. Mrs. Doheny looked almost regal in green silk with emerald jewelry. I noticed that their good looks had been captured in two larger-than-life portraits dominating the room. They were by Charles Chandler Christy. I could always recognize his portraits. He capitalized on a person's good looks and his canvases were often an improvement over real life. No wonder he demanded such high prices.

"What a lovely portrait," I said as I entered the room. "So lifelike and natural."

"I'm glad you like it," said Mrs. Doheny. "We were very pleased with Mr. Christy's work."

"I know you'll be equally pleased with Mr. Russell's." I smiled.

I untied the package I was carrying, took out the four watercolors and laid them on the lid of the custom-made gold leaf Steinway grand piano, which they had had specially made. Scattered here and there amidst the gold leaf were miniature paintings of Mrs. Doheny and the children. I knew Charlie's watercolors would show up beautifully on the gold background and would compare favorably with the family groupings painted on the piano.

"These two drawings go together for one panel and these two for the other. They tell the story of California from when it was nature's own land, to the story of the cowboy, the coming of the farmer, the coming of the oil industry. See, it ends with the oil derrick," I explained.

I watched as Mr. and Mrs. Doheny studied the drawings. I could see they were captivated.

"You know you are getting a real bargain. The two panels are actually as big as four paintings and Mr. Russell's paintings are fetching ten thousand dollars each, but since this is for you, I'm only asking thirty thousand dollars."

"Thank you, Mrs. Russell," said Mr. Doheny.

"We are very pleased with the watercolor sketches. I'm sure we will treasure the panels when they are up in my study. The price is satisfactory."

While Charlie and Mr. Doheny went into the study so that Charlie could see once more where the panels would hang, Mrs. Doheny took me around the house and showed me some of their treasures. They had just bought a Gutenberg Bible. I felt a thrill when I held it, but nothing compared to the thrill I was feeling inside knowing that I had just made a single sale for thirty thousand dollars!

As soon as we got into the car, I said, "Oh, Charlie, isn't it wonderful. Thirty thousand dollars!"

"And you made them think they were getting a bargain," replied Charlie

I saw Ted's reflection in the car's mirror. He let out a silent whistle.

"Anyone who can afford two Charles Chandler Christy portraits and a gold-leaf Steinway can easily afford thirty thousand dollars. I hope I asked enough," I said. Charlie and Ted laughed.

I think the sale and Christmas raised Charlie's spirits. He was like a little kid. He always loved Christmas. Or maybe it was the California climate that made his rheumatism so much better. Whatever it was, Charlie was painting beautifully and was even ahead of schedule on the panels. Since he was feeling so well I thought it was important that we attend the opening of his show at the Corcoran Gallery of Art in Washington,

D.C.

It was a glorious exhibit. Senator Thomas J. Walsh of Montana had sent out cards himself telling of the exhibition. A thin layer of snow covered the ground on opening night, February third, but that didn't deter the crowd. There were Senators, Congressmen, even cabinet members there to rub elbows and talk about Charlie's paintings and the genius of Charlie's work which had truly captured the West that was. But that's not all they talked about. An important bill was coming to the floor and there was one undecided congressman there. He was never alone. The pro group cornered him and tried to persuade him to vote for it. The minute they moved on, he was surrounded by the opposition trying equally hard to get him to vote against it.

There were handsome women wearing long white gloves and sequinned and beaded dresses. They smiled and waved and hugged each other as if they had been separated for years although they had probably been to an embassy tea together that very afternoon. You'd never know that some of their husbands were political enemies. I was fascinated by the show, and everyone there seemed to be equally fascinated by Charlie and his show.

After everyone had left I was too keyed up to go back to the Willard Hotel.

"Let's ask the cab to take us up to the Capitol. I'm too excited to go back to the hotel. I want to see the capitol at night with its lights reflecting on the snow," I begged Charlie. Charlie couldn't turn me down. He was excited too. We had the cab take us up Constitution Avenue. That broad boulevard flanked by big government buildings reflected the power of the city, but it was nothing compared to the Capitol's dome at night.

"Isn't it beautiful? Oh, Charlie, I'm so glad we came," I said.

We stood arm in arm. Suddenly it began snowing again. I stuck out my tongue and caught a flake. "This doesn't even taste like a Montana snowflake."

"We'd better get back to the hotel. It's been a big day," Charlie said as we got into the taxi cab.

"Charlie, it's been a wonderful day. We met some very powerful people tonight. I have a feeling that 1925 is going to be our year. I can't wait to get back to California and tell C. O. Middleton about the people we met this evening. Even he will be impressed."

It was hard to impress C. O. Middleton. He spent most of the time impressing other people. It was said that he had made and lost several fortunes before we had ever met him, that he had been both a millionaire and a bankrupt several times. I believed it. No matter how gigantic the stories, they were not as big as his ego. Right now, he was in his millionaire stage and getting richer each day building mansions for stars in Beverly Hills. He didn't know much about the building business, but his partner, Roy Marshall, did. C.O. knew how to sell.

He was born in Texas and if there ever was a

brash Texan, he was it. Some people said he left Texas for Memphis because he owed money and when he owed one hundred thousand dollars in Memphis he came on out to California for that was as far as he could go. Others said he got the one hundred thousand dollars back in a card game at the Mar Monte Hotel one night and he decided to stay in California for that was where the big spenders were. He drank his whiskey straight. He always smoked a big cigar, and he always, always was ready for a high stakes poker game.

Yet there was something about C.O. Middleton you couldn't help but like. Maybe it was because he was an original. He was his own person, and he drew people to him like bees to honey. He built a hunting lodge up in the California hills and had fifty keys made for the door. Those keys went to his fifty best friends— bankers, movie stars, an ambassador or two, doctors and artists. Charlie Russell was one of his favorite artists.

C.O. lived a life that would have been frowned upon had he been any other man. He built a home at 1406 Grand Avenue in the hills of Santa Barbara for his mistress, Lindley Anderson. He and Lindley were entertained by the cream of California society, the Hunts, the Blacks, and the Cobbs. No one seemed to care that Lindley was his wife's first cousin. His wife, Nin, didn't seem to care either. She was happy with her big house and her four children; and as long as C.O. was generous with his money, it seemed he could do as he pleased. Besides, she didn't believe in divorce. Who would take care of her? No one back in Mississippi would understand a divorce.

Lindley Anderson was nothing like I expected. I expected a brazen hussy, a painted woman. She was little and quiet and spoke with a soft southern drawl. Her big eyes reminded me of the eyes of a fawn, and when she looked at C. O. they filled with complete adoration. I think the reason she talked so softly was because she was hard of hearing and afraid that she might be shouting. She always carried around a little box connected by wires to her hearing aid. She had a quick sense of humor and giggled when Charlie teased her, saying, "I think you have your wires crossed." It became a running joke between the two of them.

I remember when we first met and she said, "I've been so looking forward to meeting the beautiful Mrs. Russell. I've heard so much about you. C.O. tells me that you handle all of Mr.Russell's exhibits, that you make all of his sales and that no one has ever bettered you in a deal. And C.O. should know since he's president of the Santa Barbara Art League and owns the Biltmore Salon. I admire you so much, Mrs. Russell. How can you be so smart?"

"Please call me Nancy," I said.

"And you must call me Lindley," she replied. "C.O. is so pleased that you all are going to build a house in California. He thinks you should spend more time here for here is where the money is, and he says Mr. Russell's paintings sell better at the Biltmore Salon in Los Angeles when Mr. Russell drops in occasionally."

"Yes, we are planning to build a house in Pasadena and spend more time in California," I replied.

"Oh, I'm so glad. I know we'll be good friends."

Charlie and I were both excited about our new home, particularly since a friend from Great Falls who had moved to California would be our builder. He owned Theisen Construction Company and we knew he was a good and conscientious builder and would do everything to please us.

I knew we couldn't build a mansion like a John Barrymore or a Wrigley of Wrigley's Gum, but I wanted it to be different and not look like just any other house since it was going to be the home of Charles M. Russell, the world-famous artist, who was not just another artist. Years earlier we had visited New Mexico on our way to Mexico. I was touched by the beauty and simplicity of the Pueblos. I thought a southwestern touch would be appropriate in Southern California. Our house had to be much more than just a house. It had to be a gallery that would show off Charlie's paintings to their very best advantage.

Over the next several months we met with our builder many times to plan our home, Trail's End. There would be a long driveway to the side of the house, extending all the way to the alley. When we had an exhibit or party, the cars would be able to line up and have easy access in and out. The front door would be on the side of the house. The studio-gallery would be forty-two by twenty-four; with spacious walls to hang Charlie's paintings. There was to be a skylight the length of the studio which would bring in natural light to shine on Charlie's paintings so one could appreciate the beautiful clear colors he used. In one corner would be a fireplace fashioned after a Pueblo kiva. Along that end of the room would be shelves where we could display Charlie's bronzes. Next to the studio-gallery, where Charlie could paint, was a small living room. Beyond was to be a walled patio with a fountain at one end and a fireplace at the other. It would be the perfect spot to entertain. I knew we would have lots of parties for friends like Bill Rogers and Bill Hart and also for prospective buyers. There's nothing that sells a painting faster than good food and the good company of a happy, enthusiastic owner.

Of course, there would be a kitchen, a large dining room, a screened-in back porch and a bathroom downstairs. Upstairs would be our bedroom suite with bedroom, sitting room and bathroom; a bedroom for Jack; a guest bedroom and bath for out-of-town patrons who needed to stay with us; and a sun room which could also serve as a guest bedroom or maid's room. We had planned our dream house.

We were renting a place at 6816 Odin in the Hollywood Hills, not far from a young director, John Ford, who had taken an interest in Charlie's paintings. When I woke up New Year's Day, 1926, I said to Charlie, "Happy New Year. This is going to be our best year ever. Everything we've worked for is going to come about. We're going to build our Trail's End. Your paintings are getting the highest price ever. Somehow, everyone knows the price of the Doheny panels and Dr. Cole, Malcolm MacKay, the Biltmore, all are clamoring for your work. Our dreams are coming true. We finally have it made."

14

The Last Summer

By spring, Charlie could hardly breathe. Each day I watched him get worse. I begged him to go to the doctor. I pleaded with him. I scolded him. I nagged him. He was being more than stubborn. I think he was scared. He would not go.

In May, Josephine and Margaret Trigg came to California to visit us. They were shocked to see how terrible Charlie looked.

"Nancy, you have got to get Charlie to the doctor. Maybe it's because you see him every day that you don't realize how awful he looks. He's sick," Josephine said.

"I've tried everything I can think of, and I can't get him to go. Maybe he'll listen to you and Margaret. He knows how much you both care for him," I answered.

"I'm outnumbered," Charlie finally said. "Three against one. All right, you win. I'll go to the doctor so long as I can go back to Great Falls and go to Dr. Edwin."

Margaret had not been well and I knew that the long, hard trip back to Great Falls would be exhausting for her as well as for Charlie. The roads left much to be desired. Besides, being cooped up in a car with Jack for several days was almost more than a healthy person could take, for Jack was never still. It was decided that Margaret and Charlie would take the train home and that the rest of us would drive. The train arrived a couple of days before we did.

When I saw Charlie, I could hardly believe my eyes. His health had deteriorated even further. His complexion was a pasty gray and each breath was labored.

I immediately went to see the doctor.

"Dr. Edwin, what's wrong with Charlie?" I cried out the minute I saw him at his office.

"That goiter of his has *got* to come out. I've told Charlie, it's continued growing and is cutting off his breathing. There's only one place to go, that's Mayo's. There are specialists there. Dr. Henry Plummer and Dr. Charles Mayo have developed a new procedure for this kind of operation. But Charlie said he won't go. He says he's not going to let anyone slit his throat," Dr. Edwin said.

I went home and two hours later I called Dr.

Edwin. "Charlie will go to Mayo's if you go with us. Oh, Dr. Edwin, will you please drop everything and go with us to Mayo's," I pleaded.

"Of course, I will, Mrs. Russell. You know everyone loves Charlie, and I'm no exception. I don't know how you talked him into going, but I'm glad you did. I'll do my part. Let me get in touch with the Mayo Clinic and set up an appointment." On Friday, June twenty-fifth, we boarded the train for Rochester. It was a smaller town than I had imagined. Because of the fame of the Mayo Clinic, I expected a metropolis. This little Minnesota town had one industry — sick people. It was obvious everywhere you looked: the people getting off the train, the people checking into the hotel, the people sitting in the hard-backed chairs at Mayo's waiting to see their doctors. They all had fear in their eyes. You came to Mayo's when you needed a specialist.

Charlie couldn't stand sitting in our room at the Kahler Hotel waiting for test results. It was even worse sitting in the lobby where everyone seemed to be waiting for his test results. The three of us decided to go for a walk. That was a mistake. We walked by the Colonial Hospital for children. Since it was a beautiful day, they had rolled many beds and wheelchairs outside. We saw face after face with the hollow-eyed, hollow-cheeked look of the very sick.

"I don't ever want to walk this way again," said Charlie.

Charlie loved children, and it didn't seem fair to

him that disease could strike those so young and innocent. The results of Charlie's tests agreed with those of Dr. Edwin. His goiter had to be removed. Charlie refused.

"But, Charlie, we came all the way up here to see what was wrong. The doctors at Mayo's are the very best. If they say it's got to be done, we have to believe them. And Dr. Edwin dropped everything to be with us. You can't let him down and disappoint him," I pleaded with Charlie.

"Mame, do you know what it feels like to think about them slitting your throat from ear to ear?" said Charlie, his voice just above a whisper.

I knew I needed to get Dr. Edwin to help me convince Charlie he needed the operation so I asked him to meet me in the lobby while Charlie took a nap. "Dr. Edwin, you've just got to do something with Charlie. I've done all I can, and he trusts you."

"I think I have the solution. Do you know Jack Flannery from Great Falls? He had that operation yesterday. As soon as Charlie wakes up from his nap, we will all go up and visit Jack. Of course, Jack will be sitting up in bed. The doctors always have their patients half-sitting up so that the small drainage tube they have inserted can drain the excess fluid and blood. Charlie won't be able to see it because of the bandage. Now, you just leave it up to me," Dr. Edwin said and he patted my hand with reassurance.

As soon as Charlie woke up from his nap, we

went to see Jack Flannery. Dr. Edwin was right. There he sat in bed with his throat all bandaged.

"I was operated on yesterday," said Jack. "And as you can see, here I am sitting up in bed, talking to you. Why, there's nothing to it."

Charlie agreed to the operation. I must have paced a hundred miles, back and forth, in the waiting room. The minutes crawled by so slowly. I looked at my watch a thousand times. I tried to force myself not to look at it until I thought segments of at least five minutes had passed. I was always wrong, but I had to do something to occupy my mind while Charlie was "getting his throat slit ear to ear."

Finally the doctor came in and said that Charlie had made it through the operation successfully. And I could see him as soon as he came out of the anesthetic.

He was sitting up in bed. There was a large white bandage around his throat. His eyes were closed. I crept across the room and took one of his hands, which was cold and ghostly white, and gave it a squeeze. His eyelids opened. He tried to smile.

The next day, Jack Flannery came to see Charlie.

"Well, I was operated on yesterday and see here I am sitting up in bed, talking to you . . . there's nothing to it . . . you son of a bitch," Charlie swore.

Each day Charlie got better. We were flooded with letters, wires, get-well cards, postcards and calls. Everyone loved Charlie, and they all wanted to wish him a speedy recovery. As Charlie's strength returned I would sit in his hospital room and read his letters and cards to him. We got a letter from Ralph Budd, president of the Great Northern Railroad, who said they had a special train, the Columbia River Special, leaving Chicago July fifteenth and coming through St. Paul on its way to Oregon. The president of the railroad would be honored to have Mr. and Mrs. Russell as his guests in his private car. He and his railroad would be privileged to escort them to Great Falls, Montana, when Mr. Russell was well enough to travel.

"Well, write him we'd be proud to ride along with him in his private car. Tell him I'm doin' fine, that there was nothin' to it, and that I'm leavin' somethin' here I don't need anyway," said Charlie.

I smiled and chuckled. "I'm so glad to see you've got your sense of humor back. That means you are getting better," I said.

The nurse entered Charlie's room just then and asked me to accompany her to Dr. Balfour's office. I assumed the doctor wanted to make arrangements for Charlie's release, or maybe they wanted payment.

The nurse knocked on the doctor's office door, then opened it as if she knew he was waiting for us.

"Mrs. Russell," he said as he stood up. "Please come in and take a seat." He motioned to a chair across from his desk.

"I'm glad you sent for me. I was just about to come to see you. Chas is so much better that I was wondering when we could go home. We've had an invitation from Ralph Budd, president of the Great Northern Railroad, to be given a ride home in his private car. I need to let them know when we'll be ready to leave," I smiled as I sat down.

"Mr. Russell came through the operation with flying colors. He should be able to leave the first of next week."

"Oh, I'll have to call Mr. Budd. The mail will take too long," I said as I started to get up to leave.

"Please wait a minute, Mrs. Russell. There is something you need to know. Mr. Russell came through the operation fine, but the tests have shown that he has serious vascular problems. His heart has been so weakened by the stress on it due to the long delay in removing the goiter that he has, at most, ninety days to live."

There was silence.

I heard my voice, "Are you sure?" It didn't sound like my voice. It was the voice of a stranger. Yes, a stranger, for this wasn't happening to me. This wasn't happening to Charlie. It must be someone else. "But it can't be true. Chas has not looked this good in ages. He can breathe better. He has more strength. His color is good. There must be some mistake."

"I'm sorry, Mrs. Russell, but I'm afraid there's no mistake," Dr. Balfour replied.

I dropped my head into my hands.

"Is there anything I can do?" Dr. Balfour asked.

"Yes, please don't tell Charlie." I said.

But somehow Charlie found out, and he asked them "not to tell Mame."

From then on we played a game. We played "make-believe" that everything was going to be all right. I wanted everything to be as always. Maybe if we pretended everything was the same, it would be.

We boarded the private car in St. Paul for our return trip to Great Falls. The car was paneled in gleaming polished walnut, the furniture covered in dark velvet. On the floor was a magnificent Oriental rug made especially for this car in China.

"Oh, Charlie, we need to have rugs made in China for our new home in Pasadena," I said.

"When are we going to get started on that house? All we've been doing is the plannin.' I'm ready to start the buildin'," said Charlie.

"As soon as we get back from Lake McDonald. I know how you love it there. And we'll ask our best friends to spend the summer with us. We'll ask Margaret and Josephine, of course, and Dr. Edwin and his wife."

"Maybe that fellow I met at Mayo's from Great Falls who'd had the same operation. We could sit around and talk to our hearts' content about our operations," said Charlie.

"I'm going to get in touch with Martha Gabrielson. She's out in California being a secretary, I think. I'll ask her if she will come up to the lake with us and keep an eye on Jack. She was wonderful with him when he was a little boy, and I'm really going to need someone this summer. I never saw a nine-year-old with so much energy. He's just never still. I certainly can't take care of him and entertain all our guests," I said as I looked out the train window at the trees, the plowed fields, the streams, the roads that all became a blur as they passed by. And I thought to myself — make believe everything is the same — make believe that this is just another summer at Lake McDonald, not Charlie's last.

I looked around at the rich surroundings of President Budd's private car and I thought about another car so long ago, a car with hard wooden benches, with blowing soot. I smelled the sour smell of dried sweat, the odor of stale food. I heard the babies crying and mothers quieting them in foreign tongues. I felt the firm shoulder of Mama under my cheek. I'd come a long way from that car. But where would I go, what would I ever do without Charlie?

Half the town of Great Falls was out to meet us when the private car rolled to a stop. Everyone was so glad to see Charlie back and looking so well. Make believe everything is fine, I said to myself. We just stayed long enough to get our things, pick up Jack, and wait for Martha to come from California before we had Ted drive us up to Lake McDonald.

The lake had never been as blue, the sky as clear, or the mountains as beautiful as they were that summer. Charlie, as always, had a saltlick out for the animals. Since he had wintered with the Bloods when they ran out of salt, he had respected the importance of salt to all living creatures. At first when the deer came to lick salt, they jumped and ran at any approach. All we would see was the white flash of a tail as it disappeared in the woods. But by summer's end Charlie had made friends with the deer, especially a fawn. He would put a lump of sugar in his hand and the fawn would gently nibble it.

As with every summer at Lake McDonald, Charlie would paint in the mornings in his studio. In the afternoon, he would often go into Apgar, or visit with our house guests on the big front porch that overlooked the lake, or play with the children. Jack loved to sail the boats Charlie made. There was a fish pond next to the lodge. On the afternoons that Charlie was "boat builder," the banks of the little fish pond crowded with children. The air was filled with shouts, laughter, and squeals of delight as each child urged on his boat to victory in a race. The biggest kid of all was Charlie who enjoyed the races more than any other spectator.

We went to Lewis House, the biggest lodge on the lake, for dinner. It was still popular with tourists but wasn't as full as usual this summer. It seemed other spots had become more popular. They still rang the gong to announce our party, which created an even bigger sensation than it had years earlier, for Charlie's fame had spread. After we were seated in the dining room, we were engulfed by tourists who wanted to meet the famous artist. Old-time friends and residents of Lake McDonald also came up to shake Charlie's hand and tell him how glad they were he was back from Mayo's. Everyone had kept up with his progress through the newspapers. Charlie basked in the warmth of friendship. He still had that magnetism that drew people to him. He used to say that when he had nothing else, he had friends.

I wanted it to be a perfect summer, an idyllic summer. But we had one terribly upsetting incident. When we went to Lewis House for dinner one evening, I looked around at Charlie's paintings and to my horror, I saw that beside Charlie's paintings were hung Olaf Seltzer's. I could not believe my eyes. I closed them. I opened them. They were still there. I went over to the paintings and I stared. It was true. John Lewis, our good friend, had hung Olaf Seltzer's paintings right next to Charlie's. I could not eat my dinner.

The next day, I went back to Lewis House and confronted John Lewis.

"How dare you hang Olaf Seltzer's paintings in the same room, much less on the same wall, with Charlie's?" I didn't wait for an answer. "He is not even in the same league with Charles Marion Russell. Seltzer is nothing but a very poor imitation. He is a copy-cat. He never had an original idea in his whole life — every theme he ever had for a picture Charlie did first. John Lewis, I thought you were our friend. How could you?" I demanded.

"Well, Olaf said he was a good friend of Charlie's and that Charlie wouldn't mind," stammered

John.

"Charlie may not mind, but I do. You either take down Olaf's pictures or I will take down Charlie's and never again set foot in Lewis House." I warned.

Of course, John took down Olaf's pictures and we continued to dine at Lewis House throughout the season.

The summer slipped by too quickly. I knew it was gone one morning when Charlie brought me my warm water and lemon juice as he had every morning for years. Charlie still liked to get up early, even at Lake McDonald. But even in the middle of summer the early morning hours were nippy and by early fall they held quite a chill.

"Here, Mame. Here's your juice," said Charlie as he handed me the glass.

I reached out from under the warm covers. "My, it's turned cold. Why haven't Ted or Cook started the fire?" I asked as I drank the warm lemon juice.

"The fire's goin' in the fireplace," replied Charlie. "It's just turned real cold. Ol' Jack Frost was paintin' it up last night."

"I guess it's time we returned to Great Falls," I said. "Oh, Charlie, I don't want this summer to end. It's so beautiful here at Lake McDonald."

"I know," said Charlie.

I knew he knew what I meant, but we both played our parts.

We returned to Great Falls. Charlie returned to

painting in his studio in the mornings and visiting with his friends in the afternoons. I returned to taking care of the correspondence and the business dealings.

Charlie was excited about a painting he was completing of Father DeSmet meeting with the Flatheads. On the morning of October twenty-fourth, he got up early as usual, prepared his breakfast, brought me my lemon juice, and went out to his studio to work. He looked better than he had in years. He was filled with vigor. It was such a beautiful October day, that we had Ted take us for a ride in the afternoon. We had some friends, the Thoroughmans, over for dinner. Charlie was in rare form and had them mesmerized with his stories. After they left, he went up to bed while I picked things up downstairs and Cook did the dishes.

I heard a loud gasp. I ran up the stairs. Charlie was sitting in Jack's bedroom at the top of the stairs staring at the sleeping boy. His face was ashen. He was gasping for breath and clutching his chest. I screamed. Cook came running.

"Tell Ted to call Dr. Edwin."

It seemed an eternity before Dr. Edwin arrived, though it was only minutes. He ran up the stairs with Ted right behind him. Dr. Edwin had his bag opened, his stethoscope out and was listening to Charlie's heartbeat all in one motion.

"Someone carry Jack out of here," Dr. Edwin motioned to Ted.

Ted picked the boy up gently and carried him

into Charlie's and my bedroom and placed him on the bed.

Charlie gasped and slumped forward. Dr. Edwin caught him in his arms. Again he listened for Charlie's heartbeat. Then slowly, very slowly, he took off his stethoscope, looked at me, and with tears rolling down his cheeks said, "He's gone."

"Oh, no! No! No!" I said. I rushed to Charlie, sat on the floor beside him and put my arms around his fallen body. I cradled him like a baby and rocked him back and forth, crying.

After a while Dr. Edwin touched me on the shoulder, then pried my clutching hands from Charlie's body. He pulled me up and led me from the room.

"I've called W.H. George and Company. The mortician is here. I also called Reverend Keller and he, too, is here. Come on, Mrs.Russell, let's go downstairs," Dr. Edwin said calmly as if he were talking to a child.

"Mrs. Russell," said a young man who suddenly appeared, his hand outstretched. "I'm Mr. George's assistant. Don't you worry about a thing. I'll take care of everything. I'll just go right upstairs and remove the deceased, then I'll call the newspapers. I'll handle everything." He smiled as if he were planning a party.

"No, you won't. You won't take Charlie anywhere. You can prepare his body for burial here, here in the home he loved. I'll not have him taken to the mortuary. Do you understand?" I demanded.

"If that's your wishes," he stammered.

"And I forbid you to call the newspapers. I will not have Charlie's death in the newspapers until I've told Josephine and Margaret Trigg. They have the right to hear it from me. Do I make myself clear?" I said.

"Yes, Mrs. Russell," the assistant said soberly.

When the young mortician went upstairs, Dr. Edwin said, "Don't worry, Mrs. Russell. I will make sure he doesn't get to the newspapers. Is there anything else I can do?"

"No, thank you. You've been most kind."

"I think you had better get some rest, for you have some difficult days ahead of you," he said as I showed him to the front door.

"I don't understand, Dr. Edwin. Charlie looked better, felt better, and was in better spirits today than he had been in ages. He was excited about a painting he was working on. We had a wonderful ride this afternoon and tonight Charlie had a glorious time entertaining our friends at dinner. He never seemed so well, then, suddenly he's gone," I began to cry again.

"Nature's funny that way. Often it gives you a spurt of energy just before it's time to leave this world." Dr. Edwin said as he patted my hand. "Just hold on to the thought that he had a wonderful day, his last day, doing what he liked most. We are all going to miss him. This town's not going to be the same without Charlie Russell. Now, I'm going to insist you go on up to bed. It's already the middle of the night." Dr. Edwin said.

"I'll go up after a while. I'm just going to sit

here in the living room," I told the doctor as I let him out. I couldn't tell him I couldn't sleep in our bed without Charlie. Charlie would never be in it again.

I don't know how long I sat in the living room before I fell asleep, curled up in the chair. When I awakened it was daylight. I remembered why I had fallen asleep in a chair in the living room. I remembered what had happened the night before. Charlie was gone. It all seemed like a bad dream. Maybe if I went upstairs I would find him in bed. Or maybe he was already painting in the studio and last night had been a nightmare. I knew I would have to go upstairs and tell Jack. I was stiff from sleeping in the chair. My joints ached, my head throbbed. I pulled myself up the stairs and went into my bedroom. Jack was still asleep. As if my gaze had the power to awaken him, he began to stir. His eyelids fluttered open, and he looked around.

"Mama, what am I doing sleeping in your bed?" he asked.

"I have some terrible news. Last night your daddy died."

There was silence. Utter disbelief was written across his small face, then he jumped out of bed, came running to me and buried his face in my skirts.

"Now, Jack, I have to go over and tell Josephine and Margaret Trigg, so you go on downstairs and have Cook fix you some breakfast."

"Can I go with you. Can I?" he asked.

"No," I said.

"But I want to see Aunt Nomee."

"Jack, do as I said. Don't be difficult. Go have Cook fix you some breakfast. You have to be a big boy now and do what I tell you."

Sniffling, Jack went downstairs.

I got my coat on and went to the Triggs.

Josephine answered my knock. She took one look at my face and she knew. She put her arms around me, and we both stood crying.

"When?" she asked.

"Last night. A little after eleven. Dr. Edwin came but there was nothing he could do. I wouldn't let anyone call the newspapers because I wanted you and Margaret to hear it from me." There, I had said it. Margaret had heard me come in and was standing in the doorway behind us.

"Oh, no," she gasped.

We went to her. Josephine helped her to a chair and then went to get her a glass of water.

"But he seemed so well. He looked so good, better than in ages," said Margaret.

"How is Jack taking it?" asked Josephine.

"He's having breakfast right now. He wanted to come with me, but I wouldn't let him. He's too young to understand all the arrangements I have to make. I've got to get in touch with the newspapers now, go to the funeral parlor, find a horse-drawn hearse, for that's what Charlie wanted. There are a thousand and one things I need to do."

"This has been a big shock to the boy. I think I'll go over there to be with him, and you won't have to worry about him while you make all the arrangements," Josephine said.

"Thank you, Nancy dear, for coming to tell us," said Margaret.

"Charlie had a world of friends, " I said. "I have to send so many telegrams. Josephine, I will have Martha help me since you are going to take care of Jack."

"You two could be of great comfort to one another," said Josephine. "I know Jack is hurt and confused. It's hard for us to understand death. Can you imagine how hard it is for a child?"

"Josephine, I have to plan a funeral that is a fitting tribute to the world's greatest artist," I said.

15

Remembering Charlie

THE HEAVY, SWEET FRAGRANCE OF ROSES, lilies, and gardenias filled the air. Mingled with their perfume was the smell of sweat as people pushed and crowded into the Episcopal Church of the Incarnation. I was seated in the front row, dressed all in black — black hat, black veil, black coat, black dress, black stockings, black shoes, black gloves. If black could have a feeling, this was it — total loss — void — emptiness. I stared at the thousands of flowers of every color and hue and thought of how Charlie loved color, and how he could capture the strange lavender rays of sunset that sometime streak across a Montana sky.

I don't know what the preacher said — something about a great artist and a great friend who would be missed by all. Women sobbed into their handkerchiefs. There were songs and prayers. We stood up. We sat down. We knelt. It was as if someone else was there in my body.

My mind was filled with a jumble of images. I remembered the shows, the openings, the reviews. I remembered the excitement of the sales and the rise in prices. Suddenly I knew that I wasn't through yet. I sat in that front pew and I vowed I would never let them forget Charlie. I would never let them forget his paintings. I had survived before, and I would again. And in some way Charlie would survive through me.

All at once the service was over. I stood up and walked down the long center aisle. People nodded to me along the way. A few stuck their hands out to shake mine. Outside I watched as the pallbearers gently placed Charlie's casket into the horse-drawn hearse as if he were asleep and a jostle might awaken him.

Charlie had hated automobiles until the day he died. To him they symbolized the demise of the horse, they were noisy, they belched fumes. He wanted a horse-drawn hearse. There wasn't one to be found in Great Falls, but we found one in Cascade. Behind the hearse pranced a big sorrel with his head held high. On his back was Charlie's saddle. Charlie's boots were stuck in the stirrups backwards. On either side of the sorrel rode two of Charlie's best friends, Charlie Beil and Horace Brewster.

I got in a long black car. The procession began. It slowly wound through the streets of Great Falls, out into the country. The procession was blocks and blocks long, strung out as far as the eye could see. This slow parade headed for Highland Cemetery, several miles outside of town. The road was lined all the way to the cemetery with men, women, and children. Stores, businesses, and schools had all been closed for the day. Everyone had come to pay their respects and to say goodbye to a friend. Everywhere people wept.

Finally the procession stopped at the side of a small hill. The place was marked by a large, natural boulder which was to be Charlie's headstone. Charlie always loved everything in nature. I got out of the car and stood by the opened grave. Again the pallbearers gingerly lifted the casket out of the horse-drawn hearse and placed it carefully on the ropes. As it was lowered into the ground, the minister began his last words.

The boulder headstone had an artist's palette made of metal bearing Charlie's name. The thumb-hole in the palette, I decided, should be drilled big enough for a bird to nest in. We had always had bird houses in the yard. Charlie would watch the birds build their nests, protect their eggs, then feed their young and when the time was right, teach them to fly. Now he would be kept company by the songs of the birds.

And Albert Trigg was buried right next door. Charlie wouldn't be alone. I remembered back when we bought the cemetery lots adjoining the Trigg lots at the time Albert died. It seemed like the right thing to do, for Charlie and Albert had been such good friends in life. When we were in Great Falls, not two days would pass without one visiting the other.

The minister tossed a handful of soil onto the lid of Charlie's casket. "Dust to dust," he said, then he bowed his head in prayer.

While he prayed, I said to myself, "Someday I will lie down beside you, darling. But until that time, I promise I will take care of the business end, and they'll not forget you."

Soon everyone was coming by and taking my hand and expressing their condolences.

It was late when we returned to Great Falls and the house on Fourth Avenue North. It, too, was filled with people. The house was too small to hold the crowd. It spilled over onto the front porch and yard. People were milling about inside and out greeting one another, reminiscing about days gone by, days they had shared with Charlie. Even though I had always known that Charlie had many friends, I hadn't realized how many. I knew the town loved him but I hadn't known how much. I tried to circulate through the entire crowd, shaking everyone's hand. Then dusk was upon us and the crowd grew thin. Slowly people left for their homes, reluctant to part. While they stayed together exchanging Charlie Russell stories then perhaps his spirit stayed among them.

I was standing in the yard saying good-bye to the last caller when Josephine came out of the house. She came to me and put her arm around me to lead me inside.

"I don't want to go in just yet," I said.

"But it's dark. Come in and have a cup of tea and something to eat," she said.

Was it her parents' English background that made Josephine think that a cup of tea would always make everything all right, would always make me feel better?

"No, I'm going to Charlie's studio," I replied.

"Do you want me to come with you?" she asked.

"No," I said. "I just want to be there with Charlie," I said as I turned to go into the studio.

I opened the heavy door and went inside. In the darkness I could pretend he was there. I closed my eyes, and I could see him sitting at the easel. I could almost hear his brush stroking the canvas. I could smell the tobacco that he took from his pocket as he rolled a cigarette.

I heard the door open. "Who is it?" I asked.

"It's me, Mrs. Russell, Young Boy."

"How did you know I was here?" I asked.

"Because I miss him, too. He was the best white man I ever knew. He was the only white man I ever knew who could think like an Indian," Young Boy said to me. "He was the only white man who trusted Young Boy. I would come to him when I was broke and ask for a loan and he would give me the money. He wouldn't make me sign no paper. He'd just say pay it back when I had it."

"And you always did," I told Young Boy.

"I'm goin' miss him, Mrs. Russell. The world's a poorer place without him."

"Thank you, Young Boy. Thank you for coming by," I said.

Then Young Boy slipped out and was gone.

The next morning I was up early. "Martha, we have a thousand things to do. You type, don't you?" I asked her.

"Of course, Mrs. Russell, but I thought you wanted me to watch over Jack and help around the house."

"This is more important, besides Jack will be in school most of the day. We need to compile a list of everyone to whom Charlie ever sent an illustrated letter. I'm going to have a book published of Charlie's letters so the whole world will know what a genius he was. Some of his best work was on those letters. But it's not the painting that is most important, it's his words. His words were almost poetry. His letters declared his philosophy. Young Boy told me last night that the world was a poorer place because Charlie Russell was gone. Well, the world is going to be a richer place once I get his letters published in a book for all to read.

I also need to find the right publisher, one with a special knowledge of color, true color. We could ruin Charlie's letters with a sloppy color job. I need to visit Charlie's most devoted buyers like the Mackays and Dr. Cole, back East. I need to organize some memorial shows for Charlie. I need to start pushing Charlie's works at the Biltmore Gallery again. When I'm out in California, I must commence with the house in Pasadena." As I said this, I was rushing around the house getting out address books, copies of correspondence and ledger books.

"Surely, Mrs. Russell, you don't plan to leave Great Falls?" asked Martha.

"Not this year. I need to stay here and make sure that Charlie's friends build him a proper tribute, one he deserves. I was thinking last night as I sat in his studio that the most appropriate monument in Great Falls would be his studio, the place that has made Great Falls famous because of the work Charlie did there," I said. "Don't you agree?"

"Agree to what?" Josephine had come in.

"To making Charlie's studio a monument to his memory," I told Josephine.

"Nancy, I think that's a wonderful idea. What better way to keep Charlie's memory alive than give the people of Great Falls his studio as a museum, dedicated to Charlie," Josephine said.

I could see the joy on her face.

"Who said anything about giving? Oh, I'll make them a good price — say, twenty thousand dollars. That's practically stealing it, but I won't give it. People only value what they pay for. If it's free they will think it's not worth anything. I'll meet with the city powers-that-be and make them my offer. Martha, have you got that typewriter set up? There are so many letters I need to write before I leave for California."

"Nancy, you're not going to California now?"

"I'm not moving right now, but I have business to take care of. I have a show to plan, a house to start," I said.

"But you can't go off and leave Jack."

"Jack's in school. I won't be moving until next year. It will take that long to get the house in Pasadena built," I said.

"I was hoping you'd stay in Great Falls. You spent your winters in California because the winters here were too harsh for Charlie. Now that he's gone . . . ," Josephine said with a hurt and puzzled look on her face.

"Josephine, don't you know anything about business? California is where the money is. There's not over ten people in Great Falls that can afford a Charlie Russell, and there are hundreds in California," I explained.

"But what about Jack? He's only ten and his daddy has just died."

"He'd be a sight worse off if he didn't have anything to eat or wear. Charlie's work keeps the roof over our heads. I can't let his reputation or prices slip. I must take care of the business. That's all I've got."

"You've got Jack. You can take care of him," she said.

She didn't understand. I went to her and gave her a hug. "Josephine, you and Martha and Ted can take care of Jack while I keep a roof over our heads. Before I go anywhere, I need to meet with the Great Falls fathers and plan Charlie's museum."

The meeting was set up. When I returned I was livid.

"I can't believe it. They wanted me to give them Charlie's studio. They wanted me to pay for its maintenance. I thought they were the Chamber of Commerce. Don't they realize how important the museum would be to Great Falls?. It would be a great attraction.

"I think I convinced them to set up a Charles Marion Russell Memorial Park Committee. I told them that I thought all four lots plus the studio and the house was well worth twenty-five thousand dollars. I said I would donate five thousand of that price and would accept twenty thousand for everything. And I would give them all of Charlie's personal effects. I absolutely insisted that they give the park to the city and that the city promise to maintain it forever. I also insisted that there would be suitable glass cases built to house Charlie's effects, and that Joe DeYong and I would be responsible for cataloging and arranging them.

"They didn't know if they could raise the twenty thousand. Now I'm more certain than ever I'm doing the right thing moving to California where people have money and will spend it," I said as I stormed into the house and slammed the front door.

"Mama, when are we moving to California?" asked Jack as he looked up from a book Josephine was reading him.

"Not this year, Jack. Not until the house is ready and I have sold some bronzes and paintings," I told him.

"Oh, Mama, are you going to leave? Please don't go," Jack cried as he jumped up and ran to me. He threw his arms around me and held tightly.

"Jack, I'm not leaving you for good. It's very important that I plan some shows right now of your father's work. It's even more important that I plan a book of his letters. In order to do this there is a great deal of traveling I'll have to do," I explained.

"Then take me with you," Jack sobbed.

"Now, Jack, you have to be a big boy. You're ten years old. You're certainly old enough to understand that I must keep daddy's name in front of the public."

He nodded his head and wiped his tears on his sleeve.

Travel I did. I went to California. Lindley Anderson and C.O. Middleton met my train. Lindley insisted I stay with her in her house on the hill overlooking Santa Barbara.

"Now, Nancy, you just let Gertrude and me take care of you. You look a bit worn out. With some rest and Gertrude's good cooking, plus California's warm sunshine, we will put some color back in those pretty cheeks," Lindley said.

I could still hear that faint southern accent that crept into her voice as she fussed around trying to make me comfortable.

"It's nice to have someone take care of me for a change, but I don't have time to rest. I have got to plan a big show here in California for the winter crowd, and I can't wait until next winter. That will be too late. Truthfully I need the money because I'm going to build the house in Pasadena that Chas and I had planned. Jake Theisman is all ready to go and can start the minute I give him the signal," I told her.

"Oh, does that mean you all will be moving to California?" Lindley clapped her hands with delight.

"Yes, Great Falls will never be the same without Chas. Oh, Chas loved Great Falls and all of his old time friends, but I never felt the same. Some of Chas's friends didn't care for me because they thought I had ruined Chas by getting him to quit drinking and spend more time painting. But that was Chas's own choice. They resented me because they thought I kept his nose to the grindstone, but everything I ever did was for Chas's good. They didn't understand that he wanted his work to be recognized. He enjoyed the fame and attention as much as I did, yet his friends were never jealous of him, they never resented him. No, they kept those feelings for me. I could feel it. Sometimes I could almost cut it with a knife.

"Do you know I offered Chas's studio, with his easel, his personal effects, in fact, just the way it was when he died, to the Chamber of Commerce of Great Falls for a measly twenty thousand dollars, and then had to browbeat them into making the deal? Those narrow minded, visionless little leaders. That studio will become the single most important thing in Great Falls. They should build a shrine to Chas. Instead, it took all of my persuasive powers to get them to promise to raise twenty thousand dollars. Oh, I could feel the resentment when I left that meeting.

"I was never accepted in Great Falls the way Charlie was. The grande dames of Great Falls, those illustrious members of the Maids and Matrons, were never going to accept me as an equal. They would always look down their noses at me because I had been a hired girl, because I had such little education, because I hadn't gone to a finishing school. Well, that's all right. As soon as the house in Pasadena is finished, I'm closing the deal with the Chamber of Commerce and moving to California. I can remember how excited I was when we built our home on Fourth Avenue North, the best street in Great Falls. I was so naive. I thought if I lived on the best street I would belong to society. Well, I never really did. But out here in California everyone accepted us. Not only did they accept us, they admired us, and not only Charlie but me," I said.

"Oh, Nancy, we all love you, and we all missed you. Everyone will be ecstatic when they hear you are moving here for good."

"I'll still be traveling a lot for I can't let Chas's work out of the public eye. You know the old saying — out of sight, out of mind. I've vowed to continue to build his reputation as an artist. I have dedicated myself to that end."

"C.O. can help you with the show here. He thinks the best place to have your very first memorial exhibition is right here in Santa Barbara and that the Art League should sponsor it. You know it will be a great success if C.O. is behind it. He's brilliant at everything he does," Lindley said.

"Did I hear my name? I couldn't agree more with the idea of having the first memorial show here in Santa Barbara or that I am brilliant," C.O. said as he burst in the room puffing on his ever-present big, black cigar.

C.O. Middleton always seemed to make an entrance. It wasn't only that he was a big man but that he washed into a room like a tidal wave.

Gertrude had quietly slipped into the room with a tray of lemonade. She had but one purpose in life, and that was to take care of Miss Lindley. And take care of her she did, with uncanny foresight.

"There you are Gertrude. How did you know we were parched? That cool lemonade will just be the finest thing I could imagine on this warm day," said Lindley.

"I can think of something finer. Bring me bourbon and ice," ordered C.O.

Gertrude was used to C.O.'s gruffness, which she tolerated because of his gentleness toward her Miss Lindley. She left the room and returned with a drink more bourbon than ice.

"Now, that's more like it," bellowed C.O. To me he said, "You just leave everything to me. I'll take care of the show in Santa Barbara, then we'll move it on to the Biltmore Salon. We should have it right after Christmas. Before Christmas people are too busy rushing around, and the rich folks from back East are always bored and looking for something to do right after Christmas. We'll give them something. We'll invite all of Charlie's old friends from Hollywood. Everyone in the Santa Barbara Art League will be there. And you can bet your boots those folks from back East will want to come rub elbows with the likes of Will Rogers and Bill Hart," C.O. said.

He was right. The show was a success. It opened in Santa Barbara on January third and ran through January fifteenth, then moved to the Biltmore Salon and ran January twenty-fourth to February twelfth. I knew how important these shows were. They were the first after Charlie's death. They had to succeed or offers for other shows would not be forthcoming.

The next thing I had to accomplish was to set up a show on the East coast. I could not neglect my book. I continued to contact Charlie's friends asking to use their letters.

I went to New York and met with the head of the Grand Central Art Gallery to plan a big commemorative show for the fall of '27, then on to Tarrytown, New York to visit Dr. and Mrs. Cole. They were valued patrons, and I felt I could count on them to continue to purchase Charlie's works from me. I also wanted to use the letters Charlie had written Dr. Cole in my book. I knew I needed to ask for these in person, for it would be hard to turn me down. I would explain that Will Rogers was going to write the introduction and that H. E. Maule, of Garden City Publishing, was going to see to it personally that a new process was used to give this book the best color ever seen. I also wanted to persuade Dr. Cole to let me use the poem that Charlie had written for him, "*Where Tracks Spell War or Meat.*" I was sure he couldn't turn me down.

I went on to see Mr. and Mrs. Malcolm MacKay. As always, I was graciously received. I wanted them to know I was personally handling Charlie's paintings and bronzes. They also promised I could use one of Mackay's Charlie Russell letters. Everyone seemed enthusiastic about the book. Each thought it would be interesting to see what Charlie had written to other fellows.

That is, everyone but Charlie's long-time friend, Frank Bird Linderman. I couldn't believe my eyes when I read his response to my letter requesting the use of several of his illustrated letters in my book.

"Can you believe this?" I asked Josephine as I opened the mail that had collected at the house in Great Falls. I had stopped over on my way to Lake McDonald. School was almost out and I wanted to pick up Jack so that we could spend the summer at Bull Head Lodge. I needed a rest. I had been traveling all over the country mending fences with old-time customers, collecting letters for the book, meeting with the publisher and overseeing the building of the house in Pasadena, which was almost finished. By fall we would be able to move in.

I repeated myself, "Can you believe this? Frank Linderman refuses to send me Charlie's letters for *Good Medicine*. He says he will send me black and white reproductions. That won't do at all! It would ruin their impact. I bet he is planning on writing a book on Charlie himself and using those letters. I bet he thinks it will lessen their importance in his book if they are used in mine.

"If he were really a good friend of Charlie's, he'd want to be a part of this legacy. Some of the most beautiful letters Charlie ever wrote were to Frank Linderman. He's never forgiven me for making Charlie finish that painting for the Prince of Wales before doing his illustrations. Always thinking of himself, and his book. Real friends are happy for you when good things happen, not mean and resentful. A good friend would want to have his letters in a book that was to be a special tribute. But he's just selfish as always." My voice shook with rage.

"Nancy, I think he became angry because he had fallen on such hard times. His wife and girls were used to a better life, and he needed to have his book ready for the Christmas sale," Josephine tried to explain.

"I even moved in next door to them in Santa Barbara to make everything better. But Mrs. Linderman never forgave me either. She couldn't stand being poor. She was too proud. Oh, I used to wish they would get an oil lease or something, then maybe she would be happy and not take it out on me," I said.

"What do you mean?" asked Josephine.

"If you are proud and poor, you hold a grudge forever. If you're proud and rich, then you can afford to forgive and forget. They never forgot. And Frank Linderman always took credit for getting Charlie the mural at the Capitol. Charlie got that job because he was the best artist. No one could have painted that mural like Charlie. I bet you when Frank Linderman's book about Charlie comes out the hero of the book won't be Charles Marion Russell. It will be Frank Bird Linderman. Well, we'll see about that. I'd planned to rest this summer at Bull Head, but instead, I'm going to hire a writer and dictate a book about Charlie. It will be better than anything Frank Bird Linderman could write, for who would know Charlie better than me?"

"I think you really should rest this summer. Take some time off and spend it with Jack," advised Josephine.

"There'll be plenty of time for resting later. Now, who do we know in Great Falls that could write an accurate book about Charlie and could come with us to the lake this summer? I know, Dan Conway. He's a good newspaperman. I liked the article he wrote on Charlie when he died. I'll call him right now," I said as I went to the phone.

16

Leaving Great Falls

"I want you to emphasize our very first meeting," I said to Mr. Conway. "I want you to write that I was visiting my friends, the Ben Robertses in Cascade, when Charles Marion Russell came riding up.

"Pardon, Mrs. Russell," said Dan Conway. "But I thought you were a hired girl at the Roberts's when you met Charlie."

"I think it is all right to take a little artistic liberty if it makes it a better story, don't you? Besides, I am paying you to write this book, and who should know the story better than I?" I asked.

We were sitting on the long porch that overlooked beautiful Lake McDonald. Every morning we sat there while I dictated the book. In the afternoons, Mr. Conway typed up his notes while I caught up with my correspondence. Martha Gabrielson and Ted were there to help out. Martha had become indispensable to me in helping me with my correspondence. When she had time she helped with Jack, who seemed to spend more and more time with Ted. Ted still had lots of family and friends in the Lake McDonald area, and Jack loved to tag along with them. This was fine with me, for it allowed me to work on the book with Mr. Conway.

"And, Mr. Conway, Charlie said a thousand times that before we met he wasn't getting but twenty-five dollars a painting and had no reputation east of Great Falls. Then he'd say, 'Today I've got a home, a son, a wife who thinks a lot of me and whom I think a lot of. They know my work in the East as much as they do in the West. I get as much as ten thousand dollars now for my paintings.'"

"Mrs. Russell, you are an amazing woman. How many other women could have done what you did?" Dan Conway said with admiration in his voice.

"Why, thank you," I replied. "Mr. Russell said over and over that I was his inspiration. He said that he still 'loved an' longed fer the old frontier and everythin' that goes with it, but would sacrifice it all for Nancy.' You know he hated automobiles. But he let me have my automobile and I let him keep his horses. It was always fifty-fifty with us. Now, I want you to stress that in your book, that we were partners."

"I will, Mrs. Russell," Conway replied.

"You might also want to mention that at all times I dressed very simply and in the most modern suits and gowns. No matter how famous we became I never ever dressed ostentatiously."

"Absolutely, Mrs. Russell. Anyone can see you have impeccable taste," Conway said as he jotted notes.

"And, Mr. Conway," I said, "I also want you to touch on Charles Russell, the philosopher, as well as the artist. He was so much more than just a painter. Although he was a magnificent painter, he was also a great philosopher because he could reveal in his paintings what he deeply believed in. I think it would be good to compare him to Remington. Yes, that's the right comparison. By that comparison, Russell, the philosopher, would stand out," I said.

"Are you familiar with the Remington painting *Missing*?" I asked. "You aren't? Let me describe it. The central figure is a lone soldier. He has been captured by the Indians. He will be missing at roll call the next morning, thus the title. His hands are tied behind his back. There is a rope tied around his neck, and he is being led away. On either side of him, are columns of Indians on horseback. He, of course, is walking. The first and foremost figure in this painting is the soldier. It is almost by second thought one notices the Indian. If you look at their faces, they all have the same face, the same identical face. Chas would never ever do that. Every Indian, man, woman, and child, was somebody to him.

"Take Chas's *Her Heart is on the Ground*. That painting of a lone squaw sitting by the body of her dead husband makes you want to weep. She has wrapped him in his buffalo robe. She has placed his shield by his body, along with his bows and arrows. She has killed his horse, to serve him in the happy hunting ground. She will come there from sunup to sundown as long as the tribe is there. No one knows how long the tribe will stay, for when the buffalo move on the tribe will follow. She has cut her hair so that everyone will know that she is mourning her beloved. She has even taken her knife and slashed her arms so that she can bleed and suffer and ache for her loss. Her baby is with her and he clings to her, dumbfounded. Every time I look at that picture, I think my heart will break. I sometimes wish that we let our widows display their suffering in such an obvious way.

"Compare that one lone, suffering Indian woman to Remington's battle scene, *Battle of War Bonnet Creek*. There are bodies of soldiers and Indians strewn all over the ground. The scene is terribly dramatic, but it doesn't bring a tear to your eye. Of course, Remington was mistaken. Not a single soldier lost his life.

"That's another thing I want you to say. Chas researched his paintings."

"I don't quite understand what you want, Mrs. Russell," said Conway.

"Don't you see? Every man, woman, and child, every cowboy or Indian was important in Chas's paintings. How many Indian children have you seen in

Remington's paintings? But it was more than that, all of God's living creatures were important. When Chas painted a longhorn steer toppling a cowboy and horse, with two riders riding to the rescue, he called it *One Down, Two to Go*. He saw it from the viewpoint of the longhorn.

"And he could make you laugh as quickly as he could make you cry. He painted a prospector who hadn't had any fresh meat in ages. High up in the mountains, he comes upon a bighorn sheep — oh, wonderful fresh meat. He shoots his prey but the body falls on a ledge that is impossible to reach. What to do? He can tie his pack horse to it and pull it up, but his pack horse might slide in the snow and lose his supplies. He certainly can't tie his mount, for to lose him would be even more disastrous. He called it *Meat's Not Meat 'til It's In the Pan*. You must write that Chas's paintings touched all the emotions."

"Charlie wasn't the *only* good story teller, Mrs. Russell. "

"I can see this is going to be a very productive summer. I feel certain you can get all the notes you'll need for our book. I hope to get it to a publisher by winter or spring. You know I'm working on a beautiful full color book called *Good Medicine*. It's Charlie's illustrated letters. It would be wonderful if they both could go to press at about the same time. Of course, I only have this summer to work with you. By fall, I must get back to Pasadena for the completion of our home, and then move," I said.

"This summer should be plenty of time. It is really a privilege working with you, Mrs. Russell, on my book."

"Beg your pardon? Don't you mean *my* book? This is my story of Charlie that you are reporting. As a good reporter, I know you'll do an admirable job."

"Of course, Mrs. Russell, and I am flattered that you chose me. I know you will be pleased with the job, and I will work tirelessly until it is finished," Conway said.

The summer flew by, the same as other summers in many ways. Friends from Great Falls came to visit, Dr. and Mrs. Edwin, Josephine and Margaret. We still took the boat up to Lewis House for dinner. We were still announced, but now it was "Mrs. Charles Russell and party." I was still exhibiting Charlie's paintings on the walls of Lewis House and making a few sales to tourists. But the tourists didn't seem as interested in Charlie's work without him there to tell them the stories behind the paintings. Charlie was a wonderful story teller. But I could tell his stories. Hadn't I heard them a thousand times? It was just going to be harder, but I could work with more dedication.

When the leaves began to turn, I knew it was time again to close up Bull Head Lodge.

17

Ross, Vera, and Jack

"PLEASE, PLEASE, PLEASE don't make me go to a military school," Jack screamed.

"Now, Jack, control yourself. You're not a baby. You're almost eleven years old," I replied calmly.

"But I hate military schools. You sent me to that horrible Page Military in California when I was eight. I hated it." Jack's voice rose to an even shriller pitch.

"You were only there for a short time. How can you judge? You were there for less than a semester. You went in the middle of the year and that's always hard. Boys have already chosen their friends. This fall you will be there at the start of school and you can be on the ground floor making friends." I knew I had to remain calm and firm.

"That wasn't it. They order you around all the time, and if you don't do what they say they confine you to your room. If that doesn't work they beat you," Jack cried hysterically.

"Paddle," I replied. "If you weren't so stubborn, you wouldn't be paddled. If you would only try to cooperate you wouldn't get into trouble. If you would only try to be nice to the other boys then they will be nice to you."

"I won't go. You can't make me. I'll stay here in Great Falls. Aunt Nomee can look after me," Jack threatened.

"Yes, Jack, I can make you go, and you will go. I'm closing the house here. It's to be turned over to the Charles Russell Memorial Park as soon as the house in Pasadena is completed and I've moved our furniture and things there," I said firmly.

Jack looked crestfallen. He knew I would not change my mind.

"There are thousands of boys all over the country who would give their eye teeth to have the opportunity of going to a private school. The educational advantages I'm giving you will prepare you to go to college and become a lawyer or enter another profession. Someday you will thank me. Besides, there is no place else for you to live to go to school. The house here in Great Falls will be closed. I'm moving everything out, and the house in Pasadena isn't ready yet."

"Can't we stay in a hotel until it's ready? Can't I stay with you and just go to a plain, normal school?" Jack pleaded.

"No, I'll be gone most of the fall. There is a big memorial exhibition opening November the eighth at the Grand Central Art Galleries in New York. It's our first show on the East coast since your father died. I've got to be there early to be sure that all the important people are invited personally to the opening," I explained.

"That's all you ever think about, isn't it?" Jack said as he stormed out of the front door and slammed it.

"Jack! Jack! Jack Cooper Russell, you come right back in here." I yelled after him. But he didn't come back. "Well, he'll be back as soon as it gets dark," I said to no one.

In a few minutes, the phone rang. "Nancy, it's Josephine. Jack is over here and he is all upset. As soon as he calms down, I'll bring him home."

"Will you please explain to him that going to a military school is not the end of the world? He might even like it," I said over the phone.

But he didn't like it. The more they pushed him, the more stubborn he became. I wrote him letters. I called him. I tried to explain that he was hurting no one but himself. The school wouldn't suffer. The officers wouldn't suffer. He would be the one. I couldn't seem to make a dent in his hard head. He finally got leave. Since the house in Pasadena wasn't finished, we spent his leave at Lindley Anderson's as her house guests.

I picked Jack up at school. He didn't say two

words in the car. It was as if he wanted to punish me for his getting into trouble at the school.

"Jack, I've had nothing but bad reports on you from your school," I said.

"It's not my school," he snarled.

"If you would only try, I know you'd like it. The commandant says it's not because you're not smart, it's just that you won't apply yourself. He tells me that you deliberately try to provoke your instructors."

"They're stupid bastards."

"Jack! Where in the world did you learn language like that?" I asked.

"At that wonderful school you shipped me off to," Jack replied.

We rode in silence the rest of the way to Lindley's house. When we got there, Jack was at first sullen and silent. But Gertrude's fussing over him and offering him his favorite cookies hot from the oven and Lindley's telling him how handsome he looked in his uniform finally brought a smile. By dinner time he was captivating everyone with his stories of the other students and teachers at his school.

I noticed how straight he sat at the table in his uniform. He did indeed look handsome. After he had gone to bed, Lindley and I sat in her parlor sipping hot tea.

"I do declare Jack has grown. Pretty soon, you'll have to beat the girls away from him with a broom if he gets any better lookin'," she said.

"I can't worry about that. I've got all I can handle trying to get him to cooperate with his teachers at school. The commandant says his attitude is terrible. If they tell him to do one thing, he'll do just the opposite. He seems to take delight in challenging authority. The more he does this, the tougher they are on him. I can't seem to make him realize that he is his own worst enemy. I don't know what I'm going to do with him," I said.

When his leave was over, and we got back in the car for me to take him back to school, he got sullen.

"Lindley is right. You do look very handsome in your uniform. I noticed how very straight you sat in your chair at the dining table," I said.

"They give you a whack across the back with a long cane if you slump over at the table," Jack replied.

"Can't you see anything good in your school? Can't you change your attitude?" I pleaded.

"I hate that place," he said.

The rest of the way we rode in silence. When Jack got out of the car, I said, "Our house will be finished and the furniture will be in place by the holidays and we'll spend our first Christmas in our new home. I promise we will have a wonderful time. I'll get you some marvelous presents in New York when I'm there for the opening of the show in November."

"The best present you could give me would be to get me out of this prison," he replied as he got out of the car at the dormitory.

I didn't have to get him out of school. He did that by himself. When I returned at the end of November from New York, there was a letter awaiting me from the commandant saying that when Jack came home for the holidays he had been instructed to bring all his things with him. He did not fit in with the school's program, and it was a waste of my money and their time to try to educate him there. They felt that I should find a school better suited for his needs.

This time Ted picked him and up along with his belongings, and brought him home.

"Hey, Mom, I'm home," Jack yelled as he burst through the doorway. "Gee, that Christmas tree looks great! I sure like it in front of that big window. I see you brought all of our favorite decorations from Great Falls. I think they look better here than they did there."

He was all smiles. I decided I wasn't going to ruin our Christmas by talking about school now. After Christmas I would tell him that I had found him another school.

When the holidays were over, I sat Jack down and told him about his new school.

"I'm not going to any old military school. I won't," he stood up and yelled.

"Sit down," I demanded. "It's not a military school. It's a boys' school on Catalina Island. Betty Rogers told me all about it. Her son Jimmy goes there and he likes it. Will and Betty are very pleased with it, and they highly recommend it. I had a dickens of a time getting you admitted in the middle of the year. I'm sure if Will Rogers hadn't recommended you personally you would never have been accepted. I thought you would be pleased about going to school with Will Rogers' son. You should be grateful that I am sending you. I think you would be thanking me for spending the money. It's very expensive, but I'm willing to sacrifice for your education," I said.

"Did you know about this when I got home from school?" he asked.

"Yes," I answered.

"How could you let me go through all the holidays thinking I was going to Woodrow Wilson Junior High, in Pasadena, when actually you were sending me away as soon as you could get rid of me?"

"I'm not getting rid of you, Jack," I answered. "You can come home on the weekends. I didn't tell you before Christmas because I knew you would act just like this and ruin Christmas for everyone by being unpleasant and ungrateful."

"Yeah, I've got a lot to be grateful for," he scowled.

"You never did thank me for the beautiful presents I brought you from New York for Christmas. You'll never know how much time I spent shopping for you. I didn't even take time to shop for myself."

"I know you're always thinking of me," Jack said. "I'll have Ted take me to the ferry for Catalina as soon as I'm packed. I'll get out of your hair as fast as I can."

"You're not *in my hair*, as you put it. I always do what I think is best for you." I went to him with my arms outstretched.

Pushing me away, he went upstairs to pack.

Jack didn't get along any better at the boy's school in Catalina than he had at the military school. Before the end of the semester the headmaster phoned me and asked if I could come see him to discuss Jack.

"Mrs. Russell, please sit down," the headmaster said as he indicated an empty chair in front of his massive desk. I noticed that the walls from ceiling to floor were lined with books. I wondered if he had read them all and decided he probably had.

"Mrs. Russell, I asked you to come because I want to discuss with you what is best for your son Jack," There was a pause. "He will not be readmitted in the fall," the headmaster said.

"Has he been causing trouble?" I asked.

"No."

"I know he is smart and can keep up with the work," I pleaded.

"Jack is an extremely intelligent young man. It's not that. Our counselor thinks that Jack needs to be home in a loving and supportive environment so he will feel secure," the headmaster said with emphasis on the word secure.

"But this school has such a wonderful reputation for education," I pleaded.

"There is a great deal more to education than academics. There is the whole person, and at this school we try to approach each individual differently and try to decide what is best for each young man placed in our trust. We have come to the conclusion that Jack would be better off at home."

In the fall, Jack attended Woodrow Wilson Junior High. He seemed genuinely happy to be home at Trail's End. At first he was filled with enthusiasm. He did his homework. He cooperated with his teachers. He even completed his chores around the house without complaining.

"I'm very pleased with your change in attitude," I said to him one evening in the living room after dinner. Jack was sitting at one of the tables doing his homework. "I would think you would like to invite some boys your own age to visit. If you got to know more of your fellow students, I'm sure you could run for a class office," I suggested.

"I wouldn't get elected. These kids have all known each other for years. I'm new in the school," Jack answered.

"That doesn't mean you shouldn't at least try to get to know them. Why don't you go out for football or baseball?" I asked.

"I don't like sports," Jack replied.

"Well, you certainly can be involved in scouting. It's a wonderful way to meet people. You need to be aggressive and make some friends," I said firmly.

The more I suggested Jack try to make friends, the more he retreated into his shell. As the months passed, whenever I tried to suggest ways in which he could become involved in school activities, he would close his book, put up his homework and go upstairs. With his first poor grade, he became discouraged.

"I don't know what I'm going to do with Jack," I said to Ted Taylor one morning after breakfast. Jack had left for school. Ted was sitting at the table having a second cup of coffee. "The more I encourage him to get out and be with people, the more a recluse he becomes. He was so excited about going to Woodrow Wilson but just one or two poor test scores have him so quickly disheartened.

"He spends all of his time after school in that workshop over the garage. I had such hopes for him in the fall when school started. I really thought he had changed, but now he is back to the same old Jack. The more I suggest he do something, the more he does the opposite. The only thing he seems to care about is building radios in the workroom."

"That's not all bad," said Ted. "How many thirteen-year-olds do you know who can put together a radio?"

"But Charlie had so many friends. Everyone loved him. How many times he said that he had friends when he didn't have anything else. I think I'll go up to Jack's school and talk to the principal, Arthur Brown. He seems like such a nice man. Children are his business. He'll surely know what to do," I said with resolve.

I made an appointment with Mr. Brown the next day. Woodrow Wilson was a new school and everything was modern and up-to-date, even the principal's office. When I walked into that office, it gave me a sense of confidence that I was doing the right thing.

Mr. Brown was a slight man who wore glasses. He had a receding hairline, but otherwise looked quite young. His quick smile and firm handshake made me feel at home immediately.

"Mr. Brown, I'm Mrs. Russell. I've come to talk to you about my son Jack. He started out the year so well. Now his grades are poor. He doesn't seem to care about anything but building radios in his workshop over the garage. The more I encourage him to make friends and join in school activities, the more he stays to himself. I just don't know what to do with him," I said.

"Mrs. Russell, Jack is near being an electronic genius. Often people who are very talented in one area tend to spend all their energies on what interests them," he replied.

"But Mr. Brown, Jack's grades are slipping. I can't seem to get him involved in school activities. I want him to be popular and get along. I know he has the ability to make good grades. It's not as if he were dumb. What's wrong with him?" I asked.

"It's been difficult for him being in so many schools these last few years. Also his father's dying must have had an affect on him."

"But I've given him everything," I interrupted.

"When one succeeds in one thing, such as Jack does in building his radios, and has experienced failure or rejection in others, it is natural to concentrate where success lies," Arthur Brown continued.

"Would you help me with Jack?" I asked.

"That's what I'm here for," he smiled.

"I mean outside school. I think you would be a good influence on Jack. I'd like for him to get to know you better. Would you and Mrs. Brown come for dinner tomorrow evening?" I asked.

"We'd be honored. I hear you have one of the finest collections of your late husband's works. I would dearly love to see it. You may not know it, but Charlie Russell is my favorite artist. My wife is very interested in American art and she will be as thrilled as I am with your invitation." Arthur Brown stood and walked me to the door of his office.

The Browns came for dinner and many dinners thereafter. Mrs. Brown was delighted to help Jack with his studies and Jack passed the eighth grade. I was relieved. Jack was thrilled when school was out and summer vacation was at hand so we could return to Lake McDonald and to Bull Head Lodge. Was it the beauty of the place, the happy memories there, or the presence of Josephine and Margaret Trigg that made Jack so excited about returning? Or was it just that school was out?

"Oh, Mom, I don't want to stop over in Great Falls. I want to go straight on to Bull Head Lodge," he whined.

"We don't always get what we want when we want it. I have business to take care of in Great Falls.

"But I want to go on up to Lake McDonald. I don't want to stay over in Great Falls. I'll just be in the way there while you set up your shrine," Jack said.

"It's not a shrine. It's your father's studio where the greatest work any American artist ever created was done. Where the story of the west was captured on canvas for all eternity to enjoy. Where the last hurrah of God's own people, the Indians, is dealt with in understanding and sympathy. Don't say you don't have time to stay over in Great Falls so we can be sure it is set up properly for the opening" I said.

"Mrs. Russell," Ted suggested, "let me take Jack on up to Lake McDonald. He can stay with me at my brother Bill's until you finish your work. You and Joe DeYong can concentrate on the studio. When you finish you can take the train to Apgar and I'll meet you."

That was exactly what we did. I let Ted know by telegram when I was arriving and he was there to meet me. I couldn't help but notice how well he looked. The air of Lake McDonald really agreed with him. At the lake he loved to wear knickers, which were all the rage, with a tweed jacket and a gray felt hat. I think he liked to impress upon his brothers that he was no longer a wild Irishman who drove around on a motorcycle, but a man of some status in the employment of a famous family.

"Ted, I don't know what I'd do without you," I said as he opened the door for me. He just smiled.

"Jack has been having the time of his life," he told me as he started the car. "He has made a new friend. There's this kid, Ross Case, who's a friend of my nephew Gene. Jack met Ross when he was over playing with Gene and they've become good friends."

"Is Ross a nice boy?" I asked.

"He's great. All the kids like him. He laughs all the time and is a joy to be around. His folks are good, honest, hard-working farmers. You couldn't find a better friend for Jack than Ross," replied Ted.

"He sounds too good to be true," I said.

"Jack has already asked me to ask you to invite Ross over to Bull Head to stay for a few days," Ted said.

"I don't know. I've asked Josephine and Margaret to come up, and I don't have any help in the kitchen," I said thoughtfully. I wanted to know a little more about Ross.

"Ross's sister, Vera, is a young school teacher who hasn't found a job. I thought maybe you could hire her to come and help out in the kitchen and keep an eye on the boys," said Ted.

"You and Jack have everything figured out. All right. I'll take your word. You might as well drive me to the Cases' or I'll never hear the end of this."

At the Cases' modest farm house a tired-looking

gray-haired lady answered my knock on the screen door.

"I'm Mrs. Russell," I said.

"Yes, ma'am, I know," she said as she wiped her hands on her apron and opened the door. She ushered me into the parlor. It had a musty smell, as if it were never used, but everything was as neat as a pin, not a speck of dust.

"I hear our boys have become good friends, and I wanted to extend an invitation to your son to come and visit us for several days at Bull Head Lodge. I think I can promise him a good time. Of course, I have to find some help since I'm already expecting house guests. Ted says your daughter Vera is without employment. Do you think she might consider helping me out?" I asked.

"I'm sure she would, ma'am. And I think Ross would be tickled to spend a few days with you," said Mrs. Case.

Just as the words were leaving her mouth a boy of about twelve came running in through the back door. He screeched to a sudden stop when he saw me in the parlor with his mother.

"This is Mrs. Russell, Ross. She's Jack's mother, and she has invited you to spend a few days at Bull Head Lodge," Mrs. Case explained.

"That's great! I'll go get my bag. It's already packed," Ross said as he ran out of the room.

I knew then that I had been ganged up on by Ted and Jack. But it had the most pleasant results imaginable. Jack was a changed boy that summer. Ross was even better than Ted described. He would do anything for me. He had a wonderful manner that made people happy just to be near him for he was so filled with joy. His sister was just the same and loved helping out in the kitchen and in the house.

"Ted, you were right. I have never seen Jack so happy. You know I think this is the first really good friend Jack has ever made and because Jack is a year older than Ross, Ross looks up to him. It's just what Jack needs," I smiled.

Summer disappeared. We had had a constant stream of guests. It was like the old days. Having the lodge filled with people brought back memories of the many summers when Charlie was there. I didn't want summer to end. When it ended we would be back in Pasadena. I would be busy again contacting prospective buyers, trying to set up shows, encouraging gallery owners to push Charlie's work, visiting with collectors — and settling Jack back in school.

I knew what I had to do.

Again I had Ted drive me to the Case farm in Holt. Again I knocked on the door and again Mrs. Case answered. Again I sat in the musty parlor and asked if Ross could come to visit us.

"But Pasadena is so far away and for a whole school year, why that's nine months! Oh, no, Mrs. Russell that would be too long. I'd miss him too much, and I know he would be homesick for his family." Mrs.

Case shook her head from side to side.

"It would be a wonderful opportunity for the boy. He's never been thirty miles from home, I bet. Just think of all the things he could see — the ocean, for one. I'd introduce him to famous and important people like Will Rogers. We'd drive through Salt Lake City on our way to California, and I would show him the Tabernacle there with its magnificent organ. It is an educational experience that might never come along again. Most parents would give anything for their sons to enjoy the travel and sights that I am offering Ross. And as far as his getting homesick, I would be happy to have Vera come along. I know she hasn't found a job teaching as yet, and I would be delighted to hire her as a tutor for Jack. She could also help out in the kitchen and around the house. She would be with Ross so he would have family near. And Vera too would share in the wonderful educational opportunities I'm offering Ross. Mrs. Case, you must think of your children."

When we left Lake McDonald, Ted and I were sitting in the front seat and the three young people were in the back. They sang songs, told jokes, and Jack and Ross played a silly game of Paper, Rock, and Scissors by the hour. The first night we got to Anaconda and stayed at the hotel there. Ross had never been to a hotel and he was so excited that each of us saw the hotel afresh through his eyes. So it was all of the way to California. Ross enjoyed everything so much that it was infectious. He couldn't believe the size of the organ in the Mormon

Tabernacle, and it grew in my eyes as he gazed at it. I could hardly wait for him to see the ocean — and I wasn't disappointed, for its vastness was even bigger when Ross looked at it.

We finally arrived at Trail's End.

"This is the most wonderful house I've ever seen," said Ross as we entered. "And, gee, those are the greatest paintings I ever saw." He looked at the bronzes. "How in the world could an animal look so real? Oh, Mrs. Russell, will you tell me about all these pictures? Will you tell me how they make these animals?"

"Of course I will," I responded. "Not only will I tell you the story behind each and every painting, but I will also share with you Mr. Russell's philosophy, which is as important as his paintings."

I never had a more attentive audience. Ross and Vera wanted to hear the stories over and over. Ross was so curious and eager to learn that he did well in school. He drew people like a magnet. When the other boys in school selected Ross as first choice on their football, baseball or handball teams, he never let them forget his best friend Jack. He and Jack were inseparable. They joined the Scouts together. They went to church together. They went to the movies together. They studied together. Jack had never been happier and had never made better grades.

But Christmas was coming and Ross suddenly had an attack of homesickness.

"It just doesn't seem like Christmas with all the

flowers blooming. At home there is always snow by now. Pa and I would always to out into the woods and get us a tree for Christmas. We made a game out of seeing who could find the best tree, then we would cut it down and haul it home. We'd set it up by the fireplace. Everyone in the family would gather to string popcorn and sing carols. I really miss them," Ross said.

"We are going to have a tree. We have beautiful decorations and you, Vera, Jack, and Ted can help put them on the tree. There will be dozens and dozens of presents. Christmas will be just as much fun out here in California, snow or no snow. There is so much you haven't seen yet that I promised your mother I would show you. You haven't been to Knott's Berry Farm. I haven't taken you to China Town or taught you to eat with chopsticks. We haven't been out to visit Will Rogers. The Rogers' have a wonderful monorail train that rides on top of the fence around the polo field. You haven't gone on the U.S.S. Catalina, over to the island. We've been invited to spend a weekend at Balboa Beach with the Browns.

"Ross, there are so many things left to do! Your mother allowed you to come so you could have these opportunities. You must forget your homesickness and think about her wishes. I tell you what— after Christmas I'll invite your mother to come visit and together we will show her the sights. How do you think she'd like going on the cable car to Mt. Lowe or taking in the Pasadena Play House?" I asked.

"Oh, she'd love it. Mrs. Russell, you're the most wonderful lady I've ever met," Ross said. "I'm going to write Mom right now and tell her what we're going to show her, if that's all right," Ross bounded up the stairs two at a time.

Ted had overheard our conversation. "That boy idolizes you. He worships the ground you walk on — as does every man you ever smiled at," he said.

Christmas came and went. Ross and Vera were thrilled with their presents. Any signs of homesickness had vanished with the anticipation of Mrs. Case's visit.

I could hear the stories I had told Ross and Vera about the landmarks in California repeated for their mother when she came to visit. They seemed proud that they knew so much and Mrs. Case was duly impressed with what they had learned.

"Mrs. Russell, you were right when you talked me into letting the children come out here. No matter how much I have missed them or longed for them, I know that this is a school year they will never forget. God bless you," Mrs. Case said as she boarded the train to go back to Holt. She took out a handkerchief and wiped her eyes before she kissed Vera and Ross good-bye.

"Ma, it's only a couple of months until June and we'll be home," said Ross.

In the car, driving home from the station, Ross said, "Ma's right. I'll never forget this year. Even when I'm old and gray I'll be able to close my eyes and see

Trail's End and all those beautiful paintings. Mr. Russell may have died, but he is still the most important person around."

In California, spring becomes summer without one being aware of it. School was out. We packed up the Lincoln and headed for Montana.

As excited as Ross had been to see California and the ocean, he was even more excited as we drove over the crest of the mountains and he looked down at Flathead Lake, for he knew he was home.

At the end of the summer I realized it was futile to try to persuade Mrs. Case to allow Ross to return with us to Pasadena. Vera was to be married and Mrs. Case was not going to let Ross come by himself. She felt he had had plenty of educational opportunities.

Ted, Jack and I climbed into the car and started west alone.

18

Ted

"DID YOU HEAR THAT CAR squealing into the driveway at two a.m.? Jack again!" I said angrily to Ted.

"Now, calm down, Nancy," Ted said reassuringly. "Jack is twenty-one years old. He's got a place of his own, even if only an apartment over the garage. He's just sowing a few wild oats."

"He's old enough to act with some sense of responsibility. He's old enough to have a job. I tried to get him to go to college. I tried to get him to study law so he could make something of himself. But, no, the only place he wanted to go was that damn technical school to tinker with his precious radios.

"How do you think he pays for those radio parts? I have told him over and over not to charge them to me, but he goes right ahead. He knows I'll be billed and I'll pay. Ted, I want you to go up to his apartment right now and have a talk with him," I insisted.

"He's a good kid. He's just having growing pains," Ted explained.

"Growing pains! He's a grown man, and he should act like one. If you aren't going to talk to him, I will," I stormed out of the house and up the outside stairway to the apartment over the garage. I banged on the door until a red-eyed, disheveled Jack finally answered.

"Good God, Mother, what do you want at this hour?" he asked.

"It's nine o'clock. Most men are at work, not sleeping off a night on the town."

"Mother, I'm twenty-one years old," Jack replied.

"Then why don't you act it? I've just received another bill from Dow Radio over on Colorado for radio parts. How many times have I told you not to charge anything to me without my permission? Do you know how tight our money is? We can't even count on the dividends from the Parker-Russell Manufacturing Company anymore. Portis decided to develop the land at Oak Hill into a subdivision. He was going to make a fortune. He put in streets, water and sewer lines. Then he decided he wanted St. Louis to annex the whole thing and now city taxes are going to bankrupt the company. What a harebrained idea. He didn't use his head, just like you don't use yours."

"That's not fair," Jack said.

"What's not fair is your charging to me what you can't pay for when I'm barely able to make ends." I said.

"It seems like you have enough to keep Ted in clothes. It seems like you have enough to pay him the kind of salary that lets him to buy a place on Flathead Lake and build a lodge. You have enough to get a new car every other year. You have enough to be on my back night and day to go to college," Jack said angrily.

"Ted earns every cent he's paid. I don't know what I'd do without him. And sending you to college would be an investment in your future so that you could get a good job. The future is going to be in the hands of college graduates." I tried to reason with him.

"Didn't you know that the soup lines are filled with college graduates? Didn't you ever hear of the Depression? Don't you know that there *are* no jobs out there? Where have you been?" Jack asked.

"You are impossible," I said as I hurried down the stairs.

I stormed into the house through the back door.

"What's wrong, Mrs. Russell?" asked Lavina, the cook.

"Everything," I said. I went into the living room and stood with tears running down my face. Ted came over and put his arms around me. I rested my head on his broad shoulder.

"What's wrong, Nancy?" he asked.

"Everything. I don't know what to do with Jack. I can't reason with him. He won't do what I tell him. I don't like his drinking. I've heard from St.Louis and the Parker-Russell Manufacturing Company is nearly bankrupt. Like everybody else in the Russell family, we've been surviving on dividends. I don't know what Tom Portis was thinking of. He had no experience in developing a suburb. And his timing couldn't be worse. The country is just beginning to pull out of the Depression. Money is still tight. I should know. I've had to work twice as hard to make a sale. People don't buy paintings when they can't put bread on the table. I've had to do everything I could to keep the prices of Charlie's paintings up. You'd think Jack would help instead of aggravating me. You'd think he'd want to contribute to the household expenses by getting a job instead of carousing about at all hours," I said with a sob.

"I'll talk to Jack," Ted said.

"I don't know what I'd do without you."

"I don't know what I'd do without you, either."

There was silence. I pulled away from the comforting shoulder and looked at Ted.

"You must have known. I've been in love with you for years, I think from the first moment I saw you at Lake McDonald," Ted said.

"But, Ted, I'm ten years older than you are," I answered.

"You are the most beautiful woman I've ever seen. When you walk into a room, you light it up with your smile. When I first saw you, I thought you were a queen, and I was more than willing to be your loyal subject," Ted said.

"You are indispensable to this household. I've tried to show you my deep gratitude by paying you well, because I didn't want to lose you," I said.

"I don't want to be indispensable to any household. I want to be indispensable to you. I want to be loved by you. I want to marry you, to take care of you. I want you to lean on me. You've shouldered the burdens by yourself long enough. I want to share them with you," Ted stepped forward and again took me in his arms.

I felt warm and comfortable.

"I've got to think this over," I said as I stepped away.

"Take all the time you want," Ted replied, "as long as the answer is Yes."

"Josephine is coming next week. I'll talk it over with her," I said.

"It's your decision, not Josephine's."

"She's my dearest friend. She has written to me every Sunday evening for years. She knows my every thought. I would want her blessing." I tried to explain.

"Ah ha, you're already leaning toward Yes or you wouldn't want her blessing, as you put it," Ted said as he started toward me.

"Ted, you're right. I am so weary of carrying all the responsibility. Not only the problems with Jack, but my father's income is almost nothing, so I have to continually loan him money. And now his brother Lafe has moved in with him and he's no better off. I can't sit back and see them starve. Now Charlie's stepmother has moved out here to California. She has completely gone through the money Father Russell left her. Because we live in this big house and I have a cook and a chauffeur she thinks I'm rolling in money and she is constantly whining. Just wait until the Parker-Russell Mining and Manufacturing Company actually goes bankrupt, and she no longer gets any more money from it. You're right. I do long to lean on somebody.

"You are like family, and you've always gotten along so well with Jack. I remember when Ross Case was living with us, and he and Jack got in a fist fight. I was hysterical when I saw Jack with his nose all bloody. You were the one who calmed me down and convinced me that everything was all right, that Ross had come from a big family just as you had and lots of times brothers decided their differences with their fists. You said that when Jack washed off the blood, he and Ross would be friends again. You were right. I realize how much I've depended on you these last ten years. And I think I knew you cared about me," I said.

"Cared about you? I've loved you. I've worshipped you. I'd do anything for you," Ted answered.

I could hardly wait to tell Josephine the news. The days crept by, but finally she arrived. I waited until nighttime when everyone had gone to their bedrooms before I knocked on her door. She told me to come in. She was sitting at the dressing table in her nightgown and robe, brushing her long hair, which she always wore up in a knot. Her hair was streaked with gray. She had taken off her pinched glasses, but the place where they rode on her nose was indented from years of wear. She was getting old, and she was a year younger than I was. But I felt like a young girl, a giddy, young girl with her heart in her throat.

"I've been waiting all day to talk to you in private, Josephine. Guess what?" I said, but I didn't wait for her to answer. "Ted has asked me to marry him. I told him I would think about it, and I've thought. I'm going to say Yes. I know he's a little younger than me, but he loves me. He says he worships me and he wants to take care of me. Oh, I yearn for someone to take care of me instead of me taking care of everyone else. I want your blessing. You're my dearest friend."

"Nancy, are you crazy? Have you completely lost your mind? My blessing? Don't you know that Ted Taylor is not a little younger than you are. He is ten years younger. What do you think people will say? What do you think people would say in Great Falls if you marry your chauffeur? You could never show your face there again."

"I don't care what people think. And I wasn't really planning on staying in Great Falls, only going through on my way up to Lake McDonald," I answered.

"Let's forget, then, about what other people

think. You have spent your whole adult life being Mrs. Charles Marion Russell. You dedicated every waking minute to making Charlie successful. He would never have had an international reputation without you behind him. You have devoted your life to him. Are you willing to throw that away? You have been Mrs. Charles Marion Russell since you were eighteen. Try that name on your lips, then see if you can replace it with Mrs. Ted Taylor. It doesn't fit. You can't throw away your lifetime's work." Josephine got up from the dressing table and sat next to me.

"But it's so lonely. I'm so tired of crawling into an empty bed. I'm so tired of carrying everyone's burdens. Ted said he would take care of me," I said.

"And how is he going to do that? He has nothing. Everything he has you have given him — even the clothes on his back. You have been supporting him — how long — ten, twelve years? And he is going to take care of you? Don't be ridiculous. Sleep with him if you want, but for heavens sake don't marry him," Josephine said firmly.

I was shocked. This suggestion from proper Josephine.

"Nancy," Josephine said, "Ask yourself who is going to carry on the legacy of Charlie Russell if you don't?"

"Well, of course, I will. I never planned to stop that. I couldn't," I said.

"Who could do it better, Mrs. Charles Marion

Russell or Mrs.Ted Taylor?" Josephine asked.

I knew she was right. There was complete silence. I got up and went to my bedroom. I lay awake all night.

The next morning I told Ted I needed to talk to him privately. We went out into the back yard and sat by the fish pond. I could hear the splashing of the water from the fountain as it fell into the pool. The birds in the aviary next to the goldfish pond were singing their hearts out. It was a gloriously sunny day. To any stranger happening on the scene, it would have appeared idyllic.

"Ted, I can't marry you," I said flatly.

He looked as if he had been hit by a sledgehammer. He let his breath out and asked, "Why?"

"I've spent my whole adult life being Mrs. Charles Marion Russell. I simply can't give that up. All I've thought about, since I was eighteen, was how to make the world aware of Charlie's genius. I've had to work even harder at it since he has been dead. Everything I see, everything I hear, everything I think, has been about one thing — how to make Charlie's work more appreciated. It's my life's blood. I couldn't live without it," I said quietly.

"But you can live without me," Ted answered.

"Please don't leave me. I count on you so much. I depend on you so. I couldn't get along without you," I said.

"Well, you are going to have to try," Ted answered angrily. "You think you're too old for me. You're not! You're still beautiful, vibrant, and alive. You have more enthusiasm and energy than a woman half your age."

"No, Ted, it's not that," I said.

"Josephine talked you out of it," he said.

"No, Josephine only pointed out the truth to me. I cannot give up my life's work." I tried to explain.

"What about me? I can't go on living under the same roof with you now that you know how I feel. What am I to do? I've worked the last twelve years for you. I devoted my life to you, and now you turn me out."

"I'm not turning you out. Just the opposite. I'm begging you to stay. Why don't you take some time off? Go up to Flathead. Work on your lodge at Blue Bay. Isn't it called Talking Waters? Listen to the water as it laps against the shore. Get away by yourself and think things over. Ted, I need you. You may come to the conclusion that it is more important to be needed than loved."

Ted took my advice and left for Flathead Lake. I was so glad that Josephine was there. She kept reassuring me that I had done the right thing, the only thing. It would have been terribly lonely without her, with Ted at Flathead and Jack living in the apartment over the garage.

"I'm so happy you could stay a little longer," I said to Josephine.

"Oh, Nancy, it's always wonderful to be with you. And you know I would do absolutely anything for you," Josephine replied.

"I know you mean that, and I do want you to do something for me while you're here. I want you to talk to Jack. He has always been so fond of you. I worry about him so. I want you to convince him he should get a job. He needs to make something of himself. I don't know what's going to become of him. He needs to settle down, marry a decent girl. He's going with a very nice girl by the name of Virginia Miller. I want you to encourage him to see more of her. Jack always listens to you. When I talk to him, it's like I'm talking to a brick wall."

"I'll be happy to talk to Jack. I've never had any trouble talking with him," Josephine said.

In the next few days it became obvious that Josephine had talked to Jack. He was taking Virginia Miller out again. He took over some of Ted's duties, including chauffeuring. He even began reading the want ads and answering some. I wondered why Josephine had so much influence on him when I didn't.

I received an invitation from Bill Hart for dinner at his magnificent home in Newhall. Jack volunteered to drive me, but I told him it wasn't necessary, that Bill had said he would send his car for me.

"Good, then that gives Aunt Nomee and me a chance to go out together for dinner, just the two of us."

He still called her that favorite childhood nickname, and she still enjoyed it.

Bill's big, black, chauffeur-driven limousine came promptly at four-thirty to pick me up. The number of automobiles on the road was unbelievable. I thought to myself, I'll bet some day every family in California will have a car. The limousine slowly snaked its way through lines of cars until we reached Newhall and then raced up the curving road to the top of the hill as if the driver were suddenly making up for lost time.

The door of the hilltop mansion was open and Bill was standing in it awaiting our arrival. He started down the steps and met me as the chauffeur opened the door. He reached into the car and helped me out, then held both of my hands.

"I was worried about you, my dear little Nancy," he said.

"It was so crowded on the roads! Charlie would have never believed that automobiles have caught on so. Remember how he used to call them skunk wagons?" I laughed.

Bill led me up the stairs to the front door, then into his magnificent dining room. We sat with the long table dividing us, but it was as if we were sitting side by side for it was a night for remembering.

"Remember when you took Charlie and me out to the ocean for the first time?" I asked.

"And you took off your shoes and stockings and walked in the waves. You giggled like a little girl."

"That was so long ago. Well, I'm not a girl any

longer," I sighed.

"Nancy, you look like a girl to me. I'll swear you're still as pretty as you were then," Bill replied. "Not like an old has-been actor."

"Bill, that's not true," I said vehemently. "I thought this evening as we drove up and I saw you standing in the doorway in your cowboy clothes what a handsome man you are. No wonder half the women in America swoon when you come on the screen. You don't look a day older than you did the first time we met."

"I need to have you come for dinner more often. Having you here is like walking back in time thirty years. Boy, we did have some good times — you, Charlie, and me."

"Yes we did."

"Remember the opening of Charlie's one-man show at the Folsom Galleries and how you got me to set up an interview with the *New York Times*?" Bill asked.

"I'll never forget. I was so excited. And that article was almost a full page. I thought I'd die from sheer joy when I saw it."

"I promised that reporter an exclusive the next time I opened on Broadway if he would go over and meet you and Charlie. I knew that once he met you, you'd have him captivated," Bill said.

"Oh, Bill, what a dear friend you've been."

"But I've never told you how much I envied Charlie. Not his talent, though Lord, he had plenty of that, but I envied him having a woman like you behind him. I wished I had married someone like you, someone I could count on. In this fickle town they love you one minute and forget your name the next."

"No one could forget William S. Hart. You're the greatest cowboy actor in the world," I said.

"See what I mean? Nancy, do you think it's too late for us?" Bill asked.

There was silence. I looked down the table, past the candlelight, to read his eyes. He was serious.

"Oh, Bill, you are one of my dearest, most precious friends. You and Charlie and I had such special times together, and I treasure them. But I will always be Mrs. Charles Marion Russell. Charlie's reputation will always be my life work."

"As I said, I always envied Charlie, and I still do. Let's have a toast to Charlie," Bill said. Then he stood and raised his glass.

After he put it down I asked quietly, "Will you still be my friend? I need you so much. I need someone to remember the good times with me. Can we still share them?"

"Of course, my dear. I will always be your friend. You can always count on me." And our conversation gently slipped back to days gone by.

After dinner the limousine took me back to Pasadena. That night I lay in bed unable to sleep. One of the voices in my head shouted, "You fool!"

19

A Will of Iron

"You really are a fool," said Lindley.

I had decided to visit Lindley Anderson in Santa Barbara. I needed to get away. I needed someone to cheer me up. It always raised my spirits to spend a weekend in her beautiful hillside home. I didn't expect to be scolded.

"How many women would give their eye teeth to be Mrs. William S. Hart and live in that gorgeous mountaintop mansion? Ted's gone back to Montana. What's Jack up to, other than racing around and wrecking up cars? Parker-Russell has finally and officially declared bankruptcy. C.O. says paintings aren't selling worth a tinker's damn, and you turn down Bill Hart's proposal. I can't believe you, Nancy."

"I thought you, of all people, would understand. I will always treasure Bill's friendship. But I can't marry. I have to be Mrs. Charles Marion Russell. How else am

I going to set up a fitting memorial to Charlie? Bill and I shared some good times together but even he understands. "

"Nancy, you need help. You need to have your head examined! But more important, I think you need some rest. My dear, you look so tired. Why don't you take a vacation? Why don't you go to your place in Balboa and just relax." Lindley got up and came over to pat my shoulder.

"I have to work twice as hard now because money is so tight," I answered.

"C.O. says that war is brewing in Europe, and when it breaks out, our shipyards will go back in full swing and our factories will be humming again," Lindley said.

"I pray there's no war. I thought the last war was fought to end all wars. I think Charlie always felt a little guilty that he was too old to serve. He did posters for the war effort, but I think deep down he wanted to be a doughboy, fighting in the trenches. And deep down I was thankful that he was too old, for he was too precious to send into that hell. Funny how we try to protect loved ones, but we can't protect them from the inevitable."

"You need to protect yourself. You need to take care of yourself. I'm serious, Nancy. I'm worried about you. You don't look well, and I've noticed that sometimes you forget the words at the end of a sentence, which is a sure sign of exhaustion."

"I'm just tired, and, I must admit, worried about Jack. I know you heard he had a car wreck while driving me and Josephine back from the World's Fair in San Diego. Thank God no one was killed. Josephine broke her collar bone. She was in a lot of pain, but it wasn't serious. Of course, she didn't blame Jack. In her eyes, Jack could never do wrong,"

"Well, we aren't going to worry about Jack, or selling paintings, or war, or anything else this weekend. We are just going to have pleasant thoughts and sit around sipping hot tea and eating cakes and relaxing. Speaking of tea and cakes, here comes Gertrude with a tray. Let's go into the garden and have tea. It is such a beautiful June day."

"Lordy, Miss Nancy, you sure are a sight for sore eyes. You don't come around much lately. Miss Lindley says you're too busy. She also says you're all worn out. Well, we're going to just pamper you all weekend and see you get a good rest," said Gertrude as she carried the tea tray into the garden.

After that weekend, I returned to Trail's End feeling better than I had in years. I had more energy. I was ready again to tackle my book on Charlie. I knew it would be as successful as *Good Medicine* had been. Dan Conway's book was not published. I didn't blame the publishers; he had spent too much time writing about himself. The only good parts of the book were the ones I dictated. Well, I had made a mistake in hiring him. That was really brought home to me when I found he was trying to peddle the book himself. I put a stop to that. I had hired him. Anything he wrote while in my employ belonged to me. This time I was going to do it right. I was going to write a book about Charlie myself. I wrote to all of his best and dearest friends and asked them to recall for me their fondest memories of times shared with Charlie. I told them that nothing they could write would upset me for Charlie and I had no secrets. I wanted this to be a true, alive, vital book. Someone named James Rankin had written me, as well as every one of Charlie's friends, saying he was writing a book about Charlie. He asked me to tell him about Charlie from a wife's viewpoint. I wrote back and told him I was more than a wife, I was Charles Russell's partner. Now I knew I had to get my book published first.

I was sitting at my desk and it was well into the evening. My left arm had gone to sleep and I had a severe headache at the base of my skull. I decided to give up my writing for the day and to stand up and stretch my legs. As I stood, white, searing pain shot between my eyes. I felt a hammer to my skull. I fell to my knees. I tried to roll over and grab the leg of my chair but I couldn't.

I don't know how long I lay there. It seemed forever. I kept repeating *Oh, dear God, make someone come in and find me. Don't let me die.* Finally I heard footsteps.

"Mother? Oh God, I think she's dead!" Jack cried.

"No—"

I heard a girl's voice. I wondered who it was, then I recognized it. It was Virginia Miller.

"I think she's had a stroke," she said, bending over me.

"What should I do?"

"Call an ambulance."

I vaguely remember being lifted on a stretcher, and the sound of the siren as we careened through the night to Huntington Memorial, where professional hands probed and examined me and finally a voice said, "You're going to be all right, Mrs. Russell." Then I blacked out.

When I woke up I tried to sit, but I couldn't. I tried to speak, but my tongue was so thick words wouldn't form. I could see Dr. Olmstead standing at the foot of the bed. He was writing on my chart.

"Well, Mrs. Russell, are you finally awake?"

I tried to ask him what was wrong, but my speech was so slurred I didn't recognize my own voice, and I didn't think he could understand me.

"You had a rough time last night. I'm afraid you had a cerebral embolism which has affected your left arm and leg. I know you find it difficult to speak. With time and proper care and therapy you'll be much improved. Now you just rest and get your strength back. In no time you'll be out of the hospital and going home."

God had answered my prayers. Jack had come in and found me. I was still alive, but I couldn't move my left arm or leg. My heavy, thick tongue was difficult to move. Was this living? I lay there and thought, Why me?

I didn't get better. I developed bronchial pneumonia. My right lung collapsed. I burned with fever. I drifted in and out of consciousness. Hours dragged into days, days became weeks. I awoke one morning and I thought I saw an apparition next to my bed. It couldn't be real. It must be my mind playing tricks on me. It looked like Ted. It wasn't a trick, for it moved. Ted walked over and took my hand, my right hand, and I could feel the warmth and pressure of his fingers holding mine.

"Nancy, I've come to take you home," he said.

I tried, in my thick speech, to tell him I couldn't walk. He seemed to understand.

"That doesn't matter. I have strong arms. I'll carry you. Now, you've got to get better so we can go back to Trail's End, where you belong. You haven't finished with — what do you call it? Your mission? You haven't built your proper memorial to Charles Russell."

Tears ran down my cheeks.

September, October, and November passed, and I grew stronger each day. Ted insisted that I be well before Christmas. On December third, I was discharged to go home. My speech had improved to the point where there was only the slightest slur, but I still couldn't walk. Ted had to carry me.

The Christmas tree was in front of the big window in the gallery-living room, as always. In years past, almost the entire floor was covered with brightly wrapped packages, but not this year. The six months in the hospital, and now the round-the-clock nurses, had terribly depleted our finances, and I knew I had another big expense. I had to convert the storeroom into a downstairs bedroom. I figured I could cut a double-wide doorway into the gallery-living room so my hospital bed could be wheeled in and out. I would fill the two outer walls of the room with windows so I could see outside and watch the birds in the aviary. I also planned a double-wide door to the outside, so I could be rolled into the back yard where I could sit in the sun next to the fish pond and listen to the fountain. I even planned a fireplace that would leave room enough for a large overstuffed chair or two. I knew this room would have to serve not only as my bedroom, but also my office. My life.

I didn't see much of Jack. I did see Florence, Charlie's stepmother. She took the streetcar out to visit me almost once a week, in order to cheer me up. But I knew the real purpose — she hinted at it often enough. If I had money enough for a chauffeur, a maid, a nurse and a new room, then obviously I had money to spare for a poor widow whose sole income from the Parker-Russell Mining and Manufacturing Company had disappeared.

Dr. Olmstead knew how worried I was about money. He also knew how deeply I desired a proper memorial to the memory of Charles Russell. He came up with the perfect solution.

"Mrs. Russell, I have suggested that Dr. Wagner, who is an active member of the Southwest Museum, and Mr. Hodge, the director, come see you," Dr. Olmstead told me on his next visit. "I think they can get their Board of Directors to buy your paintings and exhibit them at the museum. What do you think of that?"

"I'd welcome their visit," I answered.

On February fifteenth they came to see me.

"Mrs. Russell, I'm F.W. Hodge, Director of Southwest Art Musuem, and I think you know Dr. Wagner."

"Welcome to Trail's End. I'm delighted that you could come. I gather from Dr. Olmstead that we might be able to come to some mutual agreement that will be to both our benefit," I said.

"Mrs. Russell, let me tell you at the outset, I have long been an admirer of your late husband's work. I think he is one of America's greatest artists. I also know of his long-time friendship with Charles Lummis, the founder of Southwest Museum. I think it would be wonderful to have his work at our museum," Mr. Hodge said.

"I would insist that the collection be kept intact and that it be called the Charles Russell Memorial Collection," I said.

"There would be no problem with that," Mr. Hodge replied.

"I think that one hundred and forty thousand dollars is a reasonable sum. There are thirteen oil paintings, two watercolors and thirty-six bronzes. One of the bronzes is one of only four castings and the others sold for three thousand dollars each. I can show you a list of the bronzes and their prices at the Biltmore Gallery.

"There are some personal pieces I would want to keep. I would have to keep Charlie's self-portrait, *When I Was a Kid*, which hangs in the dining room, and a few others."

There was silence.

"Mrs. Russell, I thought you were going to will your collection to us," Mr. Hodge said quietly.

Another silence.

"The museum doesn't have any money," he said.

Another silence.

"Mr. Hodge, I have hospital costs, doctors' fees, nurse's salaries. I live here with my adopted son, and I have a cook and chauffeur. I cannot meet my expenses. I'm going to be compelled to sell my pieces of Charlie's work off one at a time. It has been my dream to keep the collection together, as a memorial to Charles, and I can think of no better place than the Southwest Museum to display it."

"Maybe I have an idea," interrupted Dr. Wagner. "What if we could raise the money from our Board of Directors to meet all of your living expenses for as long as you live? We would also promise to keep the collection intact, call it the Charles Russell Memorial Collection, and always to display it — What then? Would you give your collection?"

"Yes," I answered.

"We'll get with our board and get back with you. Possibly a member of our board, or a friend of the museum, will assume your expenses for the benefit of the museum," Dr. Wagner said as he left.

"So, Mother, you are going to give everything to the Southwest Museum," said Jack as he came in.

"Obviously you've been eavesdropping," I said.

He ignored this.

"Besides, I'm not giving anything away. Dr. Wagner thinks either the board or a patron of the Southwest Museum will pay our expenses. You know, right now, I don't have the income to meet our expenses, and I can't think of a better place to have a Charles Russell Memorial Collection on perpetual display."

"They get everything and all I have is one measly painting."

"You know my dream of a Charles Russell Memorial Collection. I gave you the best, my very favorite, *War Scars of Medicine Whip*. It has all the action, drama and pathos of any great Russell. How many times I've heard Charlie tell the story behind it. I gave it to you because I thought you appreciated it, and I wanted to do something special for you and Virginia. That night you found me on the floor when I had my stroke, I'm sure you saved my life. When you told me you had been coming to find me to say you were getting married, I gave you that painting as a special wedding present. I can understand why Virginia thought you should put off the wedding until I was out of the hospital, but I'm home now and I think it's time for you to get on with your life. Get married, settle down, and make something of yourself," I said.

"You are really a broken record. Well, Virginia has cooled off. I think her folks are to blame. I think they've poisoned her against me, telling her I wasn't good enough for her. That's all right. There are plenty of fish in the sea. Girls have always taken to me," Jack said.

As if to prove he was right, Jack now dated not only Virginia but lots of other girls as well. I noticed one girl was coming over more and more often. I found out her name was Betty Alexander. She and her girlfriend, Dorothy Bott, and Dorothy's boyfriend were spending more and more evenings in Jack's apartment over the garage. They would listen to the radio or play records. I could hear their laughter and their voices mixed with the sound of the music. I didn't like the looks of Jack's new girlfriend. She was pretty enough, but she was young. I knew I had to talk to Jack about her, but I didn't want to confront him. He was so stubborn. If I told him not to see her, I knew he would do just the opposite.

As I was trying to figure out the best way to handle this, we got an invitation to Jimmy Rogers's wedding. Jack's invitation was for Jack and Virginia. I'm sure Betty Rogers thought they were still engaged.

"Jack, you have to go to Jimmy's wedding, and you have to take Virginia Miller."

"I'd rather take Betty," Jack said.

"The invitation is to you and Virginia. Besides, Betty is much too young for you. How would it look for you to go to the wedding of Will Rogers' son with that child? What is she, fifteen years old?" I asked.

"She's sixteen," Jack answered.

"And how old are you? Twenty-two! You're too old for her," I snapped.

"Oh, that's great coming from you. How many times have I heard the story that you were only seventeen when you and Charles Russell first met. And didn't your uncanny brilliance in business make his international reputation? Were you too young for him? Was he too old for you?" Jack asked.

"That was different. Betty Alexander is still a child. Have you taken a good look at her? She's still wearing short white anklets like a little girl," I said.

"Have you taken a look at her? She's old enough, plus she thinks I'm brilliant because I can build a radio from scratch. She thinks I'm charming and handsome. The first time she came up to my apartment she thought it looked like a pig's sty and said she would play maid and clean it up, which she did. She had it shining and sparkling in no time. She'd do anything for me. She cares about me." Jack said.

"I care about you, too. That's the reason you're going to take Virginia to the wedding and that is final," I said.

Jack took Virginia to the wedding. I had hoped that he would see more of her and less of Betty, but it didn't work out that way.

Finally, Dr. Wagner called and said that they were still trying to find a way to pay my living expenses, and that they really wanted the Charles Russell Memorial Collection at the Southwest Museum.

"I want it there, too. I'll call my lawyer and make a codicil to my will. I'll instruct my trustees, Edgar Holland and George Miller, that if I dispose of the major portion of the artworks to a person or a museum during my lifetime then they are to deliver to that museum or person what art works come into their hands upon my death at no cost. That should help you convince a patron or the museum to agree to pay my expenses," I said.

"That's wonderful, Mrs. Russell. I think that commitment will really help me. May I ask you a question? I don't mean to be too personal, but what about your adopted son?" Dr. Wagner asked.

"He is far too immature to inherit the collection. I fear he would sell it off piece by piece and let the money slip through his fingers. My dream has been to have my collection held as one collection on permanent display in Charlie's memory," I explained.

"I guess you know your son was standing out in

the hallway listening to our conversation the other day, so I thought he might have an objection."

"It is not his to object or agree. The collection is mine." I answered Dr. Wagner. "I hope to hear from you soon." I hung up. Then I dialed my lawyer to see the codicil was added.

I waited and waited to hear from Dr. Wagner. The days dragged on. Finally he called.

"Mrs. Russell, I'm sorry to take so long in getting back to you. I didn't want to call you until I had tried every avenue I could think of. I have. The news is not good. There is no patron or friend of the museum that will pledge the money to meet your living expenses for your lifetime and the museum simply does not have the money. These are hard times. I'm so sorry," he said.

"I am too, and I want to thank you for all of your efforts on my behalf." I hung up the phone. My dream of having Charlie's memorial collection at Southwest was shattered. I picked up the bell on the table next to my bed and rang for Lavina.

"Please get Ted to push me out into the garden," I said. "I want to hear the birds."

Ted came and rolled the bed outside. We sat without speaking. Finally he said, "What's wrong, Nancy?"

"They can't come up with the money. Dr. Wagner had the nerve to tell me that times are hard. Who would know it better than I? I don't think I can take another blow," I said.

"Sure you can. You've always figured something out. You will now. You've always managed," Ted came to my bed and held my hand.

"I can't," I said.

"Yes, you can. You have a will of iron," said Ted.

"I don't know what I would do without you,"

"You are going to have to try for a few weeks. I need to go up to Flathead Lake and make some repairs on my place. One of my brothers was over there and wrote that the roof leaked. I got to get it fixed before fall, while the weather's still good. Once the snow starts, that roof will be ruined."

"It's hard to believe, when you're out here in California, how it still snows back in Montana. Didn't Arthur Brown buy a place next to yours? Oh, I can see how a Californian would fall in love with that beautiful blue lake and those mountains. How I wish I could see Bull Head Lodge again. Of course you have to go. Fix your roof and hurry back," I said.

"I will," Ted promised.

"If anything should happen to me while you're gone, remember you promised to oversee the breaking of the plaster molds for Charlie's bronzes. I trust you, Ted. That's why I put it in my will that you are the one to see to it the molds are broken. Whoever buys my collection can have one of each bronze. After that the molds must be destroyed. I will not have the market flooded with Russell bronzes after I'm gone. The casting of bronzes from those molds and the selling of them at galleries like the Biltmore have kept food in our mouths and a roof over our heads. Some of those plaster molds are in bad shape now and I'll not allow someone's greed to force them into use after I'm gone. That would harm the reputation of Charlie's bronzes. Now you have to promise me you'll have them destroyed," I implored.

"Nothing is going to happen to you while I'm gone," Ted said.

"I also put it in that codicil that the executors are to consult with you, Bill Hart, and Betty Rogers, when they dispose of my art works, whether it's to a person or a museum. All of you know of my dream for a Charles Russell Memorial, and I trust all of you to see my wishes are carried out," I said.

"Stop talking like that. Nothing's going to happen to you in the few weeks I'm up at Flathead," Ted reassured me.

"Promise," I demanded.

"I promise. This is silly. I'll be back before you know it."

"I don't know how we will get along without you," I repeated.

"Remember, I told you, you are the strongest person I know. You have a will of iron," Ted said, smiling.

"I'm nothing but a bed-ridden old woman," I

said.

"You're still the most beautiful woman I've ever seen and you can handle anything, bed-ridden or not," Ted answered.

Ted was right. Nothing happened to me.

On October sixth, Jack came into my bedroom. He was white as a sheet. "Mother," he said. "Arthur Brown just came to my apartment over the garage, banging on my door. Ted's brothers thought I should be the one to tell you."

"Tell me what?" A chill went down my spine.

"Ted fell off the roof. He broke his neck. He's dead," Jack said.

A will of iron, Ted had said. I would need it now.

20

War Scars

"I WILL RING UP REVEREND HARTSOUGH of the Michalinda Community Church and see when is the first possible time he can marry Jack and Betty," I said to the frumpy, disheveled woman who was standing at the foot of my bed. She was Betty Alexander's mother and she was red-faced with anger.

"And what are they going to live on?" she demanded. "Jack don't have any work."

"They can live in Jack's apartment over the garage. It seems apparent to me that they have already made use of it. I promise you I will not let them starve," I explained. "Now, let me call Reverend Hartsough."

It was arranged that they would be married the

coming Sunday at eight in the morning, in Reverend Hartsough's home. After Betty's mother had gone, I told Lavina to go to Jack's apartment over the garage and tell him I wanted to see him immediately.

"Betty's mother was just here. Do you know what she was here about?" I asked.

"Yes, Mother," Jack answered.

"I promised her you would do the honorable thing," I said.

"I've already asked Betty to marry me," Jack said.

"Good, because the wedding is arranged for this Sunday morning at eight in Reverend Hartsough's study in his home.

Jack looked at the floor. "Whatever you say, Mother."

"Oh, Jack, this may be the best thing that ever happened to you. If you have a wife and a baby to support, it may make you grow up, accept responsibility, and make something of yourself." Jack didn't say a word. "I can't be at this wedding since I can't even get out of this bed, but will you bring Betty by before you go to Reverend Hartsough?"

"Sure, Mother," Jack said, and he bent down and kissed me on the forehead.

Jack brought Betty by early Sunday morning, October twenty-third, 1938.

"I want to give you children my blessing," I said. "Betty, I want to give you this ring and bracelet to wear at your wedding. They are two of my favorites. In fact, I wore them for the portrait Bill Krieghoff painted of me. Now you shall have them," I said as I handed them to Betty.

She took them with a big smile. She looked beautiful that morning. She blushed and said, "Thank you, Mrs. Russell. I'm really going to try to make Jack a good wife."

"I know you will," I answered.

After they left, Lavina came in. "I hope and pray that having a wife and baby will make Jack settle down and get a job," she said. "It's a big responsibility, having a wife and baby."

But they didn't have a baby. Instead, in February, Betty had a miscarriage. Maybe it was because of her youth. She had a terrible time and was so ill. She was hospitalized for weeks.

When she came back from the hospital to the garage apartment, she was glum and despondent. I didn't blame her. Jack still didn't have work.

One evening, in order to raise Betty's spirits, I decided to have a dinner party for the three of us. I dressed in my finest. Jack carried me to the table. I looked forward to having a pleasant evening.

"If you are old enough to have a wife, you are old enough to have a steady job," I said gently, at some point in the conversation.

"I can't take much more of your nagging, Mother," Jack said. He started to get up and leave the dinner table.

"You sit right down. I haven't finished," I ordered. "You're eating my food, at my table, under my roof, and you'll listen to me."

"Mrs. Russell, I was reading an ad in the papers. The Southern California Gas Company is hiring men," said Betty.

"You can't be serious. That's for common laborers. Those are ditch diggers' jobs," I said unbelievingly. "There's no future to a job like that. Jack could do a thousand times better."

"But jobs are so hard to find. I just thought that Jack could start there. He has to start somewhere."

"You don't think at all. Neither of you thinks," I said disgustedly.

With that, Betty jumped up and ran out of the dining room, knocking over her glass of tea.

"See what you've done, Mother," Jack said as he jumped up and ran after her.

"Lavina, would you please come and clean up the tea? It will stain this good white linen cloth if not immediately attended to."

The next morning Jack came to see me. "Mother, Betty and I are moving out. We have found a little place in Altadena."

"Could you tell me what you are going to use for money?" I asked.

"You are always telling us how much it costs to have us here, how much extra it is for food, how much extra for utilities. We figure that if you gave us one hundred and fifty dollars a month, we could live in our own place in Altadena," Jack explained. "You are probably spending more than that on us staying here. Just think how much money you'll save."

"Jack, I need you here. Since Ted's death, I need someone who can drive me and do those chores that are too heavy for Lavina," I said.

"We aren't staying. Betty says it's not working out, that we need our own place. She says that two women can't live under one roof," Jack said.

"We aren't under the same roof," I said.

"It's the same. We are constantly reminded that it's your roof, your food, your table, your house. You have to be obeyed by everyone in this household. We are no longer going to be your subjects," Jack said as he stormed out of my bedroom.

I called George Miller. "I want you to get in touch with my lawyer immediately. I want to change my will. I left this house and other property to Jack to be held in trust until he was thirty-eight. I thought by then he would be mature enough to handle it, but Jack's never going to grow up. I want to revoke any and all provisions, including the right to use the house or apartment, and particularly to revoke any and all distributions of any part of my estate for Jack Cooper Russell. I have an insurance policy of which he is beneficiary and I will provide him with one hundred and fifty dollars a month for life. And that's absolutely it!" I realized that I had raised my voice until I was shouting over the phone.

"Mrs. Russell, whatever you wish, we will do. Now, be calm. I think the best avenue is just to add another codicil to your existing will as you did in '38," George Miller advised.

"I don't care how you do it, just get it done and be here this afternoon," I said as I hung up.

They were there on the afternoon of March twenty-third, 1939, and I signed the second codicil.

I didn't think Jack could do anything that could make me angrier with him but I was wrong.

Alex Cowie of the Biltmore Gallery came to see me. "Nancy, it's so good to see you looking better. I've come out to bring you a check on a bronze we sold."

"It's always so good to see you. It will give me a chance to catch up with the news. Who is selling, and who is buying?" I asked as I reached out my hand to greet him. "But you could have sent the check by mail, although I'm glad you didn't."

"I also came out to pick a bone with you. Why are you letting Standahl's Gallery handle *War Scars of Medicine Whip*?" he asked.

"What?"

"I thought we had an understanding," he continued.

"What do you mean?"

"It's right in the front window of Standahl's."

"Are you sure?" Again, I couldn't believe what Alex was saying.

"I saw it there myself. Are you telling me you didn't know?" Now Alex was the one bewildered.

"Yes, but I promise you that it won't be there long." I covered up my anger, my bewilderment, and my hurt. In a cheerful voice, I said, "Now, tell me everything you know that's going on in the art world. You are always up on the latest news. I'll ring for some tea, and we can go out by the fish pond while I catch up on all the happenings. I hope it's not too much trouble for you to roll my bed outside," I said.

"Of course not," said Alex.

We spent a pleasant afternoon and as soon as Alex was gone and I was back in my room, I sent for Lavina. "I want to get in touch with Jack immediately. Since he doesn't have a phone I will send him a telegram. That's the fastest way I know. I want you to take this wire to Western Union now. Say 'Come immediately. Important. Mother.'"

The next afternoon Jack and Betty were standing at the foot of my bed.

"What's so important?" Jack asked.

"I have never felt so betrayed. How could you?" I asked.

"Mother, I don't even know what you are talking about," Jack answered.

"Yesterday, Alex Cowie was here with the news that *War Scars of Medicine Whip* was in the window of Standahl's. How could you? I gave you one of Charlie's most wonderful paintings. I thought you would cherish such a gift. How could you put it up for sale?" I demanded.

"Mrs. Russell," interrupted Betty. "We still have bills to pay from when I was in the hospital. Poor Dr. Rogers hasn't been paid yet. We desperately need the money."

"You would stoop that low to sell one of Charlie's best without even letting me know?" I asked.

"I thought that a gift was a gift, and that the receiver could do with the gift as he chose. But, no, *your* gifts have strings attached. That's all right, Mother, I will take it out of Standahl's Gallery tomorrow. Come on, Betty," Jack said and he turned on his heel and left.

"Mrs. Russell, we really need the money," Betty whispered as Jack grabbed her hand and pulled her out of the bedroom.

I thought that was the end of it, but two weeks later I received a phone call from a Sam Rosenthal, Jr.

"Mrs. Russell, you don't know me, but I recently purchased a Charles Russell oil. I wondered if I might impose on you and have you validate its authenticity? I'm sure it's genuine, but I would feel so much better hearing it from you," said a young enthusiastic, charming voice over the phone. "I've always dreamed of owning a Russell, and now to actually have one in my possession is almost too good to believe. If it's not too much trouble, could I possibly have you look at it since, of course, you *are* the Russell authority?"

"I would be glad to. I fear I am confined to my

bed since I suffered a stroke so you will have to bring it to Trail's End," I said.

"That would be no trouble at all. I so look forward to meeting the famous Mrs. Russell," Sam said. "Would three o'clock tomorrow afternoon be convenient?"

"That should be fine," I answered.

Promptly at three Lavina showed a tall, tanned, handsome, young man into my bedroom. He was practically prancing with excitement as he took the large painting from under his arm, unwrapped it, and brought it to my bed for my inspection.

War Scars of Medicine Whip.

"It has to be a genuine Russell — the colors, the action . . ." Sam said eagerly.

After a moment or two, I said, "Indeed, it is. And one of his best. May I ask you where you found it?"

"I first saw it in the window of Standahl's Gallery. I would walk by, stop and stare at it. I dreamed of owning it. I love your late husband's work. One day it was gone. I was devastated. I thought someone had bought it. I forced myself into the gallery to ask what had happened. You can imagine my excitement and relief when I found that the painting had not been sold but the owner had taken it home from the gallery. I begged for the name and address of the owner. You can imagine how surprised I was to find out that it was none other than Charlie Russell's own son. I got his address from the gallery owner and went to see him. I told him how much I wanted that painting. I think his wife helped me convince him to sell — something about doctor's bills. Anyway, I was sure it was an original. I just wanted you to verify it. I have the bill of sale right here," Mr. Rosenthal reached in his pocket and pulled out a sheet of white paper.

It was dated March twenty-fifth, 1940. And there was Jack's signature.

"Mr. Rosenthal, that painting is very special to me. It has always been in the Russell family. Charlie painted it for a relative in St. Louis, a Mrs. Silas Bent. I bought it from her years ago because I loved it so. It has hung in this house since we moved here in 1927. I gave it to my son. I would really like to buy it back from you. I will give you a handsome profit." I pleaded.

"Oh, Mrs. Russell, I love it, too. You have so many marvelous paintings by Charlie Russell, and I have only one. This is my dream come true. I couldn't possibly part with it. I hope you understand. I idolize his work, and it brings me such joy to know that I am the owner of this wonderful painting."

"Of course I understand. You bought it in good faith and a deal is a deal," I said quietly.

After Mr. Rosenthal left, I again told Lavina to get a wire off to Jack immediately.

The next day he and Betty came again.

"What now, Mother? Why this command performance? You wired. We're here," Jack said.

"I have never been so hurt and so angry. How

could you promise me you would take *War Scars of Medicine Whip* out of Standahl's Gallery, then sell it? Isn't your word worth anything? How could you sell that painting behind my back? Don't you know how much it meant to me? Have you no feelings?" I demanded.

"I took it out of Standahl's Gallery, as I promised. Sam Rosenthal came to me and begged me to sell. It was my painting. You did give it to me, or don't you remember?" Jack said.

"And we really need the money for Dr. Rogers," added Betty.

"That's not the point," I almost screamed at her. "You have betrayed any trust I have in you, Jack."

"Come on, Betty. We don't have to stand here and listen to this," Jack said as he left hastily with Betty right behind him.

I didn't see either one of them for weeks. I still sent them a check for a hundred and fifty dollars each month. They still cashed the checks. I knew that in time our tempers would cool and they would be back, and that I would forgive Jack, but I would never forget what he had done.

Jack came back, but not for reconciliation. He came storming into my bedroom, slamming the door behind him.

"How could you, Mother? How could you lie to me all these years? How could you betray me? The great, good, righteous Nancy Russell, nothing but a liar," Jack yelled.

"What are you talking about?" I asked in bewilderment.

"Well, I finally got a good job, just like you always wanted. The pay is great. I'm working for Lockheed. Everything is gearing up with rumors of war. There's a great opportunity for advancement. Just one small catch. In order to be hired, I had to have my birth certificate. Guess what? My father wasn't a hero, gone off to fight for freedom. My mother didn't have to give me up because of the other children she had to feed. No, I'm a bastard. I'm illegitimate. How could you have lied to me all those years? How could you have deceived me?" Jack demanded.

"Jack, I did it for your own good. I was trying to protect you. It would have been a stigma that I didn't want you to bear." I tried to explain.

"Don't give me that. It was a stigma that the great Mrs. Russell thought might touch her. What would people say if they knew the great Mrs. Charles Russell had adopted a bastard. You were only thinking of yourself and Charlie's reputation,"

"Don't be silly. I was only thinking of you," I pleaded.

"You're nothing but a liar. I can't believe a word you say. I hope I never have to see you again," he said as he ran out of my room.

"Jack! Jack! Jack!" I called after him.

21

Charlie, First and Last

"Mrs. Russell, it's time for medicine," said Nurse Cartwright in her eternally cheerful voice.

"Later," I slurred.

"It's not going to do us any good to be in the hospital if we don't do as the doctor says." Nurse Cartwright put a pill in my mouth and held a straw against my lips so that I could take a sip of water.

"But I need to stay awake. I want to be awake when Jack comes. You know Jack, my son. How many days have I been here?" I asked, for one day seemed to slip into another.

"Let's see. Twenty-three days."

"Jack hasn't come today, has he?" I asked. I couldn't remember.

"Not yet. Now, let's just lie back and rest," Nurse Cartwright said as she patted my arm.

"I need to tell him I love him," I said.

"No worry now. Worry just prolongs our getting better. Think about good things. You received a call from William S. Hart today — *the* William S. Hart — and he sent flowers. Now, why don't you tell me again about the first time you met Charlie Russell. It's such a wonderfully romantic story."

"I'll never forget the first time I ever laid eyes on Charlie Russell," I began. "There he stood . . . big as life . . with blond hair hanging in his face and a Stetson hat on the back of his head . . . he had on a soft shirt and tight pants held up by a red, silk half-breed sash. His eyes took everything in and were so understanding. And his hands . . . long, strong, artistic fingers . . . and the rings. Charlie always wore three or four rings. He wouldn't have been Charlie without them . .

Afterword

Nancy Cooper Russell died on May 23, 1940 at Huntington Memorial Hospital in Pasadena, California. She was a member of the F. B. Chapter of PEO, Pasadena and an honorary member of the Benevolent and Protective Order of the Elks, Great Falls lodge number 214. After services in Los Angeles, her body was taken to Great Falls, Montana, where she was buried next to her husband Charles M. Russell. Nearby are the graves of the Trigg family and Joe De Yong and his mother.

Charles M. Russell has received numerous posthumous honors. In 1959 his statue was installed in the national Capitol's Statuary Hall representing Montana. Three of his works have been selected for Commemorative United States postage stamps. These are *Trail Boss*, from a private collection, issued in 1959 to honor Range Conservation; *Jerked Down*, from the collection of the Gilcrease Institute of American Art and History, Tulsa, Oklahoma, issued in 1964 to honor Charles M. Russell-American Artist, upon the 100th anniversary of his birth; and *Charles M. Russell and His Friends*, from the Mackay Collection, Montana Historical Society, Helena, Montana issued in 1989 to honor Montana's Statehood Centennial. His painting *Bronc to Breakfast* from the Mackay Collection was the first work by an American artist to appear on the cover of *National Geographic* (Vol. 169, No. 1, January 1986).

Jack Russell is retired from the California Highway Department and lives in Oceanside, California with his wife Helen. He served overseas in the military during World War II and later lived in Missouri, where he was stationed early in the war. He was divorced from his first wife Betty.

Josephine Trigg died in 1951. She left her house and her collection of 153 works by Charles Russell (including oil paintings, watercolors, illustrated letters and cards) to the city of Great Falls on the condition that it build a museum to honor Russell within two years of her gift. She left no money to bring this about. A Trigg-Russell Foundation was formed to raise money to build the C. M. Russell Museum, which opened on September 14, 1953.

In 1967, a public subscription campaign raised $400,000 to add 20,000 square feet to the existing 1,500 square foot museum. Another public subscription in 1981 raised an additional $3 million for a second major addition to the musuem. It opened in November, 1985.

James A. Cooper deeded his home to his brother in 1941 and died in Hondo, California in 1949.

Ella Allen Ironsides moved to Seward, Alaska in 1926 and died there on July 16, 1946. She never remarried.

Lindley Anderson married **C. O. Middleton** in the 1950s. C. O. died in 1959 and Lindley followed him in 1972.

William S. Hart never remarried. Upon his death in 1946 his Newhall, California home and adjoining property was willed to Los Angeles County. It was opened to the public in 1958.

Joe De Yong became a successful artist who established a career in the movie industry. His mother "Banty" died in 1973 and he died in 1975.

Ross Case served in the army during World War II and afterwards during the occupation of Japan. He later received a dental degree and established a practice in southern California. He is married and has two sons.

Vera Case lived in Tacoma, Washington with her husband and three daughters until her death in 1971.

Dr. Phillip Cole died in 1941 and in 1944 his wife sold his collection of Russell and Remington artworks to Tulsa oilman Thomas Gilcrease. They represent the heart of the cowboy art portion of his world-renown collection, now housed at the Gilcrease Institute of American History and Art in Tulsa, Oklahoma.

The Doheny Panels became part of the Edward Laurence Doheny Memorial Library Collection at St. John's Seminary, Camarillo, California. They are now in the collection of the Hubbard Museum, Ruidoso, New Mexico.

War Scars of Medicine Whip is in the Sid Richardson Collection, Fort Worth, Texas.

Source Notes

Articles

Newspapers

Helena Daily Herald, 25 September 1894 page 4. (death of Texas Annie Allen)

Helena Independent, 2 July 1895. (Mrs. Chadwick-Biggs marriage)

St. Louis Post Dispatch, 22 November 1903. (Opening Choral and Symphony Subscription Concert and Zoo theater opening)

Great Falls Daily Tribune, 14 September 1897. (Russells to move to Great Falls).

Great Falls Daily Tribune, 19 September 1897. (Russells move to Great Falls)

Great Falls Daily Tribune, May 13, 1906. (Ella Allen arrives)

Great Falls Daily Tribune, 8 July 1900. (Russell Building Dwelling)

Great Falls Daily Tribune, 24 June 1900. (C. S. Russell visits)

Great Falls Daily Tribune, 25 December 1910. (Allen-Ironsides marriage)

Great Falls Daily Tribune, 7 September 1899. (Ridgely-Trigg marriage)

Great Falls Daily Tribune, 9 September 1896. (Cooper-Russell marriage)

Great Falls Daily Tribune, 30 August 1900. (Charlie in New Home)

Great Falls Daily Tribune, 9 November 1916. (Little Almond Eyes and Advertisement)

Great Falls Daily Tribune, 12 November 1916. (Photo of scenery of Little Almond Eyes)

Great Falls Daily Tribune, 7 June 1914. (Britons Enraptured)

Great Falls Daily Tribune, 15 April 1923. ($30,000 for Seven Paintings)

Helena Independent, 6 December 1894. (Uncollected letter for Miss Allen, 907 Eight Avenue)

Great Falls Daily Tribune, 6 December 1925. (New Book and Account of Russell's Early Life)

Great Falls Daily Tribune, 2 March 1921. (Sale of Painting to Armstrong)

Great Falls Daily Tribune, 19 November 1916. (Clothing for Little Bear's Indians)

Choteau Montanan, 30 March 1917. (Charles Russell adopts a son)

Sentinel of Billings Montana, 18 June 1914. (Russell Returns from London)

Flathead Courier, Polson Montana, 13 October 1938. (Taylor Succumbs)

New York Times, 19 March 1911. (Cowboy Vividly Paints the Passing Life of the Plains)

Great Falls Tribune, 11 October 1914. (City's Popular Social Leader)

Leslies Weekly, 3 March 1904. (C. M. Russell, the Cowboy Artist)

Santa Barbara News-Press, 6 November 1963 (S. M. Man Recalls Bar Closing Allowing Minister to View Art)

Periodicals

Lyle S. Woodcock, "The St. Louis Heritage of Charles Marion Russell," *Gateway Heritage*, Journal of Missouri Historical Society, Volume 2, Number 4 (Spring 1982): pg. 2.

Books

Maury Klein, *History of The Louisville and Nashville Railroad* (New York: The Macmillan Company, 1972).

Keith Wheeler, *The Railroads* (New York: Time Life Books, 1973).

Dean Krakel, *Adventure in Western Art* (Kansas City: The Lowell Press, 1977).

Brian W. Dippie, *"Paper Talk" Charlie Russell's American West* (New York: Alfred A. Knopf Inc., 1979).

Mildred D. Ladner, *O.C. Seltzer Painter of the Old West* (Norman: University of Oklahoma Press, 1979).

Karl Yost and Frederic G. Renner, *A Bibliography of The Published Works of Charles M. Russell*, (Lincoln: University of Nebraska Press, 1971).

Charles M. Russell, *Good Medicine Memories of the Real West* (Garden City, New York: Garden City Publishing Co. Inc., 1929). [With an introduction by Will Rogers and a biographical note by Nancy Russell.]

Ginger Renner, *A Limitless Sky, the Work of Charles M. Russell* (Flagstaff, Arizona: Northland Press, 1986).

Austin Russell, *C.M.R. Charles M. Russell Cowboy Artist* (New York: Twayne Publishers, 1957).

Lola Shelton, *Charles Marion Russell: Cowboy Artist, Friend* (New York: Dodd, Mead & Co., 1962).

Frank Bird Linderman, *Recollections of Charlie Russell* (Norman: University of Oklahoma Press, 1963).

Ramon F. Adams and Homer E. Britzman, *Charles M. Russell, the Cowboy Artist: a Biography* (Pasadena: Trails End, 1948).

Harold G. Davidson, *Edward Borein, Cowboy Artist* (Garden City: Doubleday & Company, Inc., 1974)

John F. Stover, *The Life and Decline of the American Railroad* (New York: Oxford University Press, 1970).

Dorothy Daniels Birk, *The World Came to St. Louis* (St. Louis, Bethany Press, 1979).

Directories

Great Falls City Directories 1899, 1910 and 1926.

Boise City Directories 1899, 1902-3, 1904 and 1905.

Los Angeles Directories 1904, 1917 and 1924.

Paxton City (Illinois) Directories 1906 and 1909.

Helena City Directories 1890-91, 1891, 1892, 1894, 1911 and 1912.

Santa Barbara City Directory 1926-27.

Southern California Telephone Company Directory, Pasadena Exchange, October 1938.

Certificates, Records, and Documents

Certificates of Death

Lewis & Clark County, Montana (Mrs. T.A. Allen) Sept. 25, 1894.

Lake County, Montana (Ted C. Taylor) Oct. 6, 1938.

Cascade County, Montana (Ridgely baby girl) Aug. 8, 1902.

Cascade County, Montana (Albert Trigg) April 17, 1917.

Cascade County, Montana (Margaret Trigg) Sept. 4, 1933.

Taylor County, Kentucky (Rachael Allen) December 26, 1854.

Los Angeles County, California, District 1904, No. 466 (Nancy C. Russell) May 23, 1940.

State of Missouri, Certificate 1034 (Mary Meade Russell) June 18, 1895.

Decrees

Taylor County, Kentucky Order Book 11, page 356 (James Cooper and Texas Cooper).

Taylor County, Kentucky, Order Book 5, page 626 (James T. Allen guardianship).

Cascade County, Montana, Order Book dated October 31, 1912 (Josephine T. Ridgley and William T. Ridgley).

Deeds

Lake County, Montana Book 10 (Ted C. Taylor) Montana.

Cascade County, Montana Volume 33 (Purchase of 1219 4th Avenue North, Great Falls, Montana).

Cascade County, Montana, Volume 38 (Purchase adjoining lot 1215 4th Avenue North, Great Falls, Montana).

Taylor County, Kentucky Book 14 (Jennie K. Mann Agreement).

Flathead County, Montana Book 85-513 (Lot 1A Apgar).

Orange County, California Book 857 (113 Sapphire, Balboa, California).

Los Angeles County, California Book 2477 (725 Michigan Blvd.).

Cascade County, Montana Book 133 (City of Great Falls, Purchase of Russell studio and residence).

Taylor County, Kentucky Book 13 (Maintenance Nannie B. Cooper).

Inventories

Taylor County, Kentucky, Book 5 pg. 539 (John Bluford Mann).

Casey County, Kentucky 1882 Court Orders page 18 (James Allen-grandfather James T. Allen).

Taylor County, Kentucky, Book 1 page 518 (James T. Allen loan).

Taylor County, Kentucky, Book 1, page 540 (Sale Sorrel Mare).

Marriage Bonds and Certificates

Taylor County, Kentucky Book 8, page 356 (James A. Cooper and Texas Mann).

Marion County, Kentucky Book 1, page 74 (John B. Mann and Jane K. Parker).

Taylor County, Kentucky Book 1, page 158 (John B. Mann and Nancy Bates).

Casey County, Kentucky Book 1, page 56 (Zadock Allen and Rachael Mann).

Taylor County, Kentucky Book 10, page 123 (James T. Allen and Texas Mann).

Ada County, Idaho Book 1, page 613 (James T. Allen and Jennie Ireland).

Cascade County, Montana Book 7, page 4681 (Frank P. Ironsides and Ella Carrie Allen).

Los Angeles County, California Number 18835 (Jack Cooper Russell and Mary Elizabeth Alexander).

Cascade County, Montana Book 2, page 1121 (Charles M. Russell and Nancy Cooper).

Taylor County, Kentucky Book 11, page 116 (Joseph Morris to Carrie Mann).

Miscellaneous Records

Linden Funeral Home, Helena, Montana successor to Herrmann & Company, Mrs. T.A. Allen ledger record provided by Mrs. Carolyn Linden on June 17, 1983.

Montana Granite Company, Helena, Montana, burial records of Helena (now Forestvale) Cemetery supplied by Mr. Ken Ludtke on July 21, 1983.

Great Falls Montana Community Development Utility Connection Records of July 9, 1900 supplied on March 22, 1985.

Highland Cemetary, Great Falls Montana, lot purchase records supplied by Mr. Elmer Stewart on March 28, 1984.

Huntington Memorial Hospital Medical Records Department, Pasadena, California.

The Church of the Incarnation, Great Falls, Montana, Baptismal Records page 100.

Southern California Telephone Company May 1940 bill to William S. Hart, from collection of Seaver Center for Western History Research, Natural History Museum of Los Angeles County.

Theisen Company Contractor Plans for Studio and Residence, Michalinda, California from collection of C. M. Russell Museum, Great Falls, Montana.

Screen panels from Bull Head Lodge, Montana Historical Society, Helena, Montana.

Tax Records

Taylor County, Kentucky, Tax Rolls, 1868 thru 1890.

Los Angeles County Building Permit 69428 dated Nov. 14, 1938.

Pasadena Building Description Book 5378 dated Feb. 14, 1928.

U. S. Census Records

1900 Montana, Carbon, Cascade, Lewis and Clark Counties.
1900 Idaho, Ada County.
1900 Illinois, Ford County.
1860 Kentucky, Casey and Taylor Counties.
1880 Missouri, St. Louis County.
1870 Kentucky, Taylor County.
1880 Montana Territory, Gallatin and Madison Counties.
1860 Iowa, Jasper County.
1850 Iowa, Jasper County.
1910 Montana, Cascade County.
1870 Montana Territory, Madison County.
1850 Kentucky, Casey and Taylor Counties.
1880 Kentucky, Taylor County.

Wills

Taylor County, Kentucky, Will Book 2 page 100, John Bluford Mann.

Lake County, Montana, Will Book 18 page 44, Ted C. Taylor.

Casey County, Kentucky, Will Book 2 page 486, James Allen.

Los Angeles County, California, Nancy C. Russell dated October 14, 1939.

Interviews

Miss Evelyn Cooper, in Lebanon, Kentucky on June 30, 1985.

Mrs. Martha Gabrielson, Soho, Eugene, Oregon by telephone on November 9, 1985.

Mr. Malcolm S. Mackay, Jr. in Great Falls, Montana on March 24, 1984.

Mrs. Betty Russell Crawford in Lindsay, California on Dec. 10, 1983.

Mr. and Mrs. Carol Word in Goleta, California on Dec. 16, 1983.

Mr. and Mrs. S. H. Rosenthal, Jr. in Encino, California on Dec. 8, 1983.

Dr. Ross Case in Westlake Village, California on Dec. 20, 1982.

Mrs. Harry Carey in Carpenteria, California on February 15, 1985.

Dr. W. R. Mann in Mannsville, Kentucky on June 29, 1985.

Mr. Lyle S. Woodcock in St. Louis, Missouri on June 6, 1983 and in Great Falls, Montana on March 19, 1987.

Dr. and Mrs. Russell Edwin in Great Falls, Montana on June 22, 1982.

Mrs. Ruth Frohlicher in Great Falls, Montana on March, 29, 1986.

Dr. Otey Johnson in Ardmore, Oklahoma on May 30, 1983.

Mr. and Mrs. Frank Repetti in Pasadena, California on December 19, 1982.

Mr. and Mrs. Milton Sperling in Pasadena, California on December 9, 1983.

Mr. Ward Parker in St. Louis, Missouri on June 7, 1983.

Mrs. Francis Spurling in Mannesville, Kentucky on July 3, 1985.

Mr. & Mrs. John Stevenson in Great Falls, Montana on March 31, 1983.

Mr. Conrad Lundgren in West Glacier, Montana on March 27, 1983.

Mrs. Irma Chance McLuskie; Billings, Montana by telephone on March 4, 1985.

Mr. & Mrs. Randall Swanberg in Great Falls, Montana on April 1, 1983.

Mr. J. S. Wolff in Great Falls, Montana on April 2, 1983.

Miss Alice Calvert in Great Falls, Montana on June 22, 1982.

Mr. Earl C. Adams in Los Angeles, California on December 17, 1982.

Mr. Jack C. Russell in Oceanside, California on December 18, 1982.

Miss Verne Linderman in Santa Barbara, California on December 17, 1983.

Letters and Other Papers

James Brownlee Rankin Collection, Montana Historical Society, Helena Montana.

Letter from Mr. Ross Case to Joan Stauffer, February 15, 1984.

Mr. Charles F. Lummis Guest Register, Collection of Southwest Museum, Los Angeles, California.

Joe De Yong Collection, National Cowboy Hall of Fame, Oklahoma City, Oklahoma.

Letter from Mr. W. S. Hart to Nancy Russell, Collection of Seaver Center for Western History Research, Natural History Museum of Los Angeles County.

History of the Allen Family, compiled by Irma Chance McLuskie, Billings, Montana.

Letters from Mr. A. S. Cowie to Mrs. Charles Russell provided by Mr. Steve Rose, Biltmore Salon, Los Angeles, California.

Letter from Mrs. Nancy Russell to George W. Parker, dated February 4, 1932, Collection of Ward Parker, St. Louis, Missouri.

Letter from Mr. John D. Stephenson to Great Falls Park Board dated December 13, 1976 supplied by Mr. Stephenson on March 31, 1983.

Carbon of telegram from Mrs. C. M. Russell to Mrs. Edward L. Doheny, dated December 15, 1925, Collection of C. M. Russell Museum, Great Falls, Montana.

Letter from Mr. F. W. Hodge, Director, to Mr. Harvey Mudd, dated February 16, 1938, Collection of Southwest Museum, Los Angeles.

History of the Cooper Family provided by Miss Evelyn

Cooper, Lebanon, Kentucky.

History of the Mann Family provided by Dr. W. R. Mann, Campbellsville, Kentucky.

History of the Mann and Cooper Families compiled by Miss Francis McKnight, Campbellsville Kentucky.

Letter from Mr. A. C. Douglas to Mrs. Charles Russell dated July 8, 1929.

Oral History

Montana Historical Society, Oral History Number 25, Arthur "Punk" Ward presentation January, 1974.

Junior League of Great Falls and Great Falls Library Oral History Presentation by Dr. Edwin S. Russell on April 18, 1971.

CREDITS

Artworks by Charles Marion Russell which are reproduced as chapter opening plates are the following: Chapter 1: *Mosquito Season in Cascade*, Montana Historical Society, presented in memory of Mrs. Ben Roberts by Mrs. Charles L. Sheridan, Courtesy of Helena Women's Club; Chapter 2: *Beating Back*, Collection of Mr. and Mrs. S. H. Rosenthal, Jr.; Chapter 3: *Russell Proposing to Nancy*, National Cowboy Hall of Fame; Chapter 4: *Bear Paw Pool*, The Rockwell Museum, Corning, New York; Chapter 5: *Charlie's Idea of How Cupid Roped Him*, Courtesy of Ginger K. Renner, location of original unknown; Chapter 6: *Friend Sid*, Courtesy of the Amon Carter Museum, Fort Worth, Texas, watercolor, pen and ink, and graphite on paper, 1907, 1961.309; Chapter 7: *Friend Bob*, Courtesy of the Amon Carter Museum, Fort Worth, Texas, watercolor, pen and ink, gouache, and graphite on paper, 1907, 1961.365.1; Chapter 8: *His Legs is Warped*, Courtesy of Ginger K. Renner, location of original unknown; Chapter 9: *Contrast in Artist's Salons - Charlie Painting in His Cabin*, Courtesy of the Amon Carter Museum, Fort Worth, Texas, ink wash and graphite on paper, c. 1894, 1961.305.1; Chapter 10: *We're Coming*, The C. M. Russell Museum; Chapter 11: *Mothers Under the Skin*, The C. M. Russell Museum; Chapter 12: *Friend Sid*, Courtesy of the Amon Carter Museum, Fort Worth, Texas, watercolor, pen and ink, and graphite on paper, 1914, 1961.302; Chapter 13: *Friend Guy*, Courtesy of the Amon Carter Museum, Fort Worth, Texas, watercolor, pen and ink, and graphite on paper, 1912, 1961.364.2; Chapter 14: *Friend Bob*, Courtesy of the Amon Carter Museum, Fort Worth, Texas, pen and ink, watercolor, and graphite on paper, 1913, 1961.313; Chapter 15: *To Bill Marks*, The C. M. Russell Museum; Chapter 16: *My Dear Mr. Kilmer*, Courtesy of the Amon Carter Museum, Fort Worth, Texas, pen and ink and graphite on paper, 1911, 1961.412.1; Chapter 17: *Friend Guy* , Courtesy of the Amon Carter Museum, Fort Worth, Texas, watercolor, pen and ink, gouache, and graphite on paper, 1921, 1961.300; Chapter 18: *He Aimed and the Snake was Shattered*, The C. M. Russell Museum; Chapter 19, *Friend Guy*, Courtesy of the Amon Carter Museum, Fort Worth, Texas, watercolor and pen and ink on paper, 1912, 1961.364.1; Chapter 20, *Horses Resting*, The C. M. Russell Museum; Chapter 21: *School Marm*, Courtesy of Ginger K. Renner, location of original unknown.